D1126818

BREAD REVOLUTION

BREAD
REVOLUTION

World-Class Baking with
**SPROUTED & WHOLE GRAINS,
HEIRLOOM FLOURS & FRESH TECHNIQUES**

PETER REINHART
Photography by Paige Green

TEN SPEED PRESS
Berkeley

INTRODUCTION

Bread—well, actually wheat—is once again in the crosshairs. And not just wheat, but other grains too, depending on who you believe and what your struggles are. There are a lot of theories about diet, wheat, grains, and carbohydrates floating around and, not surprisingly, they all seem plausible. And like it or not, bread is getting the blame for a lot of ills. I have baker friends who say, "It will pass, just like the last scare." But I'm not so sure.

Fifteen years ago the Atkins diet was very popular, followed by the South Beach diet and other low-carb plans. Collectively, they took a big bite out of the bread market, and the immediate result was that Wonder Bread lost a lot of sales but somehow recovered—until recently, that is, when the parent company declared bankruptcy. In 2003, when numerous reporters at a bread conference asked me, "Is bread dead?" my reply was, "No. Bread has been with us for six thousand years; I don't think it's going away." But my less public response to my baker friends was, "There's an opportunity here. It's time to focus on whole grain breads and make them as good as the artisan loaves. This is the future." And so they did—not because of anything I said, but because it was the logical, intuitive, necessary thing to do. Yet here we are, ten years later, and thanks to the growing (and important) gluten-free movement and some recent popular books, even whole grain breads have a big bull's-eye on them. What on earth is going on? Is it possible, after six thousand years, that bread really is dead? I still say no, but once again we bakers are at a crossroads and need to ask, "What is the opportunity within all of this concern?"

ROOTS OF A
REVOLUTION

I've been thrilled and privileged to be in the midst of the American artisan bread revolution that began in the mid-1980s. Actually, its roots go back even further, as I've chronicled in earlier books, but it wasn't until the 1980s that things really took off. I remember the excitement that many of us felt as we metaphorically and literally sat at the feet of our mostly European bread heroes and learned their tricks of pre-ferments and soakers and how the relationship of time and temperature work on ingredients. The excitement of discovery was palpable as bakers and millers took field trips together to meet farmers and learn about the differences among wheat varieties and the influences of *terroir*.

Soon, schools of thought emerged, with disciples of various bread masters working their way through dogmatic beliefs, arguing about the virtues of poolish versus biga, yeast versus wild yeast, mixing versus folding, and high-protein versus low-protein flours. They faced off at competitions and in the marketplace and railed against the mainstream. Then they softened—integrating, expanding, and sharing their repertoires with each other and creating new schools of thought. American teams excelled at the Coupe du Monde de la Boulangerie (the World Cup of Bread or, as we call it, the Bread Olympics). American bakers, who had been cross-pollinating each other's approaches with growing stores of knowledge and expertise, became internationally influential. The home baking movement grew exponentially through the advent of baking websites and award-winning bread books, each adding a new technique or breakthrough method and posing questions that were previously taboo, such as, "Do we really need to knead?" and, "Can bread that's partially baked and frozen and then rebaked be as satisfying as a freshly baked loaf?"

Over the years I've become friends with a lot of bakers, millers, and farmers. It's a wonderful community of earthy, spiritual, generous, and above all hardworking people. It's also a community of creative, resourceful, and resilient people. Six thousand years is a long lineage; bread and makers of bread are not going away. But I will say this: during bread's six-thousand-year saga, bread bakers have always been reinventing themselves and their craft.

This brings us to the current moment—the opportunity at hand. If you've followed me through my literary journey with bread, you know that I'm fascinated by new frontiers and revolutionary turning points, whether cold fermentation, new ways to make whole grain breads, or even unconventional methods for making gluten-free bread. Early on, I learned that answers come by asking the right questions: what-if questions and questions that others are too timid or narrowly focused to ask. Some people have the tenacity to do one thing over and over again until they do it better than anyone else. They establish benchmarks and signposts for those who follow in their path. Others, more restless in spirit, step onto paths less traveled and forge new frontiers. Sometimes they go too far and disappear for a time—or forever. But some-times they stumble upon fertile ground and become the pioneers for the next wave.

While I admire beyond words those who can relentlessly drill down deeper and deeper in their Zen-like quest for the perfect loaf, I tend to be even more fascinated by and drawn toward those adventurous souls who yearn for something not yet seen. I've lived in each world at different times, and I believe both are essential aspects of the journey. But at this crucial time and crossroads in the history of bread, I especially delight in exploring the as-yet-unknown and in meeting others who, each in his or her own way, expand the boundaries of what is possible. In this book, I've applied some of what I've learned from them to create new recipes and formulas, and I also share some of their recipes, insights, and stories.

Some of the things these bakers are exploring address current questions related to health and nutrition, some focus on flavor, and some are responses to global, environmental, and holistic concerns. Each is a piece of the puzzle of how bread, glorious in its tradition, symbolism, and significance, is relevant at this time. As you'll see in the following pages, I think it is. In fact, I think bread is having, as it has so often throughout history, yet another revolutionary moment.

THE FRONTIER AT HAND: SPROUTED GRAIN FLOUR

In fall 2009 I got a call from Joe Lindley, the owner of Lindley Mills, located in Graham, North Carolina. I knew of Lindley Mills mainly as an independent, private-label organic mill whose most well-known client was King Arthur Flour. I was already using Lindley Mills flours at a pizza restaurant in Charlotte where I was a partner, and we were very happy with them. Lindley's multigrain blend was unique in that it was milled into a very fine powder, which gave it the ability to form fairly strong gluten bonds despite containing a number of gluten-free grains. For pizza dough, having a strong gluten network is critical for allowing the dough to stretch without ripping, so this flour was a revelation. However, I did have one concern: it resulted in a crust that was slightly drier, lacking the creamy texture of classic white dough. That said, it was still the best whole grain pizza dough I'd had to that point.

Toward the end of that restaurant's time, Joe Lindley called and asked if I'd be willing to try a new flour made with sprouted wheat that he was developing, called Super Sprout. He'd also developed a sprouted gluten-free flour blend that he called Sprouted Ancient Grain, made with sprouted amaranth, quinoa, millet, sorghum, and buckwheat. Like many people, I'm a fan of Ezekiel and Alvarado Street breads, which are both made with sprouted wheat kernels, so I asked Joe if his new flour was like what they used.

He said, "No. At those places they sprout the wheat, then grind the sprouts into a wet pulp and then add other ingredients and mix it into a dough. The grain never actually becomes flour. With mine, I sprout the grain, then stabilize and dry it, and then mill those sprouted kernels into flour that can be bagged, stored, and shipped just like regular flour. It's a totally different product."

"But doesn't sprouting the wheat compromise the gluten and damage the starch?" I asked. After all, millers had often warned me about this kind of starch damage. Although all flour has some starch damage that arises during harvest and storage, and also from the pounding the grain takes during the milling process, it falls within an acceptable range. Sometimes, during overly wet growing seasons or if stored wheat kernels are exposed to too much moisture prior to milling, starch damage can exceed acceptable levels. The resulting flour is either ruined or is considered inadequate for bread, as determined by its falling number (see Glossary, page 14).

Using sprouted wheat, or any sprouted grain, to make flour seems to go against the conventional wisdom. In fact, the way Ezekiel and other bakeries that use sprouted wheat pulp get around this is by adding a relatively large amount of pure gluten, called vital wheat gluten, to the dough to provide structure. This allows the dough to bake up into what looks and tastes like bread made from regular flour.

Joe said, "You'd think sprouted wheat flour wouldn't work for bread, but for some reason it does, and I'm not totally sure why. I need you to try this and tell me if I'm crazy, but the breads I've made from it are really good, and I haven't needed to add any vital wheat gluten to it to make it work."

A few days later, I received two boxes from Joe: one containing twenty-five pounds of Super Sprout wheat flour, and the other containing the Sprouted Ancient Grain blend. Joe advised me that the Super Sprout flour required greater hydration than regular whole wheat flour. "It really sucks up the water," he said, then added, "I think the key to what makes it work for bread is that I'm using the best-quality high-protein wheat I can find. And that isn't always easy, especially in the organic realm."

As most bakers know, all wheat is not created equal. Plus, during growth and processing it's subject to a number of factors that can create differences even in the same strain of wheat, such as amount of rainfall or irrigation, temperature, humidity, and soil quality. Hard wheat, aka high-protein wheat, can also vary in performance depending on whether the protein balance in the kernels is tilted more toward gliadin or glutenin, the two proteins that ultimately create gluten.

It was time for me to play with this flour and see for myself what Joe was getting so excited about. I mixed up a small batch of basic dough with about 85% water to Super Sprout flour. The water was quickly absorbed, and within a few minutes the dough seemed fairly firm—a little too firm actually. So I worked in some more water and ended up with a very soft, sticky dough that felt similar to ciabatta dough. When I did the math, I had used 14.6 ounces (416 g) of water, which, by weight, is 91.25% of the 16 ounces (454 g) of flour. That's a lot! A typical white flour ciabatta has only about 75% to 80% water. Then, at five-minute intervals, I did a version of kneading involving four stretches and folds. Little by little, the dough firmed up into a supple, very tacky, pillow-like beauty. It had what I like to call bounce.

About three hours later—after a ninety-minute first rise, shaping, and a sixty-minute final rise, followed by thirty-five minutes of baking in my home oven on a baking stone, I tasted quite possibly the best 100% whole wheat bread I'd ever had. No sugar or honey, no oil, no pre-ferment, and no long, extended fermentation—just flour, water, salt, and yeast. Suddenly, the artisan playbook no longer applied, and this was just my first attempt. I had been prepared to add oil and honey, and maybe milk, to the second go-round, as I would for a standard 100% whole wheat dough, but even without these the bread was soft, moist, and creamy or, as some bakers say, custard-like. This mouthfeel, which I prize in bread, is usually the result of long fermentation and a very hot oven. It can also be accomplished by including fats, sugar, and eggs in the dough, but the holy grail of artisan baking is to get these qualities without resorting to enrichments, as is sometimes achieved in the best baguettes,

levains, and ciabattas. It's difficult to accomplish, though not impossible, with 100% whole wheat flour, and doing so usually entails using ample pre-ferments.

Later, I made several doughs using a combination of Lindley's gluten-free Ancient Grain blend and the Super Sprout flour to create a multigrain version, finally settling on 20% Sprouted Ancient Grain to 80% Super Sprout. Eventually, I even came up with ways to use the ancient grain blend without any wheat at all, resulting in 100% gluten-free dough. In all cases, the natural sweetness and tenderness of the sprouted grain obviated the need for sweeteners or oils, though for loaf pan breads, soft dinner rolls, and sweet doughs, I did add some enrichments.

I was having a lot of fun with this flour, and I began to realize that I was standing on the threshold of the next frontier in bread. In the pages that follow, I'll take you on my journey of discovery into this bread frontier. Along the way, I followed sprouted grain flour as if it were a breadcrumb trail, leading me to pulp made from sprouted grains, to millers and bakers who had controversial perspectives on baking with whole grains and wild yeast, and even back into the gluten-free world, which I explored in *The Joy of Gluten-Free, Sugar-Free Baking*. Along the way, I visited some arcane corners populated by unusual flours made from grape skins and seeds or from coffee cherries (the fruit that encloses coffee beans). It all adds up to an exciting time for bakers, ushered in by the emergence of sprouted grain flour and proving, once again, that bread is far from dead. Welcome to the new bread revolution!

CHAPTER 1
TUTORIAL

This chapter provides basic information that you'll need to make the recipes throughout this book, including definitions and a step-by-step photo tutorial of the techniques and methods used. The recipes will sometimes refer back to these pages, but once you've made a few of them, you'll internalize most of the information here.

Although the instructions in this book are easy enough for even beginning bakers to understand, the recipes and formulas do presuppose that you have some prior bread baking experience and understanding of baking terminology. For example, in my earlier book *Peter Reinhart's Artisan Breads Every Day*, I introduced a technique called the stretch and fold. This method is also used throughout the present book (and described in detail on page 20). I didn't invent the stretch and fold; it has been used by bakers for many years, probably for centuries. It has recently become popular, with artisan bakers using it in place of long mixing cycles, and now it shows up in many bread books. If you haven't encountered this or some of the other mixing, shaping, and baking techniques called for in the recipes, please refer to pages 19 to 29 for details on handling, shaping, and proofing dough and setting up your oven for hearth baking.

You'll also notice that the recipes make frequent use of a technique that I call "the oil slick method." As simple as it is, it nevertheless took twenty years of professional baking before I awoke to it and started lightly oiling the work surface rather than dusting it with flour. It isn't required, and you can still use flour if you prefer, but it will make your life a lot easier. Again, refer to the section beginning on page 20.

Chapter 2 is devoted to naturally leavened (aka wild yeast) sourdough starters, and you should read through it before making any of the breads that call for a starter. As you become familiar with this approach, you may become a sourdough fanatic and possibly a mad scientist. In each of my recent books, as my own knowledge has grown, I've added to the ongoing conversation about how to make and use sourdough—a conversation that may continue through the next six thousand years of bread making.

Throughout the book are responses to recipe testers' most frequently asked questions, some of which may be questions of yours as well:

TOOLS AND INGREDIENTS

You don't need a lot of tools to make great bread at home, but there are a few that are essential and others that are useful and can ease the process. You definitely don't need to run out and purchase every nice-to-have tool in order to get started. You really only need some mixing bowls, baking pans, a large mixing spoon, and rubber spatulas or something similar.

My two absolutely favorite tools are a plastic bowl scraper and a metal pastry blade. Of course, you'll also need an oven, but the type of oven doesn't matter—all ovens can bake bread as long as they are fairly accurate. Almost everything else you'll need is probably already in your kitchen. You can add tools over time, but build your inventory slowly and consciously, as there are few things lonelier than fancy equipment sitting idle and unused.

Ingredients can also be divided into need to have and nice to have. Flour is obviously necessary, as is salt and, for many of the breads, yeast. Oil, milk, sweeteners, vegetable spray oil, and the like are called for fairly often, but these are usually present in home pantries. Some of the recipes do call for specialty ingredients, so read the ingredient list closely before starting. In addition, this book often calls for ingredients that may not be readily available to you, such as sprouted grain flour and whole-milled wheat flour. While I believe that many of these will become increasingly available in the near future, for now you may need to order some of these ingredients. The Resources section (page 240) will direct you to suppliers for these.

I've covered equipment and standard ingredients extensively in my previous books, so here I'll just share a few pointers and briefly address ingredients new to this book.

TOOLS

BAKING STONE. There are many brands and thicknesses of baking stones. Typically, the thicker the stone, the more heat it will absorb and radiate back into the oven—and any baked goods therein. You can now even find versions made from solid steel or cast aluminum, and both work very well.

BANNETONS. These proofing baskets, made from bent wood, are expensive and can be hard to find, but they do make for nicely shaped loaves.

BOWL SCRAPER. A flexible plastic bowl scraper is very inexpensive, yet it's also one of the most useful tools. It's especially handy for easing dough out of bowls and off of work surfaces without tearing the dough.

CLOCHE. A cloche is a covered baking dish that simulates hearth baking, trapping moisture to create big oven spring. You can improvise one using a cast-iron Dutch oven or something similar.

COUCHE. Also known as proofing cloths, *couches*, which are usually made of linen, are used to gently support shaped loaves as they rise and help them retain their shape. You can improvise using lint-free sheets, pillowcases, or a white tablecloth.

DIGITAL SCALE. I highly recommend using a digital scale to take the guesswork out of measuring. Opt for one that displays both ounces and grams.

INSTANT-READ THERMOMETER. There are many brands of instant-read thermometers available, some with a digital display and others with a temperature dial. The probe should reach into the center of the loaf and quickly determine the internal dough temperature.

LOAF PANS. These come in various sizes, usually 4 to 5 inches wide and 8 to 10 inches long. The loaf pan breads in this book will work in any of these sizes, and either metal or glass is fine.

MEASURING CUPS AND SPOONS. I recommend measuring most ingredients by weight. But for small amounts, measuring spoons may be more useful than a scale.

MIXING BOWLS. It's best to have a number of mixing bowls in various sizes to accommodate different volumes, and for ease in mixing dry and wet ingredients separately. I prefer using stainless steel bowls, but glass bowls are also fine, albeit more fragile.

MIXING SPOONS. Either wooden or metal mixing spoons are fine for bread.

OVEN. Of course, an oven is essential for baking, and just about any type will work: gas or electric, conventional (radiant heat) or convection (with moving air), and even wood-fired. If you have a convection oven you'll generally need to lower the baking temperature in these recipes by 25°F to 50°F (14°C to 28°C).

PASTRY BLADE. Also called a bench blade or bencher, this flat, rectangular stainless steel blade is ideal for dividing doughs and scraping work counters.

PEEL. A long, flat-handled wooden or metal paddle, a peel is used for sliding dough onto a baking stone and removing it once baked.

pH PAPER. When you are making sourdough starters and breads, pH paper can help determine the acidity level of your dough. It is available at many pharmacies and from baking supply companies. And while nice to have, it's not essential.

PLASTIC WRAP. Yes, it's a disposable product, but plastic wrap will prevent a skin from forming on dough.

PROOF BOX. Although these doughs can rise nicely at room temperature in a covered container, a temperature- and humidity-controlled proof box offers more control and consistency. There are now small portable proofers available, but you can also improvise your own using ice chests or microwave boxes with a cup of boiling water to provide warmth and humidity. Even a dishwasher can be used to create a warm, humid box, as can an oven with a pilot light or light bulb.

SCORING KNIFE. Many implements can be used to score loaves before baking, so you don't really need a dedicated scoring knife (*lame* in French). You can use a double-edge razor blade mounted on coffee stirring sticks, or a sharp steak knife or bread knife.

SEED OR SPICE GRINDER. For grinding small seeds, a dedicated electric seed or spice grinder works better than a blender. In a pinch, you can use an electric coffee grinder—if you clean it well both before and after use.

SHEET PANS. The most useful size for home ovens is about 12 by 17 inches.

SILICONE BAKING MATS. Reusable nonstick pan liners are a nondisposable alternative to parchment paper for lining sheet pans. However, I recommend against using them on baking stones because the very high heat will wear them out quickly.

STAND MIXER. Many good brands are available. For bread making, it's best to choose one with a heavy-duty motor to decrease the chances of overworking it.

WIRE COOLING RACKS. These are helpful to have on hand as bread cools more quickly on racks, which prevents moisture from being trapped underneath the loaf.

INGREDIENTS

BREAD FLOUR. Choose unbleached bread flour if possible, preferably between 12% and 13% protein.

BUTTER. The recipes in this book (and almost all baking recipes) call for unsalted butter, as this allows closer control of the amount of salt in a recipe.

EGGS. The standard for baking is to use large eggs, which weigh approximately 1.75 ounces (47 g). I usually figure that one egg is approximately 1.25 ounces (35 g) egg white and 0.5 ounce (14 g) yolk, but this can vary from egg to egg.

MILK. Milk serves a number of functions in baking, from hydration to contributing to tenderness, flavor, crust color, and nutrition. As a general rule, for most of the formulas in this book you may substitute nondairy milks such as rice, almond, flaxseed, or hemp milk, and can also use any richness level from skim to whole, unless otherwise specified. In many cases, you can even use water in place of milk for a leaner version.

OILS. Any high-quality vegetable oil will work in most of the recipes. I prefer olive as well as grape seed oil, which is generally GMO-free and easy to digest, and tastes good. However, if you have a favorite oil whose flavor complements the bread you are making, feel free to use it, since it will provide the same functionality in terms of fat.

SALT. The size of salt grains determines the weight per teaspoon, with finer grinds weighing more per teaspoon. Even kosher salt comes in various sizes depending on the brand, so weighing the salt is essential. Most of the recipes in this book were developed using standard table salt, but you can use any type as long as you weigh it or know the equivalency in teaspoons.

SPROUTED GRAIN FLOURS AND SPROUTED GRAINS. These products are becoming increasingly available at natural food stores and even well-stocked supermarkets. If they aren't yet available to you locally, see the Resources section (page 240) for online vendors.

SWEETENERS. Syrups, such as honey and agave nectar, are heavier than dry sugar, so keep that in mind when substituting. Liquid stevia is highly concentrated, with 1 teaspoon (3 g) equaling 1 cup (227 g) of sugar or a sucralose sweetener such as Splenda. When substituting for sugar, I prefer liquid stevia over sucralose. You can also substitute honey or agave nectar unless otherwise specified, and many of the recipes provide quantities for these substitutions.

VEGETABLE SPRAY OIL. For the recipes in this book, you can use pan spray made with either vegetable or olive oil.

WHOLE WHEAT FLOUR. An exciting new development in the world of whole wheat flour is the recognition of the difference between whole-milled versus reconstituted whole wheat flour. (For more details, see chapter 5.)

YEAST. The three types of yeast most commonly available are compressed fresh yeast (which is moist and crumbly), active dry yeast (which is granular and must be dissolved in warm water first), and instant yeast (which has the smallest granules and can usually be added directly to the flour in a recipe). The recipes in this book specify instant yeast. If you want to substitute active dry yeast, increase the amount by 25%. If substituting with fresh yeast, use three times as much by weight.

GLOSSARY

This isn't an exhaustive glossary of baking terms; rather, it's a list of some of the important terms used in this book. In some instances, where terms may have a number of definitions or have been used in other books in a different way, the following definitions clarify how the terms are used in this book.

ANCIENT GRAINS. This term can apply to both wheat and nonwheat grains and refers to strains that existed prior to the development of modern hybrids. For wheat, this means strains such as spelt, emmer, einkorn, and Khorasan wheat (aka Kamut, a trademarked name). Nonwheat ancient grains include amaranth, barley, buckwheat, millet, quinoa, sorghum, teff, and even corn, oats, and rice if they are heirloom, non-hybrid strains. More information is on page 50.

BACTERIAL FERMENTATION. In contrast to yeast fermentation, this refers to the action of various strains of bacteria as they feed on sugars, breaking them down to release flavorful acids and esters. It is the primary source of sourdough flavor.

BAKER'S MATH. See the sidebar on page 18.

ENZYMES. Chemical proteins naturally found in all plants and animals, enzymes function to catalyze reactions, often breaking down complex molecules into more basic forms. Some enzymes break down proteins (protease enzymes), and some break down starches or carbohydrates (amylase enzymes). These two types of enzymes are critical to fermentation and digestive processes.

FALLING NUMBER. This refers to how long it takes for a stick to fall through a mixture of flour and water, a measure used to determine flour quality in terms of level of enzyme activity and starch breakdown. The lower the number, the faster the stick falls. For bread, most bakers and millers prefer a falling number over 250 and even as high as 400. Below 250 usually means there's too much starch damage, making the flour unsuitable for creating good bread structure.

FERMENTATION. Fermentation is a metabolic process in which sugars are converted into gases, alcohols, and acids. (See *Bacterial fermentation* and *Yeast fermentation*.) Bakers often use *ferment* to refer to the first, bulk rising of dough, whereas *proof* is used to refer to the rising of shaped loaves.

FLOAT TEST. A method for determining whether enough gas has been created during proofing is to see if a piece of dough, such as a shaped bagel, will float when placed in a bowl of water. It can also be used to test a piece of sourdough starter to see whether it has enough activity to leaven a dough.

FORMULA. See the sidebar on page 18.

GLUTEN. A strong protein made by the bonding of two smaller proteins—glutenin and gliadin—gluten gives dough its elasticity and extensibility and also traps gases to create air bubbles in the rising dough and baked bread. Gluten occurs mainly in wheat, rye, and, to a smaller extent, barley.

LEAVEN. As a noun, *leaven* refers to any ingredient that causes a dough to rise. It can be biological (yeast), chemical (baking soda or baking powder), or physical (gas or air). As a verb, *leaven* means to cause to rise or, as its root implies, to enliven.

LEVAIN. *Levain* is a French term for a natural leaven or starter made with wild yeast and bacteria, rather than commercial yeast (which the French call *levure*). It can be either firm or wet (if wet, it's a sponge). Levain may also refer to a specific type of bread, pain au levain, which is raised primarily with a levain starter.

MALTING. When seeds of any type are soaked in water, they begin to sprout. In the process, natural enzyme activity releases maltose and other sugars stored as starches in the seed. Therefore, malting is closely akin to sprouting. (Because the enzymes are still active at this point, this type of malted grain is known as diastatic, because the diastase, or amylase, enzymes are still viable.) But in baking and brewing, malting may also refer to roasting the partially sprouted grain to various degrees of darkness to create other flavors. Roasting denatures the enzymes, resulting in nondiastatic malt, which has no enzyme activity.

MASTER FORMULA. See the sidebar on page 18.

MOTHER STARTER. This is a natural leaven that's kept and fed, or refreshed, perpetually and from which other, smaller amounts of starter can be made for use in specific doughs.

PREBIOTICS. Prebiotics are foods that serve as nourishment for healthful bacteria (probiotics) in the digestive system, such as fiber and enzyme-rich products.

PRE-FERMENT. A generic term, pre-ferment refers to any dough that's made in advance to be added to a subsequent dough to improve flavor and texture. Types of pre-ferments include biga (a firm dough made with a small amount of yeast but without salt, of Italian origin); poolish (a wet sponge made with a small amount of yeast but no salt, of Polish origin and named and adopted by the French); sponge (a faster method using a higher amount of yeast in a wet batter); *pâte fermentée* (a piece of old dough from a previous batch added to a subsequent dough, named by the French); and wild yeast or sourdough starter, aka levain (a naturally leavened pre-ferment).

PROBIOTICS. Probiotics are beneficial bacteria and microorganisms in the digestive system. They are also present in yogurt and other cultured foods.

PROOFING. *Proofing* is a term that refers to proving yeast is alive when activating the yeast in warm water or when raising (fermenting) dough. Bakers usually use the term *fermentation* for the first, or bulk, rise, and *proofing* for the final rise. I follow that convention in this book, but the two terms are interchangeable.

RECIPE. See the sidebar on page 18.

RECONSTITUTED MILLING. This is a method of making whole wheat flour in which the bran and germ are separated from the endosperm early in the process and then added back in later. There is controversy as to whether all of the recombined portions are from the original batch of wheat that was separated or from other batches, and also as to whether the wheat performs the same as it would if left whole (see *Whole milling*).

ROOM TEMPERATURE. Room temperature is generally considered to be 70°F (21°C). If your home's ambient temperature is higher or lower than that, the fermentation times of your doughs may be either faster or slower than indicated in the instructions.

SCOOP AND SWEEP MEASURING. This method of measuring dry ingredients by volume rather than weight, such as with cups, involves scooping the ingredient up in a measuring cup, overfilling it, and then using a flat tool, such as a bowl scraper, to sweep off the excess and obtain an even measure. (See page 17 for more information.)

What's the best way to scoop flour so that a cup is likely to match the listed weight?

Volume measures are never as accurate as weights because of variations in how people scoop flour (and other ingredients), and also because the coarseness of the flour, the brand, and even humidity can all affect density and therefore volume accuracy. But if you're going to use volume measures, here's the method that should be most accurate: First, lightly aerate or fluff the flour with a whisk or even just a large spoon to break it up a bit so it isn't densely packed (don't sift, as that will overdo it). Then scoop the flour into your measuring cup, filling it over the rim. Sweep off the excess with a straight edge, such as a bowl scraper, a metal pastry blade, or even the back of a table knife. Don't pack the flour in this step; just let the sweeping do the job. The amount should be pretty close to the weight measure, but you may have to adjust the dough with more flour or more liquid as you mix. Therefore, when using volume measures it's especially important to follow the cues in the recipe instructions. The rule of thumb is always to let the dough dictate what it needs. In fact, even if you weigh ingredients accurately, the variability between types and brands of flour may necessitate adjustments.

If I don't have a scale, how do I accurately measure the salt?

There are many different forms of salt, and they vary in density. Therefore, weight measurements are always more accurate than teaspoons because a weighed ounce or gram will yield the same amount of sodium chloride regardless of how large or dense the salt crystals are. This will ensure that the ratio of salt to flour is correct. Further, a teaspoon is only as accurate as the spoon and the person doing the scooping, so it will always be approximate at best. However, if you must use volume measures, you need to know that the weights for salt listed in this book are for table salt, which typically weighs about 0.25 ounces (7 g) per 1 teaspoon. Scoop and sweep salt for the best accuracy, just as when measuring flour. Unless you are weighing it, I don't recommend using flaky sea salt, because these vary so widely depending on brand, crystal size, and density. If you'll be using a different form of salt, here are some details that can help you decide how much to use:

- **Table salt or fine sea salt (most brands):** 1 teaspoon = 0.25 ounce or 7 grams

- **Morton kosher salt:** 1 teaspoon = 0.21 ounce or 6 grams

- **Diamond kosher salt:** 1 teaspoon = 0.11 ounce or 3 grams

If you use volume measures for salt, always taste the dough and make notes to help you settle on standard adjustments to use in the future based on the type of salt used. Too much or too little salt can adversely affect the dough's flavor, fermentation time, and structure of the dough. That said, for people on salt-restricted diets, it's okay to decrease the amount of salt by as much as 50%, but if you do so, also decrease the yeast slightly (by about 10%) and note the resulting fermentation times, since yeast acts more quickly in the absence of salt.

Recipes, Formulas, Master Formulas, and Baker's Math

Although the terms *recipe* and *formula* are sometimes used interchangeably in cookbooks, for bakers they have distinct meanings, and even among bakers opinions differ as to what those meanings are. Here's what I mean when I use those words in this book: *Recipe* refers to the measurements of ingredients for a specific batch size and includes instructions. *Formula* refers to the ratio of each ingredient, by weight, to the total weight of flour, regardless of the batch size. *Master formula* refers to a formula template that can be used to create a number of bread variations. Examples in this book include Sprouted Whole Wheat Bread (page 63), and Sprouted Wheat Quick Bread or Muffins (page 58), which can be modified by adding a variety of ingredients or shaping the dough differently. In fact, almost all of the recipes in this book are so versatile that they could qualify as master formulas, providing a starting point for exploration and variations.

The ingredients for each recipe are presented in a table that includes a column for percentage, indicating the ratio between each ingredient and the total weight of flour. Armed with this information, you can use baker's math to calculate different batch sizes. Bakers are vitally interested in these ratios because they provide a concise synopsis of the type of bread being made. These ratios can't be determined based on volume measures because different ingredients have different densities.

In this book, you will see both recipes and formulas. If you decide to expand or even tweak a recipe, you can use the formula to help you make adjustments. I've explained this in great depth in some of my previous books, so rather than repeating all of the details here, I'll just recap the most important points:

- In formulas, the most important reference point is the total weight of the flour, which is always 100%: the number on which the ratios of all other ingredients are based. To determine this ratio, divide the weight of the ingredient by the total weight of the flour. If the recipe includes more than one type of flour, the total weight of all the flours equals 100%. For example, in a recipe that uses 1,000 grams of flour (35.27 oz) and 20 grams of salt (0.7 oz), dividing 20 by 1,000 reveals that the ratio of salt is 0.02, or 2%.

- Based on the formula, you can easily scale up a recipe. Say you'd like to triple the batch of the hypothetical bread in the previous bullet point. So you'd use 3,000 grams of flour. Then, you can multiply the total flour weight by 2% to determine how much salt you'll need: 3,000 x 0.02 = 60. Therefore, you'd need 60 grams of salt.

- In formulas that use more than one kind of flour, such as a combination of whole wheat, rye, and bread flour, each flour is treated as an ingredient, with their total equaling 100%. So if the total weight of flour should be 1,000 grams and you want to use 700 grams of whole wheat flour, the other two flours would have to add up to 30% of the total flour. If you choose to use 50 grams of rye flour (5% of the total flour weight, or 50/1,000), then you would use 250 grams of bread flour (25% of the total flour weight, or 250/1,000).

- Some bread books present the ratios based on *all* of the ingredients, including those in any pre-ferments and starters. This is a good way to do it, especially for professional bakers, but for home bakers I think it's easier to consider the pre-ferments as separate ingredients, rather than breaking out their flour and water and aggregating it with the total amounts of those ingredients. The formulas in this book are set up that way, with only the flour in the final dough constituting 100%, and pre-ferments and starters being listed like salt, yeast, and other ingredients, with a ratio to the flour in the final dough.

SPROUTED GRAIN. This refers to grain of any type that has been sprouted only just until the shoot begins to show. Then it is either dried or pulped. Once dried, it can be milled into flour. (See also *Malting* and *Sprouted pulp*.)

SPROUTED PULP. Once grain has been germinated and sprouted, it can be milled into a pulp that can be used to make bread dough. This is the method used for Ezekiel and Alvarado Street breads, as well as Giusto's Vita-Grain bread. (For more details, see chapter 4.)

STARTER. *Starter* is another word for a pre-ferment made with either commercial or natural, wild yeast.

WHOLE MILLING. This is a milling method in which all components of the whole grain are milled to create flour, with minimum separation of bran, germ, and endosperm.

YEAST FERMENTATION. Yeast is a microscopic fungus that causes fermentation by acting upon sugars, mainly glucose, to release carbon dioxide and ethyl alcohol. The most common bread yeast is from the species *Saccharomyces cerevisiae*, though many other species show up in sourdough starters.

WORKING WITH DOUGH

Mixing and shaping dough can be done in many ways, whether by hand or machine. The current rage is to "properly undermix" the dough and then gently strengthen it by performing a series of stretches and folds followed by intervals of resting the dough. The intervals can range from just a few minutes up to an hour, depending on the dough and the philosophy of the baker. Commercial artisan bakeries often use what is called the improved mixing method, first articulated by the great baking teacher Raymond Calvel. It begins with mixing slowly and gently for 4 to 6 minutes to hydrate the ingredients and begin developing the gluten. This is followed by mixing more quickly and intensively for 2 to 4 minutes to fully organize the gluten. Other popular techniques include the autolyse, which consists of a first mixing cycle without salt—and sometimes even without yeast—followed by a brief rest, perhaps 20 minutes, before adding the remaining ingredients and mixing at medium speed for 4 to 8 minutes.

Most of the breads in this book are made using a short first mix followed by a series of stretch and fold sequences with short intervals between them. These methods aren't necessarily set in stone. The formulas are very flexible in terms of how they can be prepared. The photos that follow demonstrate the mixing and shaping methods I suggest, but if you have a good foundation in baking science and a preferred method of your own, feel free to use alternative techniques.

STRETCH AND FOLD

Lightly oil the work surface and place the dough on it. With wet or oiled hands, reach under the front end of the dough and stretch it out, then fold it back onto the top of the dough. Do this from the back end and then from each side. Then flip the entire mass of dough over and tuck it into a ball. The dough should be significantly firmer, though still very soft and fragile. Place the dough back in the bowl, cover the bowl, and let it sit at room temperature for 5 to 10 minutes. Repeat the stretch and fold process, then return the dough to the bowl again, cover the bowl, and let it sit at room temperature for 5 to 10 minutes more. Do this twice more. The entire process should be completed in less than 40 minutes. After the final stretch and fold, you can begin timing the first fermentation cycle or place the covered dough in the refrigerator, depending on the specific instructions in the recipe.

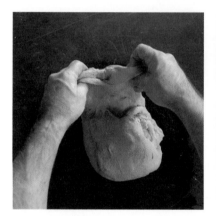 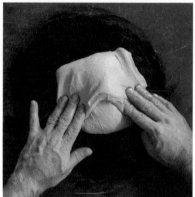 

Stretch and fold

SHAPING

Once the dough rises, you'll need to shape it before letting it proof at room temperature. I suggest these common loaves as a starting point, but there are many options and I encourage you to experiment once you are comfortable with these shapes.

Boules

To shape a boule, gently pat the risen dough into a rectangle, then bring all four corners together in the center. Squeeze the corners to seal them and tighten the skin of the dough to create surface tension. Use your hands to rotate the dough on the counter and make a tight, round ball. Using either the edge of your hand or your thumbs, press firmly on the bottom crease to exert pressure and tighten the surface. Flour a proofing basket or line a sheet pan with parchment paper, then dust it with flour, semolina, or cornmeal. Transfer the dough to the prepared proofing basket, seam side up, or place it on the prepared pan, seam side down, to proof.

Bâtards

To shape a classic bâtard, gently pat the risen dough into a thick rectangle. Fold the bottom half to the center and press with your fingertips to hold the dough in place and seal the seam. Fold the top half to the center and once again press with your fingertips to seal the seam. Roll the top half of the dough over the seam to create a new seam on the bottom of the loaf. Pinch the new seam closed with your fingertips

Shaping a boule

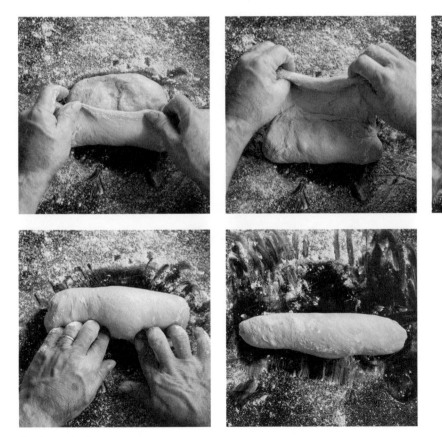

Shaping a bâtard

Shaping a sandwich loaf (page 24)

or the edge of your hand to create surface tension on the outer skin, making a tight loaf. Gently rock the loaf back and forth to extend it to the desired length, typically 6 to 12 inches. To create a torpedo shape, taper the loaf slightly at each end with increased hand pressure while rocking the loaf. Transfer the shaped loaf to a floured proofing cloth or an oiled sheet pan, seam side down, cover, and proof.

Baguettes

To shape a baguette, start by making a bâtard, as described above, then let it rest for 5 to 10 minutes. Repeat the same folding process: bottom to center, top to center, then pinching to create a seam. Seal the new seam with your fingers, thumbs, or the heel of your hand. It should create a tight surface tension. Then, with the seam side underneath, gently rock the loaf back and forth with your hands, moving out toward both ends and increasing the pressure at the ends to slightly taper the loaf. Repeat this rocking as needed until the baguette is the length of the sheet pan or baking stone. Transfer the shaped baguette to a floured proofing cloth or sheet pan that has been lightly misted with vegetable spray oil, cover, and proof.

Sandwich Loaves

To shape a sandwich loaf, flatten the dough into a 5 by 8-inch rectangle. Working from a 5-inch side of the dough, roll up the length of the dough. Pinch the final seam closed using your fingertips or the back edge of your hand. Gently rock the loaf to even it out. Don't taper the ends; keep the top surface of the loaf even. Put the loaf in an oiled pan, seam side down so it touches both ends of the pan; cover and proof.

Rolls and Buns

For round dinner rolls: Place a 2-ounce (56.5 g) piece of dough on the work surface, cup your hand around it, then rapidly rotate the dough in a circular motion, as if trying to push it through the work surface. If need be, wipe the work surface with a damp towel to create traction to help you round the dough into a tight, smooth ball. Transfer the rolls to a parchment-lined sheet pan, cover, and proof. For pull-apart rolls, assemble any number of rounded balls of dough on a parchment-lined pan, just touching, so they'll rise into one another. After they bake, the rolls will easily pull apart.

Q & A

How important is it to have the exact size of loaf pan called for?

Some of the recipes call for 4½ by 8-inch loaf pans. It isn't advisable to use smaller pans, unless making mini loaves, but if you only have larger loaf pans, they should work just fine. But the loaves may take longer to bake than specified and will probably not be as tall (or you can slightly increase the weight of the dough).

Do I need to adjust baking temperatures if using a convection oven?

Convection ovens are much more efficient than conventional ovens. However, many new convection ovens have two speeds of convection, so there is no single rule that assures a proper adjustment. My suggestion is that for convection ovens that offer a low setting, use that setting and decrease the temperature by 25°F (14°C). If the convection is very powerful, decrease the temperature by 50°F (28°C). The baking time is usually shorter in a convention oven than in a conventional oven, even with the reduced temperature, so you'll have to monitor the process and use the cues in the recipe to determine doneness.

How can I achieve a crisper crust?

After baking, turn off the oven and leave the bread in the oven for 5 to 10 minutes longer to drive off more moisture. If the crust is getting too dark, cover the bread loosely with aluminum foil. Alternatively, you can put baked, cooled bread in a hot oven (450°F / 232°C) for 5 minutes to recrisp the crust prior to serving.

For hoagies: Divide the dough into 4-ounce (113 g) pieces for 7-inch rolls or up to 8-ounce (227 g) pieces for foot-long rolls. Flatten each piece of dough with your hand, then form it into a 4-inch torpedo shape, or a 7-inch torpedo shape for foot-long rolls, much as you would a bâtard (see page 20). Let each piece of dough rest as you move on to the other pieces. When you return to the first torpedo, gently roll it back and forth to extend it out to about 7 inches, or 13 inches for a foot-long roll. The roll should have only a very slight taper at the ends. Place the rolls on a sheet pan lined with parchment paper or a silicone mat, spacing them about 2 inches apart. (The rolls may shrink back about 1 inch as you pan them.) Mist the tops of the rolls with vegetable spray oil, cover, and proof.

Bagels

To shape bagels, prepare a sheet pan by lining it with parchment paper or a silicone mat, then mist it with vegetable spray oil or lightly coat it with oil. Divide the dough into 6 to 8 equal pieces. (A typical bagel is about 4 ounces or 113 grams before baking, but you can make them smaller or larger. If you make more than 6 bagels, you may need to prepare two sheet pans.) Form each piece into a loose ball by rolling it on a clean, dry work surface with a cupped hand. (Don't use any flour on the work surface. If the dough slides around and won't ball up, wipe the surface with a damp paper towel and try again.) There are two methods to shape the balls into bagels.

The first method is to poke a hole through the center of the ball to create a donut shape. Holding the dough with both thumbs in the hole, rotate the dough with your hands, gradually stretching it to create a hole about 2 inches in diameter.

The second method, preferred by professional bagel makers, is to use both hands (and a fair amount of pressure) to roll the ball into a rope about 8 inches long on a clean, dry work surface. (Again, wipe the surface with a damp towel if necessary to create sufficient friction on the work surface.) Taper the rope slightly at each end and moisten the last inch or so of the ends, if needed. Place one end of the dough in the palm of your hand and wrap the rope around your hand to complete the circle, going between your thumb and forefinger and then all the way around. The ends should overlap by about 2 inches. Squeeze the overlapping ends together by closing your hand, then press the seam into the work surface, rolling it back and forth a

Float Test for Bagels

Remove the bagels from the refrigerator 60 to 90 minutes before you plan to bake them to test for readiness. Immediately check whether the bagels are ready for baking using the float test: Place one of the bagels in a small bowl of cold water. If it sinks and doesn't float back to the surface, shake it off, return it to the pan, and wait for another 15 to 20 minutes, then test it again. When one bagel passes the float test, they're all ready to be boiled. If they pass the float test before you are ready to boil and bake them, return them to the refrigerator so they don't overproof.

few times to seal. Remove the dough from your hand, squeezing it to even out the thickness, if need be, and creating a hole about 2 inches in diameter.

Place each shaped bagel on the prepared sheet pan, then mist with vegetable spray oil or brush with a light coating of oil. Cover the entire pan with plastic wrap and refrigerate overnight or for up to 2 days. (You can also proof the unshaped dough in an oiled bowl overnight and then shape the bagels on baking day.) Proof until they pass the float test, approximately 60 to 90 minutes, before boiling and baking.

PROOFING

After the dough is shaped, it usually needs anywhere from 1 to 2 hours at room temperature to rise, or proof (longer for some sourdough breads). You can accelerate the rising process by placing the dough in a warm place (see *Proof Box* on page 13). But if the dough warms up too quickly, the yeast ferments at a wildly uncontrollable pace. This can easily overferment the dough and ruin both the flavor and the color of the bread, so be careful! Whichever proofing method you use, when the dough has fully risen, gently transfer the dough onto a peel or the back of a sheet pan dusted with semolina, flour, or cornmeal, then proceed with scoring and baking.

Bannetons and Couches

Bannetons are baskets used to provide structure for dough as it proofs, and *couches* (which literally means "bed" or "diaper") are the linen proofing cloths many bakeries use for freestanding loaves. If you don't have professional bannetons or *couches*, you can improvise with standard kitchen equipment such as stainless steel or glass mixing bowls for bannetons and a white tablecloth or old pillowcase for a *couche*. The size of the bowl depends on the size of the loaf, but as a rule of thumb, the bowl needs to be twice as large as the piece of dough going into it to accommodate the rise.

To proof in a bowl, line a stainless steel or glass mixing bowl with a smooth, lint-free cloth napkin, scrap of fabric, or towel. Mist the fabric with vegetable spray oil, then lightly dust it with flour. Place the loaf in the bowl, seam side up, and mist the top with vegetable spray oil. Cover with flaps of the fabric or a separate cloth.

To proof in a cloth, lightly mist the surface with vegetable spray oil and dust with flour before transferring your loaves onto the cloth, spacing them about 3 inches apart. With the loaves placed, bunch up the fabric between the loaves to make walls to support the dough, then cover with more cloth or plastic wrap.

Sheet Pans

To proof on a sheet pan, line the pan with parchment paper, mist with vegetable spray oil, and dust with cornmeal, semolina, or flour. Mist the shaped dough with vegetable spray oil and loosely cover with plastic wrap or a towel.

SCORING

Scoring bread releases some of the trapped gas, which helps create proper crumb, and it makes for attractive loaves. To score loaves, wait until just prior to baking, then place the shaped dough on the back of a floured sheet pan or baking peel. Using a razor blade, *lame,* or serrated knife, score the loaf about ½ inch deep. If using a razor blade, keep the back end up so it doesn't drag through and tear the dough. I often tell my students to say the word *slit* when they make the cut to emphasize an action like slitting open an envelope over any other notion of cutting. The cut shouldn't go straight down but rather be on an angle, so that it's almost parallel to the surface of the bread. If you prefer to use a sharp serrated knife or another type of blade, remember to let the knife do the work and resist the urge to press down on the dough.

HEARTH BAKING AND CREATING STEAM

A number of the breads in this book are designed to be baked at high temperatures, preferably on a hearth of some type. A baking stone is the most popular option for home hearth baking, but not everyone has one. If you don't have a baking stone, it's perfectly okay to bake on a sheet pan. You also need steam to enhance oven spring and put a shiny, crackly crust on the bread. There are many ways to create a blast of steam, but my preferred method is to use a steam pan.

To prepare your oven for hearth baking, put a baking stone or sheet pan on the middle rack of the oven and a steam pan on the bottom. For the steam pan, you can improvise by using a sheet pan with a 1-inch rim, a casserole pan with taller sides, or a cast-iron frying pan. Preheat the oven for at least 45 minutes to fully heat the baking stone.

When you're ready to bake, slide the shaped dough onto the preheated baking stone, then lay a kitchen towel over the oven's glass window to protect it from any potential backsplash. Wearing an oven mitt to prevent burns, pour about 1 cup of hot water into the preheated steam pan. (I like using a watering can because of the control and distance the spout provides.) Using a spray bottle such as a plant mister, you can also spritz the oven walls a couple of times to create additional steam.

CHAPTER 2
A SOURDOUGH PRIMER

Every time I write a bread book, I find it necessary to update my previous instructions on how to make and work with sourdough starters. One reason is that I keep learning more about the world of natural leavening, and another reason is the natural variability in the world of microorganisms. What worked in the past for a starter or what works in some regions may not work in your neighborhood.

After perfecting what I thought was the simplest, most foolproof method for my book *The Bread Baker's Apprentice*, I discovered that it didn't always work. For many readers, the first stage of preparing the starter, creating a seed culture, wasn't proceeding as I'd said it would. I never had that problem, but based on emails I received (and continue to receive even now), the problem is apparently pretty widespread. In response, a team of amateur sleuths and passionate home bakers, led by chemist Debra Wink of Columbia, Missouri, tackled the problem on the King Arthur Flour website a few years ago in a discussion group called the Baking Circle. (This discussion is preserved in the King Arthur archives online, if you'd like to read it in full.)

The short story is that Debra put the starter under a microscope and came up with the theory that the cause of the problem was leuconostoc, a strain of lactic acid bacteria that generates a lot of carbon dioxide (as yeast does) but also temporarily interferes with the growth of wild yeast. Based on this discovery and feedback that I received from hundreds of home sourdough bakers, I've continued to tweak the method to make it as reliable as possible while also being flexible enough to work with different flours and in both firm starters and wet sponges.

This chapter offers my latest update, built upon what I've written before. However, if you use a different method or already have an established mother starter on hand, feel free to stick with what works for you.

UNDERSTANDING SOURDOUGH STARTERS

By *sourdough*, I mean dough leavened naturally, with wild yeast and bacteria, as opposed to dough leavened by commercial yeast. Breads leavened with sourdough starters have a number of appealing qualities, some related to flavor and some that are more romantic and evocative. There's something compelling about capturing wild yeast and bacteria and harnessing their ability to raise dough; it's very craft-like and artisanal.

Wild yeast starters go by any number of names, such as levain, chef, mother, madre, barm, wild yeast sponge, or simply sourdough starter. Because a sourdough starter must be fermented in advance, it functions very much like other types of pre-ferments as a flavor enhancer, while also often carrying most or all of the responsibility for leavening. However, the flavor of bread made with a sourdough starter is distinctive because a sourdough starter has a more complex flavor profile than a pre-ferment made with commercial yeast, such as a sponge, biga, or poolish. Therefore, sourdough starters are sometimes used in conjunction with commercial yeast to serve as a flavor booster more than as a leaven, such as in some rye breads.

The acidity generated in a sourdough starter is important for both flavor development and control of enzymatic activity in the dough. Many people also believe sourdough starters help with digestibility, as the naturally occurring yeast and bacteria essentially predigest the grains, making it easier for the body to break them down further.

There are many classic versions of sourdough bread, though they aren't always referred to as sourdough. Pain au levain, for instance, a classic French bread, is typically made using both natural leaven (*levain*) and a small spike of commercial yeast, which helps speed the process just enough to reduce the sourness. (Unlike Americans, the French prefer a less sour flavor profile and one Frenchman told me he thought of American sourdough as "ruined bread.")

The Science of Sourdough Starters

Before discussing considerations about sourdough starters when baking with sprouted flours, and before getting into the details of making a starter, I'd like to hone in on the science within a sourdough starter so you can understand the forces at play. The most common misperception about sourdough starters is that wild yeast is what causes the sour flavor, but there's actually a more complex microbial drama taking place. Various strains of wild yeast are living side by side with various strains of bacteria, and the bacteria cause the sour flavor as they metabolize sugars and convert them into lactic acid or acetic acid. I use the plural *strains* because wild yeast is not just one specific species, such as *Saccharomyces cerevisiae*, an organism in both commercial yeasts and the family of wild yeasts. "Wild yeast" refers to an indeterminate and variable number of strains, mostly within the species category *Saccharomyces exiguus*.

From a functional standpoint, the role of the wild yeasts is to leaven and slightly acidify the bread via production of carbon dioxide and ethyl alcohol, while the function of the bacteria is to acidify and flavor the dough and, to a lesser degree, create some carbon dioxide. The acidifying work of the bacteria lowers the pH level of the dough to create an environment ideal for the growth of the desired strains of wild yeast. As the dough becomes more acidic, commercial yeast, cultivated in the controlled conditions of a laboratory, doesn't survive, whereas wild yeast does. (In addition, acidity also controls the population of certain strains of bacteria, including leuconostoc.) Thus, the yeasts and bacteria exist in a state of symbiotic reciprocality that allows them to harmoniously share the same environment and food source while supplementing each other's work. In the process, different strains of bacteria interact with various strains of yeast to create different flavor compounds. This explains why breads made in various parts of the world may have different flavors even when made with the exact same formula and ingredients.

In essence, a sourdough starter is simply a medium in which microorganisms colonize and multiply, all the while creating important by-products, including alcohol, carbon dioxide, lactic acid, and acetic acid. In other words, dough fermentation. To harness this power, bakers use the amount of starter necessary to raise the final dough, which can range from 15% up to, in some instances, 100% of the weight of flour in the final dough. In most bakeries, it's usually in the range of 20% to 33%.

As you can see, this microbial world is very complicated. It's also very fortunate, as this complexity manifests itself in the final flavor of well-made bread, with a similar dynamic being at play in the creation of great cheeses, beers, and wines.

USING SOURDOUGH YEAST STARTERS WITH SPROUTED GRAIN FLOUR

As we explore the next frontier of bread, we must find the best ways to utilize sourdough starters with sprouted grain flours, which are inherently high in enzyme activity. This opens up a host of new questions: in particular, whether it's possible to make a sourdough starter with sprouted grain flour; and if so, whether this results in a superior final dough. I'll address those issues here, and what I have to say might surprise you.

As noted earlier, doughs made with sprouted grain flour don't benefit from the use of a pre-ferment as much as conventional doughs do. The flour is already preconditioned (though not technically pre-fermented) by the sprouting process, releasing its flavor. So why use a sourdough starter in sprouted flour breads? The main reason is that bacterial fermentation produces complex acidic flavors that are often beloved in bread. (See The Science of Sourdough Starters, page 33.) Therefore, a sourdough starter provides a level of complexity that sprouted flour can't attain on its own.

As mentioned, fermentation by bacteria and wild yeasts acts upon conventional, nonsprouted flour in a way that makes it more digestible. Sourdough bread is generally considered more healthful and more easily assimilated than commercially yeasted bread, and it seems that the longer the fermentation, the easier it is to digest. There's a growing community of serious sourdough bread enthusiasts who fervently believe that sourdough bread made via a long, super slow rising process is the only healthy bread, and they're probably correct, to a point. But when bread is made from sprouted flour, we don't need that benefit; the enzymatic activity initiated by the sprouting process accomplishes the same goal. So, in the end, it's all about flavor, as is often the case when it comes to food.

You may wonder whether you can make a wild yeast starter using sprouted grain flour. I've experimented with this, and I've found that it is possible, but it's tricky because there's so much enzyme activity in sprouted flour that it doesn't stand up well over the long duration required to building up the population of microorganisms. Although it certainly feeds and supports the microorganisms, sprouted flour more quickly loses its structural integrity. Therefore, I suggest beginning with nonsprouted flour and then later, when the time comes to make the final dough, possibly switching to sprouted grain flour to build an intermediate or final starter.

All of this science may seem unnecessary, but I assure you that understanding the underlying details will help you feel more confident in making and using your own starter. So let's begin. First I'll provide instructions for an all-purpose mother starter, one that can be used in any of the breads that call for natural starter or levain. Then, at the end of this chapter, I'll take you on a brief journey into another new frontier: a raisin wild yeast starter (see page 43). Later, in the Epilogue (page 225), I'll introduce you to yet another method for making starters—one that's so far on the outer edge of the bread revolution that it needs its own chapter.

MAKING A SEED CULTURE

There are many ways to make a seed culture. The simplest is with just flour and water, and while it generally works, it doesn't always develop on a predictable schedule. I've seen methods online that call for everything from onion skins, wine grapes, plums, or potatoes to milk, buttermilk, or yogurt. These can all serve as fuel for the microorganisms, and all will work for making a seed culture. But in the end, a starter (and bread in general) is really about fermented flour. So my goal is to use flour to create the conditions in which the appropriate organisms can flourish.

The following method produces a versatile starter that can be used to make both 100% sourdough breads and mixed-method breads, leavened with a combination of wild yeast starter and commercial yeast. The starter can be made from whole wheat flour, white flour, or whole rye flour. (Rye bread fanatics tend to keep a rye-only starter, but I've found that a wheat starter works just as well in rye breads.)

At this first stage, you aren't making the starter that goes into the final dough, but rather a "seed" starter used to create another starter: the mother starter. In most bakeries, the mother is used to build yet another starter, the levain, also called the chef in some bakeries, or simply the final starter. That's the one that goes into the final dough. For the purposes of small-batch home baking, you can generally use your mother starter as the final starter as long as it's been refreshed within the past 2 to 3 days.

THE PINEAPPLE JUICE SOLUTION

To avoid the timing problems of some of my earlier instructions, and to reflect the work of Debra Wink and her many cohorts in the King Arthur Baking Circle, I now use what I call "the pineapple juice solution" when creating a seed culture. Pineapple juice isn't the only acidic ingredient that can control leuconostoc bacteria, but it is reliable and can also reduce the time required to get a seed culture going by a couple of days. Other acidic fruit juices can do the same. Some of my recipe testers have reported great success with orange juice or diluted lemon juice.

Of course, you can also use water, but the pineapple juice introduces enough acidity to encourage the growth of wild yeast earlier in the process. If you prefer to use water, it's best to go with filtered or spring water to minimize chlorine, but I've made it with regular tap water too. Aerating the starter at least once every 8 hours by stirring it vigorously is helpful for stimulating the growth of wild yeast, as yeast multiplies more rapidly in the presence of oxygen. Being conscientious about stirring a starter can do wonders for a seed culture that's slow to develop.

Opinions are divided on whether it's necessary to use pineapple juice after Day 1. It probably isn't, but it won't hurt to use it on Day 2, and in some instances, it may serve as added insurance against overgrowth of leuconostoc. That said, it's fine to forgo the pineapple juice and simply use water after Day 1.

The four phases of seed culture (clockwise from top left)

A FEW WORDS ON TIMING

As you embark on the process below, be aware that, even with the pineapple juice solution, the timing of the various phases is approximate and can be greatly affected by the time of year, ambient temperature, and aeration. At cool temperatures, it may take twice as long for the seed culture to become active, and at warm temperatures it can happen very quickly. If the process seems to be taking longer than predicted, don't abandon it. Carry on, faithfully stirring the mixture at least once every 8 hours.

Another benefit of aeration is that it protects the seed culture from invasion by microorganisms that cause molds, which tend to settle on the surface and grow on the sides of the container. But if you stir regularly, the desired microorganisms will be distributed throughout the seed culture, enhancing their ability to destroy or control the invaders. This is especially important during the dormant phase, when it appears that nothing is happening.

Speaking of the dormant phase, don't be fooled by bubbling during the first day or two. This doesn't mean the starter is active; rather, it's probably evidence of leuconostoc or other bacteria. The starter will soon go through a seemingly dormant phase in which you might think something has gone wrong. This is just a transitional period during which the starter is slowly acidifying and the wild yeast and lactic acid bacteria are slowly multiplying. Again, continue to aerate faithfully, and wait for the signs of well-established fermentation, probably 5 to 9 days into the process.

If progress remains slow, you can repeat the Phase 4 step, or you can simply extend the waiting period between phases by a day or two. Often the key is to give the seed culture more time. In the end, the microbial good guys prevail.

PHASE 1 SPONGE (DAY 1)

NOTES:

• You can substitute white flour, but if you do, increase the amount by 1 tablespoon (0.3 oz / 8.5 g). This also applies to Phase 2.

• The temperature of the liquid doesn't matter (as long as it's not hot), and this remains true throughout the process.

• To make lemon water, combine 3 parts water with 1 part lemon juice.

INGREDIENT	VOLUME	OUNCES	GRAMS	%
whole wheat or whole rye flour (see at left)	3½ tablespoons	1	28.5	100
unsweetened pineapple juice (or filtered or spring water, orange juice, or lemon water; see at left)	¼ cup	2	56.5	200
TOTAL		3	85	300

Because the aim is to create a population of desirable microorganisms, all tools and bowls should be sanitized in advance, either in boiling water or in a dishwasher. In a small bowl, stir together the flour and juice with a spoon or whisk until the flour is fully hydrated, resulting in a sponge with the consistency of thin pancake batter. Cover the bowl with plastic wrap or a lid (not too tightly, so that the mixture can breathe). Leave the mixture out at room temperature for 48 hours, stirring it with a spoon or whisk several times each day, at 8-hour intervals, to aerate it. There will be few or no bubbles or other signs of fermentation during the first 24 hours. Bubbles should begin to appear within 48 hours, but even if they don't, move on to Phase 2.

PHASE 2
SPONGE (DAY 3)

INGREDIENT	VOLUME	OUNCES	GRAMS	%
whole wheat or whole rye flour	3½ tablespoons	1	28.5	100
unsweetened pineapple juice or filtered or spring water	2 tablespoons	1	28.5	100
Phase 1 Sponge	all	3	85	300
TOTAL		5	142	500

Add the new, Phase 2 ingredients to the Phase 1 sponge and stir with a spoon or whisk to distribute and fully hydrate the flour. Again, cover with plastic wrap or a lid and leave out at room temperature for 24 to 48 hours, stirring with a spoon or whisk several times each day. There should be signs of fermentation (bubbling and expansion) during this period. When the mixture becomes very bubbly or foamy, continue to Phase 3. If there isn't any bubbling after 48 hours, continue to stir at 8-hour intervals until the mixture begins to bubble. This may take a couple of extra days, but in most circumstances the bubbling will occur within 48 hours.

PHASE 3 DOUGH
(DAY 4 OR 5)

INGREDIENT	VOLUME	OUNCES	GRAMS	%
whole wheat or unbleached bread flour	⅓ cup	1.5	42.5	100
filtered or spring water	2 tablespoons	1	28.5	67
Phase 2 Sponge	all	5	142	334
TOTAL		7.5	213	501

Add the new, Phase 3 ingredients to the Phase 2 sponge and stir with a large spoon. Because of the reduced percentage of water, the sponge will become thicker, but it will still be very wet and sticky. Again cover with plastic wrap or a lid and leave out at room temperature for 24 to 48 hours, stirring with a wet spoon at least twice each day. Within 48 hours the mixture should be very bubbly and expanded. If not, let it develop for another day or two, stirring at 8-hour intervals, until it becomes active. If the Phase 2 sponge was very bubbly prior to this feeding, it could become active and bubbly in less than 24 hours. If so, proceed to Phase 4.

PHASE 4 DOUGH
(DAY 5 OR LATER)

INGREDIENT	VOLUME	OUNCES	GRAMS	%
whole wheat or unbleached bread flour	7 tablespoons	2	56.5	100
filtered or spring water	3 tablespoons	1.5	42.5	67
Phase 3 Dough	half	3.75	106	188
TOTAL		7.25	205	355

Discard or give away half of the Phase 3 dough. Add the new, Phase 4 ingredients to the remaining Phase 3 dough and stir with a large spoon. The seed culture will become firmer, but still be slightly sticky or very tacky. Again, cover with plastic wrap or a lid and leave out at room temperature until bubbly and foamy, with an aroma similar to apple cider vinegar. It should register between 3.5 and 4.0 if tested with pH paper, and should swell and nearly double in size, though it may fall when jostled. Completion of this phase can take anywhere from 4 to 24 hours. If there are few signs of fermentation after 24 hours, stir the seed culture as before or knead it, and continue to leave it out at room temperature, covered, until it rises. Once fermentation has reached this point, you can proceed to the next step, building the mother starter, or you can refrigerate the seed culture for up to 2 days before proceeding.

MAKING A MOTHER STARTER

Once you've established a seed culture, you need to convert it into a mother starter. This is the starter you'll keep perpetually in your refrigerator and use to make doughs. (In previous books I sometimes referred to this starter as a *barm*, but I've since learned from my wild yeast guru, Monica Spiller, that the term *barm* is more properly used for starters made with mashed [scalded] grain as the growth medium.)

To build your seed culture into a mother starter, you'll use a portion of it to inoculate a larger batch of flour and water and make a firm piece of dough. Although the seed culture is full of wild yeast and bacteria, its structure has been weakened by acidity and ongoing enzyme activity. To make the mother starter strong enough to function in the final dough, you'll use three times as much flour, by weight, as seed culture. Hydration will be 67% the weight of the new flour, to create a firm mother starter. (You could also use up to 100% water for a sponge starter, but the formulas in this book are based on using a firm mother starter at 67% hydration.)

A little seed culture goes a long way, so the following instructions call for discarding or giving away about half of the seed culture. (You can save somebody else a few days of work by giving them half of yours.) If you'd prefer to keep a larger mother

Does it matter whether I keep a wet sponge mother starter or a firm dough mother starter?

Q & A

Some people prefer a wet sponge because it's easy to rebuild: simply stir in new flour and water with a spoon. I used to follow this approach, but now I prefer to keep a firm mother starter. Despite requiring some kneading or mixing with a dough hook, it's also fairly easy to rebuild. The reason for my preference is that it holds its structural integrity longer than a sponge. Also, I like the flavor of a firmer starter; it seems slightly tangier and more acidic. However, if you prefer keeping a sponge starter at, say, 100% hydration (equal parts water and flour by weight), then you'll need to decrease the amount of water in the final dough accordingly. Since most of the formulas in this book use high-hydration ratios, the amount of adjustment will probably be only a matter of a tablespoon or two of water.

starter on hand, perhaps if you bake often or tend to bake larger batches, you can convert the entire seed culture into a mother starter by doubling the weight of the new flour and water. This will give you more than 3 pounds (1.36 kg) of starter. However, most home bakers prefer keeping a smaller batch.

MOTHER STARTER

INGREDIENT	VOLUME	OUNCES	GRAMS	%
unbleached bread flour or whole wheat flour	2⅔ cups	12	340	100
filtered or spring water	1 cup or 1 cup plus 2 tablespoons if using whole wheat flour	8 or 9 if using whole wheat flour	227 or 255 if using whole wheat flour	67 or 75
Phase 4 Seed Culture	about half	3.25	92	27
TOTAL		23.25 or 24.25	659 or 687	194 or 202

1 Combine all the ingredients in the bowl of a stand mixer fitted with the dough hook or in a large bowl. If using a stand mixer, mix on low speed for 1½ to 2 minutes; if mixing by hand, stir with a large spoon and then knead by hand until the flour is hydrated and a coarse, shaggy ball of dough forms. It will be slightly sticky.

2 Let the starter rest, uncovered, for 5 minutes, then mix or knead for 1 to 2 minutes, until the starter is fairly smooth and all the ingredients are evenly distributed. It should feel like soft bread dough; if using unbleached bread flour, the starter will be softer and more supple than if using whole wheat flour, which is more absorbent.

3 Mist a large bowl or container with vegetable spray oil and put the starter in the bowl. (The bowl or container should be large enough to contain the starter after it doubles in size.) Cover loosely with plastic wrap or with a lid and leave out at room temperature for 4 to 12 hours, until the starter is nearly double in size. It should have a pleasant aroma similar to apple cider vinegar and register 4.0 or less if tested with pH paper. If the starter hasn't risen much within 12 hours, reshape it into a ball, return it to the covered bowl, and leave it out for 4 to 12 hours longer. Eventually, it will spring to life.

4 When the starter is about double in size, degas it by kneading it for a few seconds. Then shape it back into a ball, return it to the container, cover, and refrigerate. It is now ready to use for building final dough or intermediate starters, such as levains. After a few hours, once the mother starter has cooled, vent any carbon dioxide buildup by opening the lid briefly, then cover the container tightly. The mother starter can be used directly as a final starter for up to 3 days or for building an intermediate starter for up to 7 days. To use it after these times, refresh all or part of it to make a new mother starter as described below.

REFRESHING THE MOTHER STARTER

If you haven't used the mother starter in the time frames outlined above, if it starts to get mealy, or if you're using it and running low, you'll need to refresh it. (This is also called feeding or rebuilding.) To do so, discard all but 3.25 ounces (92 g), and use the saved portion as a seed culture, repeating the process above. You can use more of the old mother starter if you want; just be sure to increase the amounts of new flour and water by the same ratio. For that matter, you can even begin with as little as 1 ounce (28.5 g) of starter, rebuild in increments over a couple of feedings, at a ratio of 4 to 1 or even 5 to 1 flour to starter. This is a good thing to do when you haven't used your mother starter for a while and plan to start baking bread again.

For example, you can use 1 ounce (28.5 g) of mother starter, 1 cup (4.5 oz / 128 g) of flour, and 6 tablespoons (3 oz / 85 g) of water. This will produce about 8 ounces (227 g) of dough that you can ferment as described above to create a new mother starter. You can then build all or part of that into an even larger piece by using the same ratios: 100% flour, 67% to 70% water (or up to 75% if using whole wheat flour), and 20% to 25% starter. For example, to build 7 ounces (198 g) of newly refreshed starter into a larger starter, you can add up to 35 ounces (992 g) of flour and about 24.5 ounces (695 g) of water, resulting in over 4 pounds (1.8 kg) of starter, probably more than you need unless you're making a number of loaves.

After a mother starter spends a few weeks in the refrigerator unrefreshed, its proteins and starches start to break down. The result is a starter with the structural strength of potato soup. This is okay, because the microorganisms are still viable though somewhat dormant (and maybe even a little drunk). Discard all but 1 ounce (28.5 g) of the old starter and build it back in stages using the 4-to-1 or 5-to-1 process described above. In a day or two, you'll have a strong and refreshed mother starter.

One final note on refreshing: The acidity of a mother starter should be between 3.5 and 4 on the pH scale. If you have pH paper, you can use it to test the pH of a small piece of starter. However, acidity is caused mainly by bacteria, and it doesn't serve one of the key functions of a starter: to provide leavening. For recipes leavened using solely sourdough starter, you must also see signs of growth in the starter, indicating that the yeasts are active and capable or reproducing. In a healthy starter, the yeast and bacteria are in a state of coexistence, with the exact composition being largely determined during the seed culture stage, and then maintained in the mother starter. However, temperature variations and long dormancy periods can affect the yeast more adversely than the bacteria, so it may be necessary to refresh an old starter with a few feedings to sufficiently bolster the yeast population.

AN ALTERNATIVE: RAISIN WATER

I've recently discovered an interesting method for making a wild yeast starter using raisins and water but no flour. This unique liquid starter is sometimes referred to as yeast water or raisin water. Jeffrey Hamelman, author of *Bread: A Baker's Book of Techniques and Recipes*, wrote about it in the Bread Bakers Guild of America newsletter (a great resource; see page 240 for details). After reading his article, I started looking into it on the Internet and found a number of variations for how to make it. The idea is to create a starter that has plenty of wild yeast but not a lot of bacterial fermentation, allowing for naturally leavened breads without a lot of lactic acid. This starter creates a distinct flavor profile that's very pleasant.

Interestingly, raisin skins do harbor a lot of wild yeasts, but few of these strains are used in bread baking. Debra Wink, who's establishing herself in the American baking community as a go-to person on matters of yeast and bacteria biochemistry, commented in the same newsletter that the yeasts found on raisins and grapes are primarily wine-producing yeasts, such as *Hanseniaspora* (aka *Kloeckera*) and other obscure strains, and very little *Saccharomyces cerevisiae* (the species used for commercial bread yeast). According to Debra, the wine yeasts require more vitamins than the raisin water can provide, and they also don't like acidity, which wild strains of *S. cerevisiae* can tolerate. As a result, there's a little fermentation from the wine yeasts at the beginning, and then the activity settles down a bit until *S. cerevisiae* and other wild bread yeasts catch up and the wine yeasts die off. By the fifth or sixth day, the raisin water starts to get potent with the right kinds of yeast, and the lactic acid bacteria, which have been held at bay because there's no flour for them to feed on, don't have much of a chance to get in on the action.

After reading about how others create these starters, I experimented and came up with my own method. In the end, it's all about raisins, water, and time. The method below indicates a certain timeline for development of sufficient microbial activity. However, in cooler temperatures, it could take as long as 8 or even 10 days for the yeast to become established. Just keep stirring or shaking as directed until the raisin water is bubbly.

The resulting raisin water can be used to create a firm starter that you can use in any recipe calling for a natural sourdough starter. You'll get all of the rise without the sour tang. You can also keep some or all of the firm starter as a mother starter. However, as you use this mother starter and refresh it with flour, it will gradually become more acidic, transitioning into a regular (tangy) sourdough starter.

RAISIN WATER

INGREDIENT	VOLUME	OUNCES	GRAMS
organic raisins	¼ cup	1.5	42.5
water (preferably filtered or spring)	1 cup plus 3 tablespoons	9.5	269
TOTAL		11	311.5

1 Put the raisins and 3 tablespoons (1.5 oz / 42.5 g) of the water in a sterilized jar or container and stir or shake to combine. Cover loosely with a lid, plastic wrap, or a towel. Put the jar in a warm place or a sunny part of the house and stir or shake it every 8 hours for 2 days.

2 On the third day, add ½ cup (4 oz / 113 g) of the water and continue shaking or stirring at 8-hour intervals.

3 On the fourth day, add the final ½ cup (4 oz / 113 g) of water and continue shaking or stirring at 8-hour intervals.

4 On the fifth or sixth day, when the water is bubbly, the raisins are floating to the top, and a whitish mold has formed on them, the seed culture is ready to use. Strain the liquid into a bowl, discarding the raisins and any sediment that has settled to the bottom. Use immediately, or refrigerate for up to 3 days before building the final starter.

FINAL STARTER

INGREDIENT	VOLUME	OUNCES	GRAMS	%
Raisin Water	¾ cup	6	170	66
whole wheat or unbleached bread flour or sprouted whole wheat flour	2 cups or 1⅔ cups	9 or 7	255 or 198	100
TOTAL		15 or 13	425 or 368	166

Mix and ferment as for Mother Starter (page 40).

CHAPTER 3
SPROUTED FLOUR BREADS

In the spring of 2010, a few months after my initial experiments with Joe Lindley's sprouted grain flour (see page 3), I met Peggy and Jeff Sutton at a baking summit in Denver, Colorado. The Suttons also have a sprouted mill: To Your Health Sprouted Flour Co. Unlike Joe, who I'd characterize as a miller who happens to sprout grain, the Suttons impressed me as sprouters who happen to mill. They operate out of Fitzpatrick, Alabama, a small farming community on the outskirts of Montgomery, and their expanding business is rapidly adding new jobs to the local economy. Unlike Lindley Mills, which currently makes only two sprouted grain flours (though one of them is a blend of five ingredients), the Suttons produce a line of about twenty different sprouted grain and bean flours, including spelt, yellow corn, blue corn, rye, amaranth, barley, black bean, and quinoa.

When I visited the Suttons in Fitzgerald in 2013, Peggy told me, "At first, I was baking for friends and farmers' markets out of my home. But the supply of sprouted grain flour was limited, so I created my own sprouting system using canning jars and tubs with screened lids. I dedicated one room of our new barn to sprouting, another to drying the sprouts, and another to grinding the sprouts into flour with a small stone mill. Before long, demand for my sprouted flour outgrew this system, so I took over Jeff's barn completely. Eventually he built *another* new barn behind the house, and we moved the operation over there. Three years ago we ran out of room again, so we took the plunge and built this facility on some of our farmland. A few weeks ago we held a dedication ceremony for yet another new building, which will house an entirely gluten-free milling and packaging operation. The demand just keeps growing, and so does our operation."

As Peggy toured me around the two buildings, I saw millet soaking in dozens of large buckets, hundreds of pounds of corn kernels revolving in mechanically operated sprouting tumblers, and perhaps thousands of pounds of sprouted wheat and spelt air-drying in rooms dedicated to that purpose. Compared to some mills I've visited, the Suttons' operation is relatively modest, processing about 5,600 pounds of sprouted flour per day, but it's miles beyond where they were when I first met them in Denver. These days, they're providing flour for large bakeries, such as the Whole Foods Market Bakehouses, and they also supply the flour for a few prestigious private-label packagers. In addition, Internet sales via their website continue to enjoy rapid growth, spurred on by word of mouth and Peggy's blog.

When the new facility is complete, they'll be able to increase production to 10,000 pounds per day, nearly double their current volume. I asked if that will be enough to keep up with the demand, and Jeff said, "Probably for a short while, but we're already looking at building out more of the property. We'll just keep putting up new buildings as the demand rises."

I told the Suttons about my concern that large flour companies will simply wait for them to create the market and then swoop in with deeper pockets and try to steal it away. While they share that concern, they pointed out that it takes a lot of work to do it right. They're hoping that the big companies will just buy the flour from them, rather than try to make it themselves. Time will tell. It's difficult to know what will happen, especially since sprouted flour is still a niche market. But, as we've seen with craft beer, farmstead cheese, and other artisan producers, there is a pattern of big companies sweeping aside innovators.

FROM SPROUT TO MASS MOVEMENT

To Your Health Sprouted Flour Co. and Lindley Mills aren't the only producers of sprouted flour, though they are among the larger companies at the moment. Other players already in the game include Arrowhead Mills, Essential Eating Sprouted Foods, and Shiloh Farms, as well as Canadian companies such as One Degree Organic Foods and Anita's Organic Mill. (See the Resources section for other suppliers and contact information.) Clearly, sprouted foods are no longer a cult phenomenon or my own secret little discovery, and it's only going to get bigger.

Joe Lindley has been milling high-quality organic flour for nearly forty years. His first sale was made on July 4, 1976, a year after he bought back and restored the family's abandoned mill, which sits on the site of the 1781 Battle of Lindley's Mill, which took place during the Revolutionary War. He told me that he's been seeking better ways of milling flour to achieve maximum flavor and nutrition ever since he reestablished the mill, but it wasn't until about 2007 that he discovered the possibilities of sprouted flour. He now believes that this will be his most important contribution to the world of flour, and he's prepared to stake his future on it, though he will continue to mill traditional organic flour for his regular customers.

I think the Suttons feel the same way. Peggy Sutton and Joe Lindley have only met each other once, at the annual Asheville Bread Festival, where I introduced them in 2011. However, I view them as kindred spirits, even though their personalities are very different. Like every other miller I know, both are genuinely nice, and both are driven by their sense of mission yet are not evangelical or pushy. I think their patience must be governed by an inner knowing that their products speak for themselves and will eventually win the day. Besides, both are growing their businesses as fast as they can while, wisely, not getting too far ahead of themselves.

This brings me to the obvious question: Why are they so willing to stake their future on sprouted flour, and why have I become such an advocate of this new approach? As usual, it starts with flavor. Flavor always rules when it comes to economic viability in the world of food. However, there's much more to commend sprouted grain flours.

WHY SPROUTED GRAIN FLOUR IS THE NEXT FRONTIER

The statement with which I am most associated in the bread world is probably this: "The baker's mission is to evoke the full potential of flavor trapped in the grain." In previous books, I've described how bakers use various fermentation and mixing methods to accomplish this. In brief, the flavor trapped in the grain mostly resides in the sugars within the starch, and other potential flavors can be evoked from the grain through fermentation, both fungal (via yeast) and bacterial.

Twenty years ago, few American bakers knew about tricks such as using pre-ferments and harnessing enzyme activity to release simple sugars from starches. Now it seems as if these tricks are common knowledge, and the current generation of superb bread books continues to advance the ongoing discovery process. But sprouted flour is new territory; it's different from anything previously seen in the artisan bread movement. And what I especially love about it is that it can accomplish everything we strive to achieve through the use of pre-ferments and extending fermentation time, and it does so before the grain is even turned into flour!

Another benefit of using sprouted flour is that it means using the whole kernel—the entire grain or seed. And by germinating grains and seeds we actually enhance their nutritional benefits, allowing us receive the maximum nutritional benefit inherent in the grain. When a seed is germinated by soaking in water, this activates enzymes that initiate the transformation of the germ into a viable growing organism. To support that process, the nutritional value of the seed improves. In addition, sprouting softens the bran, reduces its phytic acid, renders it less bitter, and makes the grain's minerals more bioavailable. And when those grains or seeds are ground into flour, the resulting bread tastes better, is higher in nutrients, and is also easier to digest, allowing the body to access more of its nutrients.

Anecdotal reports also indicate that some people who are usually sensitive to wheat can tolerate sprouted wheat without typical reactions, such as indigestion or rashes. However, this is not yet hard science and must be subjected to rigorous testing. And it definitely doesn't apply to people with celiac disease or others who are highly sensitive to wheat.

Sprouting and Drying Grains for Flour

Before the recipes, I'll briefly review the process of sprouting seeds and preparing them for milling. If you've ever grown bean or alfalfa sprouts you'll instantly recognize the early steps in this method:

1. Rinse the seeds in fresh, cool water. Some seeds, including quinoa, are coated with a bitter resin, and these require two or three rinses.

2. Cover the seeds in fresh water and let them sit at room temperature for about 3 to 5 hours.

3. Drain the water and rinse and drain the seeds again. The germination process has begun.

4. Rinse the seeds again before retiring for the night, and let them drain in either a strainer, a jar fitted with a screened lid, or any container that allows the water to drain away.

5. The following morning (or later if the room is cool), you should see the beginning of a sprout: a nub breaking through the skin, or bran, of the seed. Technically, the seed is a sprout as soon as the nub appears, but the ideal time to move to the drying step is when the nub splits into two thin shoots. At this point the seeds have become vegetables and are much more digestible.

6. Dry the sprouts on a screen or perforated pan, setting up a fan to blow air across the surface. Alternatively, you can use a food dehydrator, but don't put them in a gas oven, as even just the pilot light can generate too much heat and denature the enzymes. Moving air is really the key, whether at room temperature or slightly warmer. The shoots will shrivel back into the seeds as they dry out. About 12 hours later, the seeds will be as dry as they were before you soaked them. They are now ready to be milled into flour. It's as simple as that.

TECHNICAL CONCERNS

Although the nutritional profile of sprouted flour is clearly superior, artisan bakers have rightly been concerned about whether the gluten quality of the wheat is compromised by the enzyme activity and release of natural sugars caused by sprouting. Would the resulting dough hold together when rising and still provide enough starch to fill the body of the loaf?

As I'll discuss later in the book, there are already methods for using sprouted grain pulp (also known as sprouted mash) to make popular, delicious, and commercially successful breads. However, those breads usually include a substantial amount of vital wheat gluten. Independently, both Peggy Sutton and Joe Lindley discovered that if they source their grain carefully and select high-quality, high-protein wheat, their sprouted whole wheat flour performs well with no need for supplemental gluten. (That said, some commercial bakeries do spike their sprouted flour doughs with a bit of vital wheat gluten to ensure consistent performance and loaf size.)

In addition, the natural enzyme activity triggered by soaking and germinating the seeds can enhance the performance of dough. Some of the enzymes remain active in the dough and continue to release sugars from the starches while the dough is fermenting, in the process feeding yeast and bacteria and promoting rapid fermentation. So whereas a dough made with standard, nonsprouted flour might require many hours of slow fermentation or supplementation with a pre-ferment to release so much flavor, similar results can be achieved much more quickly with sprouted flour. In most cases, all that's required is about 1½ hours for the first rise and 1 to 1½ hours for a final rise after shaping. I think the resulting flavor is as good as that of breads made with long-rising doughs—and actually even better, as you'll discover when you make some of the recipes in this chapter.

Q & A

Where can I get sprouted grain flour?

Sprouted grain flours are showing up on baking shelves in supermarkets nationwide, usually in small bags, from brands including Arrowhead Mills and One Degree. For more information on buying these flours directly from millers by mail order, see the Resources section on page 240.

Will pre-ferments, such as a poolish, biga, or sponge, improve breads made with sprouted flour? How about the overnight cold fermentation technique?

The purpose of pre-ferments is to condition flour through long, slow fermentation, coaxing more flavor from the grain and developing acidity. This preconditioned dough is added to the final dough to, in essence, age it and imbue it with more flavor. Overnight cold fermentation is another way to lengthen the development time to evoke more flavor. Because sprouted flour is already preconditioned, with flavor being released during the sprouting process, breads made with sprouted flour will taste much the same whether made with or without pre-ferments or cold fermentation.

There's no harm in using pre-ferments and overnight cold fermentation, but they aren't necessary. The one exception is wild yeast sourdough starters (which in essence are another type of pre-fermented dough). One of the functions of a sourdough starter, aside from raising the dough, is to introduce specific acidic, tangy flavors created by bacterial fermentation. So when making sprouted flour sourdough breads, you do need to use a sourdough starter to achieve the flavor complexity that it provides. (For more on starters, see pages 32–34.)

Can I use the Dutch oven baking method for some of these breads even if you don't call for it?

Yes. This method of baking, made popular by Jim Lahey (*My Bread*) and Chad Robertson (*Tartine Bread*), is always an option, especially for breads made with wet, high-hydration doughs. I'm fond of baking in a cloche (clay baking pot), rather than a Dutch oven. The recipes in this book most suited for that baking method are Sprouted Whole Wheat Bread (page 63), Sprouted Pain au Levain (page 66), Whole-Milled Lean Dough French Bread (page 165), and High-Extraction Pain au Levain (page 183).

What are ancient grains?

The term *ancient grain* is a little confusing, since all grains are ancient or come from ancient strains. However, the term has come to signify heirloom varieties or grains that have undergone little or no intentional crossbreeding or hybridization. For wheat, this includes einkorn, emmer, spelt, and Kamut (aka Khorasan wheat). However, the term *ancient grain* also refers to a whole gamut of other grains, such as buckwheat, quinoa, amaranth, millet, sorghum, and even rice, corn, barley, and oats—some of which aren't even technically grains!

Are ancient grains gluten-free? And if they are, how does this impact bread making?

Because many so-called ancient grains are gluten-free (only wheat, rye, and barley naturally contain gluten-forming proteins), the term *ancient grain* (see opposite) often gets lumped in with *gluten-free*, but this is imprecise at best. Amaranth, buckwheat, corn, millet, oats, quinoa, rice, sorghum, teff, and wild rice are all gluten-free.

Because they don't contain gluten, they tend to weaken the gluten structure of doughs made with wheat. For this reason, unless you're purposely making a gluten-free product, I suggest using no more than 20% gluten-free flour in place of wheat flour in a recipe. For more on gluten-free baking, see page 190.

Can I substitute one kind of ancient grain flour for another?

For the most part, yes. Joe Lindley has created a five-grain ancient grain blend, but other companies, including To Your Health Sprouted Flour Co., sell a variety of individual sprouted flours, and you can use

these to create your own blends. Feel free to mix and match or make substitutions as long as you stay within the same proportional ratios.

Can I use regular whole grain flour in place of the sprouted flour in these recipes?

In theory, nonsprouted flour can be substituted for sprouted, but the two don't perform in exactly the same way. If you study chapter 5, on whole grain and whole-milled bread, you'll see that the recipes using nonsprouted flours almost always

utilize pre-ferments or cold fermentation to release the full flavor potential from the grain. Therefore, I don't recommend substituting nonsprouted for sprouted flour in any of the recipes in chapter 3 without also modifying the fermentation process.

Can sprouted and nonsprouted flours be combined in some recipes?

Yes, and some bakeries are already doing exactly this. But for the purposes of this book, I've mostly separated the two types of flour, using only one or the other in any given recipe. However, there's no reason why you can't add sprouted flour to a

nonsprouted mix. One of the goals of this book is to give you the tools to create your own variations. After you experiment with the recipes here, you can apply similar methods to create an infinite number of variations.

Can I make a sourdough starter using sprouted flour?

While you can make a mother starter using sprouted flour, I recommend against it. Sprouted flour has so much enzyme activity that it tends to overripen quickly, breaking down into a mush within a few days. The yeast and other microorganisms are still viable, but the dough has no gluten structure, so it has to be rebuilt over

a couple of feedings before it can be used. Therefore, I suggest keeping a traditional mother starter, made with bread flour or whole wheat flour, and converting a portion of that into a sprouted starter shortly before you'll use it. For more on sourdough starters, see chapter 2.

SPROUTED WHEAT PANCAKES

MAKES 5 LARGE PANCAKES OR 16 SILVER DOLLAR-SIZE PANCAKES

I thought it best to start off with a recipe that's very simple and quickly demonstrates the attributes of sprouted flour. If I'm not mistaken, once you try it, you'll immediately seek out a bulk supplier for your sprouted flour pantry. These are the best pancakes I've ever eaten, period. They're so naturally sweet and creamy that you really don't need butter or maple syrup on top. But since that might be tampering with sacred ritual, I'll leave it up to you. This same batter can be used in a waffle iron to make fabulous waffles; see the variations at the end of the recipe for details.

BATTER

INGREDIENT	VOLUME	OUNCES	GRAMS	%
sprouted whole wheat flour	1 cup plus 1 tablespoon	4.5	128	100
salt	¼ teaspoon	0.06	1.5	1.1
baking soda	½ teaspoon	0.11	3	2.3
sugar, honey, or agave nectar	1 teaspoon	0.25	7	5.5
buttermilk	1½ cups	12	340	266
egg, slightly beaten	1	1.75	50	39
unsalted butter, melted	2 tablespoons	1	28.5	22
TOTAL		19.67	558	435.9

1 In a medium bowl, stir together the flour, salt, baking soda, and sugar (if using honey or agave nectar, add it to the buttermilk in the next step). In a separate bowl, whisk together the buttermilk, egg, and melted butter, then pour into the flour mixture. Stir with a large spoon just until the flour is hydrated; don't overmix. The result will be a fairly thin, pourable batter; it will thicken slightly as it sits, so don't add more flour. Transfer the batter to a measuring cup with a pouring spout (or leave it in the bowl and portion it with a ladle).

2 Preheat a nonstick skillet or griddle over medium heat.

3 Put about 1 teaspoon of butter or oil in the hot pan, just enough to thinly coat the surface. Lower the heat to just below medium. Pour in batter to make pancakes of the desired size. You may need to tilt the pan to spread the batter into an even circle. Cook until the bottom is rich golden brown and bubbles form on the top, 2½ to 3 minutes for larger pancakes, and less for smaller pancakes. Flip and cook until the other side is golden brown, about 2½ minutes.

4 Serve hot, or keep the pancakes in a warm oven at about 200°F (93°C) while cooking the remaining pancakes.

CONTINUED

Variations

SPROUTED WHEAT FLOUR WAFFLES: You can cook this batter in a waffle iron. If making waffles, I recommend doubling the recipe, since the waffle iron gobbles up a lot of batter. Also, separate the eggs. Add the yolks to the batter, and whip the whites until stiff, then fold them into the batter for additional aeration. To cook, follow the instructions for your waffle iron.

SPROUTED MULTIGRAIN PANCAKES: Replace about ¼ cup (1.1 oz / 30 g) of the sprouted whole wheat flour with an equal amount of any combination of other sprouted flours, such as corn, buckwheat, millet, sorghum, or quinoa.

BLUEBERRY PANCAKES: Add 1 cup of fresh or frozen blueberries (or other fresh berries) to the batter.

SPROUTED WHEAT OR SPELT QUICK BREAD

MAKES 1 LOAF

Peggy Sutton, founder of To Your Health Sprouted Flour Co., has been making variations of this bread for years, both for her family and to sell at local farmers' markets. You can make it with any kind of sprouted flour, even gluten-free sprouted flours, as long as the total weight of flour remains the same. This version showcases sprouted wheat or sprouted spelt flour, the latter one of Peggy Sutton's best-selling alternative flours. Because this bread is leavened only with baking soda, it falls in the category of chemically leavened breads, more commonly known as quick breads. The acidity of the buttermilk is necessary to activate the baking soda and generate carbon dioxide to raise the dough. If you prefer a more highly leavened bread, you can also add 1 tablespoon of baking powder, but try it first with only the baking soda. This master recipe lends itself to a wide range of variations, and you'll find a number of suggestions at the end of the recipe. While you can bake this in muffin pans, it will not be as sweet as you may be hoping. Try the next recipe for muffins (page 58).

BATTER

INGREDIENT	VOLUME	OUNCES	GRAMS	%
sprouted wheat flour (or sprouted spelt flour)	3 cups plus 3 tablespoons (or 3 cups plus 6 tablespoons)	13.5	383	100
salt	1 teaspoon	0.25	7	1.8
baking soda	2½ teaspoons	0.5	14	3.7
buttermilk	2 cups	16	454	119
eggs, slightly beaten	3	5.25	149	39
honey	6 tablespoons	4	113	30
unsalted butter, melted	¼ cup	2	56.5	15
TOTAL		41.5	1,176.5	308.5

1 Position a rack in the middle of the oven and preheat the oven to 350°F (177°C). Mist a 4½ by 8-inch loaf pan with vegetable spray oil; alternatively, brush the pan with melted butter, then dust with sprouted flour. You can also bake this bread in an 8-inch or larger round cake pan. In that case, cut a round of parchment paper to fit into the bottom of the pan and then prepare the pan as above.

2 In the bowl of a stand mixer fitted with the paddle attachment, or in a large bowl, stir together the flour, salt, and baking soda (on low speed if using a stand mixer). In a separate bowl, whisk together the buttermilk, eggs, honey, and melted butter, then pour into the flour mixture. Mix or stir until the flour is hydrated and all the

CONTINUED

ingredients are well combined, about 1 minute. The result should be a thick, soupy batter. Transfer the batter to the prepared pan.

3 Bake for 45 minutes, then rotate and bake for 30 to 45 minutes longer, until the top is golden brown and springy to the touch and a toothpick inserted in the center comes out clean. If the top is golden brown but the center seems doughy or too soft, tent the pan with aluminum foil, lower the temperature to 325°F (163°C), and continue baking until a toothpick comes out clean.

4 Let cool in the pan for at least 30 minutes. Run an icing spatula or something similar around the edges to separate the bread from pan, then transfer the bread to a wire rack. Let cool for at least 30 minutes longer before slicing and serving.

Variations

APRICOT ALMOND QUICK BREAD: When mixing the final batter, add 1 tablespoon (0.42 oz / 12 g) almond extract, 1 teaspoon (0.14 oz / 4 g) vanilla extract, and about ½ cup (3 oz / 85 g) chopped dried apricots. Sprinkle about ½ cup (1.65 oz / 47.5 g) sliced or slivered almonds over the loaf before baking.

CINNAMON RAISIN QUICK BREAD: When mixing the final batter, add 2 tablespoons (0.55 oz / 15.5 g) ground cinnamon, 1 tablespoon (0.42 oz / 12 g) vanilla extract, 1 teaspoon (0.07 oz / 4 g) cinnamon oil (optional), and 1 cup (6 oz / 170 g) raisins.

LEMON POPPY SEED QUICK BREAD: When mixing the final batter, add 1½ table-spoons (0.55 oz / 15.5 g) lemon extract, 1 teaspoon (0.07 oz / 4 g) vanilla extract, 1 tablespoon (0.75 oz / 21.5 g) ground dried lemon peel or the grated zest of 1 lemon, and 1 tablespoon (0.32 oz / 9 g) poppy seeds, or more to taste.

ROSEMARY WALNUT QUICK BREAD (PICTURED OPPOSITE): When mixing the final batter, add 1½ teaspoons (0.16 oz / 4.5 g) ground dried rosemary, 1½ teaspoons (0.03 oz / 1 g) rosemary leaves (fresh or dried), and ½ teaspoon (0.05 oz / 1.5 g) ground sage. Sprinkle ½ to ¾ cup (2 to 3 oz / 56.5 to 85 g) coarsely chopped wal-nuts over the loaf before baking.

HERBED QUICK BREAD: When mixing the final batter, add 1½ teaspoons (0.03 oz / 1 g) dried dill weed, 1 teaspoon (0.02 oz / 0.5 g) dried tarragon, and ½ teaspoon (0.007 oz / 0.2 g) each oregano, basil, and thyme.

SPROUTED WHEAT QUICK BREAD OR MUFFINS

MAKES 1 LARGE LOAF OR 12 TO 18 MUFFINS | **MASTER FORMULA**

Quick breads and muffins are essentially the same product in two different formats. There are many ways to make them, but in the end, they're
all chemically leavened, using baking powder, baking soda, or both, rather
than yeast. The recipe below is a template you can use to make any number of variations. I've included several suggestions for variations, but feel
free to experiment and come up with your own creations once you become
comfortable with the recipe. You'll notice that I've included sprouted spelt
flour and sprouted wheat pastry flour as options. Either will work well, and
both are becoming increasingly available.

BATTER

INGREDIENT	VOLUME	OUNCES	GRAMS	%
sprouted wheat flour (or sprouted wheat pastry flour or sprouted spelt flour)	3¾ cups (or 4 cups)	16	454	100
baking powder	1 tablespoon plus 1 teaspoon	0.75	21.5	4.7
baking soda	1¼ teaspoon	0.25	7	1.5
salt	¾ teaspoon	0.19	5.5	1.2
brown sugar (or honey or agave nectar)	1 cup plus 2 tablespoons (or ¾ cup plus 1½ tablespoons)	9	255	56
buttermilk	2 cups	16	454	100
eggs, slightly beaten	3	5.25	149	33
vegetable oil or melted unsalted butter	¾ cup	6	170	37
vanilla extract	2 teaspoons	0.28	8	1.8
Streusel Topping (optional; see sidebar page 60)				
TOTAL		53.72	1,524	335.2

1 Position a rack in the middle of the oven and preheat the oven to 350°F (177°C).
Prepare a 4½ by 8-inch loaf pan or a 12-cup muffin pan. For a loaf pan, generously
mist with vegetable spray oil; alternatively, brush the pan with melted butter, then
dust with sprouted flour. For a muffin pan, line the muffin cups with paper liners, then
mist the liners with vegetable spray oil.

2 In the bowl of a stand mixer fitted with the paddle attachment, or in a large bowl,
stir together the flour, baking powder, baking soda, and salt (on low speed if using
a stand mixer). Stir in the sugar (if using honey or agave nectar, add it to the buttermilk in the next step). In a separate bowl, whisk together the buttermilk, eggs,

CONTINUED

oil, and vanilla extract, then pour into the flour mixture. Mix or stir until the flour is hydrated and all the ingredients are well combined, about 1 minute. The result should be a thick batter, which will thicken further as it sits. Transfer the batter to the prepared pan, filling a loaf pan to within ¾ inch of the rim and muffin cups to just below the rim. Sprinkle the streusel topping over the top if desired.

3 Bake for 20 minutes for muffins or 30 minutes for a loaf, then rotate and bake for 15 to 20 minutes longer for muffins, or 25 to 35 minutes longer for a loaf, until the top is golden brown and springy to the touch and a toothpick inserted in the center comes out clean.

4 Let cool in the pan for at least 15 minutes for muffins or 30 minutes for a loaf. Turn out onto a wire rack and let cool for at least 10 minutes longer for muffins or 30 minutes longer for a loaf before serving.

Variations

When making some of these variations, you may end up with extra batter. You can bake it in an additional muffin pan, a mini loaf pan, or even ovenproof ramekins. Stored in a covered container, the batter will keep for 3 days in the refrigerator or 3 months in the freezer.

BLUEBERRY QUICK BREAD OR MUFFINS: When mixing the final batter, add up to 3½ cups (about 18 oz / 510 g) fresh or frozen blueberries to the final batter. If using frozen blueberries, toss them in ¼ cup (about 1.1 oz / 30 g) sprouted flour before adding them, to prevent clumping and sinking.

Streusel Topping

½ cup (about 2.1 oz / 60 g) sprouted flour (any type)

½ cup (4 oz / 113 g) white or brown sugar

⅛ teaspoon (0.03 oz / 1 g) salt

¼ teaspoon (0.02 oz / 0.5 g) ground cinnamon (optional)

¼ cup (2 oz / 57.5 g) unsalted butter

In a small bowl, stir together the flour, sugar, salt, and cinnamon. Melt the butter, then pour it in and stir until evenly distributed. Use your fingers to break the mixture into fine crumbs. If it's too warm to crumble, wait for it to cool, then crumble it again. Alternatively, use cold butter and pulse all the ingredients in a food processor until the texture resembles fine cornmeal.

CRANBERRY QUICK BREAD OR MUFFINS (PICTURED ON PAGE 59): Replace ½ cup (4 oz / 113 g) of the buttermilk with ½ cup (5 oz / 142 g) thawed orange juice concentrate, and, optionally, add ½ teaspoon (0.07 oz / 2 g) lemon or orange extract to the buttermilk mixture. When mixing the final batter, add 2½ cups (about 9 oz / 255 g) fresh or frozen cranberries.

BANANA QUICK BREAD OR MUFFINS: Mash 3 or 4 ripe bananas and add them to the buttermilk mixture, along with 1 teaspoon (0.14 oz / 4 g) banana extract, if you have it on hand. Optionally, when mixing the final batter, add 1½ cups (6 oz / 170 g) coarsely chopped toasted walnuts or pecans (see page 101 for toasting instructions).

POPPY SEED QUICK BREAD OR MUFFINS: Add up to 1 cup (5 oz / 142 g) poppy seeds to the flour mixture. Optionally, add 1 teaspoon (0.14 oz / 4 g) lemon extract to the buttermilk mixture.

ZUCCHINI QUICK BREAD OR MUFFINS: Add 4 cups (16 oz / 454 g) grated zucchini to the buttermilk mixture. Optionally, when mixing the final batter add 1½ cups (9 oz / 255 g) raisins and 1½ cups (6 oz / 170 g) coarsely chopped walnuts or pecans (toasted if you like; see page 101).

CARROT QUICK BREAD OR MUFFINS: Add 2 teaspoons (0.18 oz / 5 g) ground cinnamon to the flour mixture. Add 4 cups (16 oz / 454 g) grated carrots and ¼ cup (2.5 oz / 71 g) molasses to the buttermilk mixture. When mixing the final batter, add 1½ cups (9 oz / 255 g) raisins and, optionally, 1½ cups (6 oz / 170 g) coarsely chopped walnuts or pecans (toasted if you like; see page 101).

CHOCOLATE CHIP QUICK BREAD OR MUFFINS: When mixing the final batter, add 2½ cups (15 oz / 425 g) chocolate chips.

CHOCOLATE CHERRY QUICK BREAD OR MUFFINS: When mixing the final batter, add 2½ cups (15 oz / 425 g) chocolate chips and 3 cups (26.5 oz / 751 g) fresh or frozen sour pie cherries, or 2 cups (12 oz / 340 g) dried cherries.

APPLE BRAN QUICK BREAD OR MUFFINS: Add ½ cup (2 oz / 56.5 g) wheat bran or oat bran to the dry ingredients. Increase the buttermilk to 2½ cups (20 oz / 567 g) and add ¼ cup (2.5 oz / 71 g) molasses to the buttermilk mixture. When mixing the final batter, add 2 large apples, peeled and chopped into ½-inch pieces, and 1 cup (6 oz / 170 g) raisins.

SPROUTED WHOLE WHEAT BREAD

MAKES 1 LARGE LOAF, 2 SMALLER LOAVES, OR UP TO 15 ROLLS | **MASTER FORMULA**

This master dough can be used to make bread in any shape or size. It showcases the natural sweetness and tenderness of sprouted whole wheat flour without any added oil, fat, or other enrichments, such as milk, eggs, or sweeteners. Sprouting the wheat changes it so much that many of the "rules" for artisan breads, such as using pre-ferments and long, slow rising times, are unnecessary. The aims of those techniques can be achieved in less time with sprouted flour because the sprouting phase has already accomplished what pre-ferments and long fermentation typically do.

I suggest that you make this bread before attempting any of the more elaborate recipes that follow. This will familiarize you with the flavors and performance of sprouted whole wheat flour. In fact, it may be the only recipe you need for everyday breads, as it works equally well as a loaf pan bread and a crusty hearth bread.

DOUGH

INGREDIENT	VOLUME	OUNCES	GRAMS	%
sprouted whole wheat flour	3¾ cups	16	454	100
salt	1 teaspoon	0.25	7	1.6
instant yeast	1½ teaspoons	0.16	4.5	1
water, at room temperature	3¼ cups	14.5	411	90
TOTAL		30.91	876.5	192.6

1 In the bowl of a stand mixer fitted with the paddle attachment, or in a large bowl, stir together the flour, salt, and yeast (on low speed if using a stand mixer). Add the water and mix or stir until the flour is hydrated and a coarse, wet dough forms, about 1 minute. Don't add more flour, as the dough will thicken while it rests.

2 Let the dough rest, uncovered, for 5 minutes. Then switch to the dough hook or use a wet spoon or wet hands and mix for 1 minute, on medium-low speed if using a stand mixer. The dough should be smooth but still very soft and sticky (similar to ciabatta dough). Add flour or water only if necessary to achieve that texture; the dough will firm up as you continue to work it.

3 Spread about 1 teaspoon of vegetable oil or olive oil on a work surface. Using a wet or oiled bowl scraper or rubber spatula, transfer the dough to the oiled area. Lightly oil your hands, then stretch and fold the dough as shown on page 20, folding it over itself four times: once each from the top, bottom, and sides. The dough will

CONTINUED

NOTE: If it is more convenient for you to use an overnight method, put the covered bowl of dough in the refrigerator immediately after the final stretch and fold. The next day, remove it from the refrigerator 2½ hours before you plan to bake. Shape the cold dough and proof it at room temperature until it increases in size by 1½ times, then bake as directed.

firm up slightly but still be very soft and somewhat sticky. Cover the dough with the mixing bowl and then, at intervals of 5 minutes or up to 20 minutes, perform three additional sequences of stretching and folding. For each stretch and fold sequence, lightly oil your hands to prevent sticking. The dough will firm up a bit more with each stretch and fold. After the final fold it should be soft, supple, and tacky and have a springy or bouncy quality when patted.

4 Oil a large bowl and put the dough in the bowl. Mist the top of the dough with vegetable spray oil and cover the bowl with a lid or plastic wrap; if using plastic wrap, stretch it tightly over the bowl rather than laying it directly on the dough. Ferment the dough at room temperature for 1½ to 2 hours, until double in size. (This time can be shortened by using a warm proof box set at about 90°F / 32°C.)

5 Oil the work surface again and use an oiled bowl scraper or rubber spatula to transfer the dough to the oiled area. **For hearth loaves,** prepare two bannetons or a *couche* as described on page 26. Divide the dough in half and shape each piece into a boule or bâtard as shown on page 21, then put the shaped loaves in the prepared proofing vessels. **For pan loaves,** mist two 4½ by 8-inch loaf pans with vegetable spray oil. Divide the dough in half and shape the pieces into sandwich loaves as shown on pages 23 and 24, then put the shaped loaves in the prepared pans. **For rolls,** line two sheet pans with parchment paper or silicone mats. Divide the dough into the desired number of pieces and shape as desired (see page 24). Put half of the rolls on each lined pan.

6 Mist the top of the dough with vegetable spray oil, then cover it loosely with plastic wrap. Proof for 1 to 1½ hours at room temperature, until the dough increases in size by 1½ times. When poked with a finger, it should spring back within a few seconds; if it holds the dimple, it's risen for too long. (Because the dough is so hydrated, it's fragile and will fall if you proof it until double in size. It's better to bake it while it's still on the rise.)

7 To bake a hearth loaf, about 45 minutes before you plan to bake, prepare the oven for hearth baking with a baking stone and steam pan as shown on page 29, then preheat the oven to 450°F (232°C). Transfer the shaped loaf to a floured peel (or keep it on the sheet pan for baking). Score the top as desired (see page 29). Transfer the loaf onto the baking stone (or put the sheet pan on the baking stone). Pour about 1 cup of hot water into the steam pan. Bake for 15 minutes, then rotate and bake for 15 to 20 minutes longer, until the loaf is golden brown on all sides and sounds hollow when thumped on the bottom. The internal temperature should be about 200°F (93°C). Transfer to a wire rack and let cool for at least 30 minutes before slicing and serving.

8 To bake pan loaves, preheat the oven to 375°F (191°C); steam is optional. Bake for 25 minutes, then rotate and bake for 25 to 40 minutes longer, until the bread is golden brown all around, the side walls are firm and not squishy, and the loaf sounds hollow when thumped on the bottom. The internal temperature should be at least 190°F (88°C). Let cool in the pans for at least 10 minutes, then transfer to a wire rack and let cool for at least 20 to 30 minutes longer before slicing and serving.

9 To bake rolls, preheat the oven to 400°F (204°C); steam is optional. Bake for 12 minutes, then rotate and bake for about 10 to 15 minutes longer, until the rolls are golden brown and sound hollow when thumped on the bottom (they will soften as they cool). The internal temperature should be about 190°F (88°C). Transfer to a wire rack and let cool for at least 10 minutes before serving.

SPROUTED PAIN AU LEVAIN

MAKES 1 LARGE LOAF OR 2 SMALL LOAVES

Classic French pain au levain is a naturally leavened crusty hearth bread typically made with a combination of white bread flour and a small amount of whole grain flour. Therefore, you'll currently find nothing like the following recipe under the name *pain au levain* in France, unless the sprouted flour movement hits Paris while this book is being printed. However, this version captures the full spirit of its namesake while also being the closest you're likely to get to producing a San Francisco sourdough bread using sprouted whole wheat flour.

The main difference between pain au levain and San Francisco sourdough is the absence of whole grain flour in the latter. In addition, San Francisco sourdough bread is, well, more sour. There are two reasons for this. First, in San Francisco (and a few other places around the world), there is a strong presence of a particular lactic acid bacteria—*Lactobacillus sanfranciscensis*—that lends a very tangy flavor to the dough. It's too tangy, it seems, for the French, whom I've heard refer to it as "spoiled" or "ruined" bread. The second reason is a trick that French bakers use to minimize sour flavor notes: spiking the dough with a small amount of commercial yeast—just enough to boost the levain, or natural leaven starter. In the following recipe, I offer two options: a pure, starter-only version (a true sourdough bread) and a version spiked with commercial yeast. Also, you can either build a fresh starter, as described below, or you can use a piece of your mother starter as long as it's been refreshed within 3 days of making the final dough.

LEVAIN

NOTE: The amount of water required will vary depending on the type of flour used. For whole wheat flour you may need only 6 tablespoons (3 oz / 85 g), and for bread flour you may need only 5½ tablespoons (2.75 oz / 78 g).

INGREDIENT	VOLUME	OUNCES	GRAMS	%
Mother Starter (page 40), recently refreshed (see sidebar)	2 tablespoons	1	28.5	25
sprouted whole wheat flour (or whole wheat flour or unbleached bread flour)	¾ cup plus 3 tablespoons (or ¾ cup plus 2 tablespoons)	4	113	100
water, lukewarm (95°F / 35°C; see note)	7 tablespoons	3.5	99	88
TOTAL		8.5	240.5	213

Put the starter in a small bowl and add the water to soften it. Add the flour and stir until a coarse ball of dough forms. Turn it out onto a lightly floured work surface and knead by hand for about 1 minute, until a smooth dough forms and the starter is evenly distributed. Mist a medium bowl with vegetable spray oil and put the dough in the bowl. Mist the top of the dough with vegetable spray oil and cover the bowl with plastic wrap. Ferment the dough at room temperature for 4 to 8 hours, until double in size. Use immediately or refrigerate for up to 3 days.

FINAL DOUGH

NOTE: You can increase the amount of yeast to as much as 1 teaspoon (0.11 oz / 3 g) if you want a faster-rising, less sour bread. Generally, the slower the rise, the more complex the flavor. For a full-on sourdough bread, omit the yeast altogether.

INGREDIENT	VOLUME	OUNCES	GRAMS	%
Levain or recently refreshed Mother Starter (page 40)	¾ cup	3.25	92	20
water, lukewarm (95°F / 35°C)	1¾ cups	14	397	87
sprouted whole wheat flour	3¾ cups	16	454	100
salt	1¼ teaspoons	0.32	9	2
instant yeast (optional; see note)	¼ teaspoon to 1 teaspoon	0.03 to 0.11	1 to 3	0.2 to 0.7
TOTAL		33.6 to 33.68	953 to 955	209.2 to 209.7

1 In the bowl of a stand mixer fitted with the paddle attachment, or in a large bowl, stir together the starter and water to distribute the starter. Add the flour, salt, and yeast. Mix or stir until a coarse, wet dough forms, about 1 minute.

2 Let the dough rest, uncovered, for 5 minutes. Then switch to the dough hook or use a wet spoon or wet hands and mix for 1 minute, on medium-low speed if using a stand mixer. The dough should be smooth but still very soft and sticky. Add a bit more flour or water if necessary to achieve this texture; the dough will firm up during the stretch and fold process.

3 Spread about 1 teaspoon of vegetable oil or olive oil on a work surface. Using a wet or oiled bowl scraper or rubber spatula, transfer the dough to the oiled area. Lightly oil your hands, then stretch and fold the dough as shown on page 20, folding it over itself four times: once each from the top, bottom, and sides. The dough will firm up slightly but still be very soft and somewhat sticky. Cover the dough with the mixing bowl and then, at 20-minute intervals, perform three additional sequences of stretching and folding. For each stretch and fold sequence, lightly oil your hands to prevent sticking. The dough will firm up a bit more with each stretch and fold. After

CONTINUED

NOTE: Because sour-
dough breads can take a
long time to rise, it may
be more convenient to
spread the process over
two days using an over-
night method. To do so,
put the covered bowl of
dough in the refrigerator
immediately after the final
stretch and fold (for pure
sourdough with no added
yeast, give the dough
about 2 hours to begin
fermenting before chilling
it). The next day, remove
it from the refrigerator
3½ hours before you plan
to bake. Shape the cold
dough and proof it at
room temperature until
it increases in size by
1½ times, then bake as
directed.

the final fold it should be soft, supple, and tacky and have a springy or bouncy quality when patted.

4 Oil a large bowl and put the dough in the bowl. Mist the top of the dough with vegetable spray oil and cover with a lid or plastic wrap; if using plastic wrap, stretch it tightly over the bowl rather than laying it directly on the dough. Ferment the dough at room temperature until double in size, 3 to 5 hours, or 1½ to 2 hours if using the optional yeast. (Either time can be shortened by using a warm proof box set at about 90°F / 32°C.) If the dough hasn't doubled in size in the suggested time, you may need to extend the fermentation to as much as 8 hours, but it will eventually rise.

5 Oil the work surface again and use an oiled bowl scraper to transfer the dough to the oiled area. **For hearth loaves,** prepare two bannetons or a *couche* as shown on page 26. Divide the dough in half and shape each piece into a boule or bâtard as shown on pages 20 to 21, then put the shaped loaves in the prepared proofing vessels. **For pan loaves,** mist two 4½ by 8-inch loaf pans with vegetable spray oil. Divide the dough in half and shape the pieces into sandwich loaves as shown on pages 23 and 24, then put the shaped loaves in the prepared pans.

6 Mist the top of the dough with vegetable spray oil and cover it loosely with plastic wrap. Proof at room temperature until the dough increases in size by 1½ times, 2 to 3 hours, or 1 to 2 hours if using the optional yeast. When poked with a finger, the dough should spring back within a few seconds; if it holds the dimple, it's risen for too long. (Because the dough is so fully hydrated, it's fragile and will fall if you proof it until double in size. It's better to bake it while it's still on the rise.)

7 To bake a hearth loaf, about 45 minutes before you plan to bake, prepare the oven for hearth baking with a baking stone and steam pan as shown on page 29, then preheat the oven to 450°F (232°C). Transfer the shaped loaf to a lightly floured peel (or keep it on the sheet pan for baking). Score the top as desired (see page 29). Transfer the loaf to the baking stone (or put the sheet pan on the baking stone). Pour about 1 cup (240ml) of hot water into the steam pan. Bake for 20 minutes, then rotate and bake for 15 to 30 minutes longer, until the crust is golden brown and the bread sounds hollow when thumped on the bottom. The internal temperature should be 200°F (93°C). Transfer to a wire rack and let cool for at least 30 minutes before slicing and serving.

Refreshing and Using Your Own Mother Starter

For those of you who already have a starter, whether whole wheat, rye, or white, you can use it in this recipe and its variations. Simply use your mother starter (the one you keep perpetually in your refrigerator) to make a fresh "final" starter, or, if your mother starter has been refreshed within the past three days, you can use it as your starter in the final dough. The key is to build the final starter using a 70% ratio of water to fresh bread flour (75% water if you are using whole wheat flour, or 88% if you are using sprouted wheat flour). In the sourdough primer I recommended not using sprouted flour for your mother starter because I found that it broke down more quickly than a regular starter, but for your final starter you can introduce sprouted flour if you desire. Since any starter has already achieved a full breakout of sugars and flavor esters through long, slow fermentation, it is not necessary to use a sprouted flour starter, but it is an option if you prefer. For single loaf recipes, the amount of starter is so small that it is usually easier to use a piece from your refreshed mother starter.

8 To bake pan loaves, preheat the oven to 375°F (191°C); steam is optional. Bake for 30 minutes, then rotate and bake for 25 to 40 minutes longer, until the crust is golden brown and the bread sounds hollow when thumped on the bottom. The internal temperature should be 190°F (88°C). Let cool in the pans for at least 10 minutes, then transfer to a wire rack and let cool for at least 30 minutes longer before slicing and serving.

Variations

MULTIGRAIN: You can replace up to 20% of the sprouted whole wheat flour, by weight, with other sprouted flours. If you do so, decrease the amount of water by about 2 to 4 tablespoons (1 to 2 oz / 28.5 to 56.5 g), as needed.

NONSPROUTED: You can replace some of the sprouted whole wheat flour with an equal amount, by weight, of conventional, nonsprouted flour, but you'll need to decrease the water amount accordingly, with the amount depending on what kind of flour you substitute. If using whole-milled wheat flour (see page 157), you shouldn't need to adjust the amount of water very much, if at all.

SPROUTED RYE BREAD

MAKES 1 LARGE LOAF, 2 SMALL LOAVES, OR UP TO 18 ROLLS | **MASTER FORMULA**

Great rye bread is always more challenging to make than wheat bread because rye flour has less gluten and much more pentosan gum, which makes it difficult to get an open crumb structure. Historically, rye is an important grain because it's heartier than wheat and can survive and thrive in many places where wheat can't. It certainly holds a venerable place in Eastern European and Scandinavian bread making. Although rye breads have perhaps waned in popularity in the United States in recent decades, the bread world is seeing a revival on the rye front, with bakers such as Chad Robertson and Jeffrey Hamelman demonstrating just how versatile and wonderful rye can be. Now, with sprouted rye flour becoming easier to obtain, it's time for a new rye revolution too. Here's a sprouted version of a *seigle* rye, a bread in which rye constitutes more than 50% of the final flour. Feel free to adjust the ratios up or down as you explore the potential variations of this master formula.

Also, note that adding instant yeast is an option. As with many sourdough recipes, you can spike the dough with commercial yeast to shorten fermentation times and reduce the sour flavor. In the case of rye bread, the acidity of the sourdough starter is important for controlling the higher enzyme activity of the rye and preventing collapse of the dough during baking (referred to by bakers as starch attack). Therefore, the total amount of starter in the following formula is higher than in the sourdough levain on page 66. As with that recipe, you can either build a fresh starter, as described below, to use in the final dough or you can use a piece of your mother starter as long as it's been refreshed within 3 days of making the final dough.

SPROUTED RYE FINAL STARTER

INGREDIENT	VOLUME	OUNCES	GRAMS	%
Mother Starter (page 40), recently refreshed	2 tablespoons	1	28.5	25
sprouted rye flour (or sprouted whole wheat flour or whole wheat flour or rye flour)	1 cup plus 2 tablespoons (or ¾ cup plus 3 tablespoons or ¾ cup plus 2 tablespoons)	4	113	100
water	7 tablespoons	3.5	99	88
TOTAL		8.5	240.5	213

CONTINUED

In a small bowl, stir all the ingredients with a large spoon just until a coarse ball of dough forms. Turn it out onto a lightly floured work surface and knead by hand for about 1 minute, until a smooth dough forms and the mother starter is evenly distributed. If using sprouted rye flour, the dough won't be as firm as with sprouted whole wheat flour, but it should come together to make a thick, sticky dough. This is fine. Mist a medium bowl with vegetable spray oil and put the dough in the bowl. Mist the top of the dough with vegetable spray oil and cover the bowl with plastic wrap. Ferment the dough at room temperature for 4 to 8 hours, until it doubles in size or swells noticeably (the expansion can vary depending on which flour you use, as rye flour won't rise as much as wheat). Use immediately or refrigerate for up to 3 days.

FINAL DOUGH

INGREDIENT	VOLUME	OUNCES	GRAMS	%
Sprouted Rye Final Starter or recently refreshed Mother Starter (page 40)	all	8.5	240.5	53
water, lukewarm (95°F / 35°C)	1½ cups plus 2 tablespoons	13	369	81
sprouted rye flour	2½ cups plus 1 tablespoon	9	255	56
sprouted whole wheat flour	1⅔ cups	7	198	44
salt	1¼ teaspoons	0.32	9	2
instant yeast (optional)	1 teaspoon	0.11	3	0.7
TOTAL		37.93	1,074.5	236.7

1 In the bowl of a stand mixer fitted with the paddle attachment, or in a large bowl, stir together the starter and warm water to distribute the starter (on low speed if using a stand mixer). Add the flour and salt, and for a faster-rising, less tangy version, the yeast. Mix or stir until a coarse, wet dough forms, about 1 minute.

2 Let the dough rest, uncovered, for 5 minutes. Then switch to the dough hook or use a wet spoon or wet hands and mix for 1 minute, on medium-low speed if using a stand mixer. The dough should be smooth but still be very soft and sticky. Add a bit more flour or water if necessary to achieve that texture; the dough will firm up during the stretch and fold process.

3 Spread about 1 teaspoon of vegetable oil or olive oil on a work surface. Using a wet or oiled bowl scraper or rubber spatula, transfer the dough to the oiled area. Lightly oil your hands, then stretch and fold the dough as shown on page 20, folding it over itself four times: once each from the top, bottom, and sides. The dough

- If you play with the ratio of wheat and rye flour, note that the more rye flour, the more difficult the challenge, especially if you want to try to achieve an open crumb structure. If the bread is to open up in the oven, the dough must be fairly wet, and you'll need to handle it carefully. Also, the oven heat must be quite high for hearth breads; you might start the oven at its highest setting and then lower it to the designated temperature right after the steaming process. This can help create initial oven spring, especially with wet doughs.

- For an overnight method, put the covered bowl of dough in the refrigerator immediately after the final stretch and fold (or after 2 hours if not using commercial yeast). The next day, remove it from the refrigerator 3½ hours before you plan to bake. Shape the cold dough and proof it at room temperature until it increases in size by 1½ times, then bake as directed.

will firm up slightly but will still be very soft and somewhat sticky. Cover the dough with the mixing bowl and then, at 20-minute intervals, perform three additional sequences of stretching and folding. For each stretch and fold sequence, lightly oil your hands to prevent sticking. The dough will firm up a bit more with each stretch and fold. After the final fold it should be soft, supple, and tacky and have a springy or bouncy quality when patted.

4 Oil a large bowl and put the dough in the bowl. Mist the top of the dough with vegetable spray oil and cover with a lid or plastic wrap; if using plastic wrap, stretch it tightly over the bowl rather than laying it directly on the dough. Ferment the dough at room temperature for 3 to 5 hours, or 1½ to 2 hours if using the optional yeast, until double in size. (Either time can be shortened by using a warm proof box set at about 90°F / 32°C.) If the dough hasn't doubled in size in the suggested time, you may need to extend the fermentation to as much as 8 hours, but it will eventually rise.

5 Oil the work surface again and use an oiled bowl scraper or rubber spatula to transfer the dough to the oiled area. **For hearth loaves,** prepare two bannetons or a *couche* as shown on page 26. Divide the dough in half and shape each piece into a boule or bâtard as shown on pages 20 to 21, then put the shaped loaves in the prepared proofing vessels. **For pan loaves,** mist two 4½ by 8-inch loaf pans with vegetable spray oil. Divide the dough in half and shape the pieces into sandwich loaves as shown on pages 23 and 24, then put the shaped loaves in the prepared pans. **For rolls,** line two sheet pans with parchment paper or silicone mats. Divide the dough into the desired number of pieces and shape as desired (see page 24). Put half of the rolls on each lined pan.

6 Mist the top of the dough with vegetable spray oil and cover it loosely with plastic wrap. Proof at room temperature until the dough increases in size by 1½ times, 2 to 3 hours, or 1 to 2 hours if using the optional yeast. When poked with a finger, the dough should spring back within a few seconds; if it holds the dimple, it's risen for too long. (Because the dough is so fully hydrated, it's fragile and will fall if you proof it until double in size. It's better to bake it while it's still on the rise.)

7 To bake a hearth loaf, about 45 minutes before you plan to bake, prepare the oven for hearth baking with a baking stone and steam pan as shown on page 29, then preheat the oven to 450°F (232°C). Transfer the shaped loaf to a lightly floured peel (or keep it on the sheet pan for baking). Score the top as desired (see page 29). Transfer the loaf to the baking stone (or put the sheet pan on the baking stone). Pour about 1 cup of hot water into the steam pan.

CONTINUED

Bake for 20 minutes, then rotate and bake for 15 to 20 minutes longer, until the crust is golden brown and the bread sounds hollow when thumped on the bottom. The internal temperature should be 200°F (93°C). Transfer to a wire rack and let cool for at least 30 minutes before slicing and serving.

8 To bake pan loaves, preheat the oven to 375°F (191°C); steam is optional. Bake for 15 minutes, then rotate and bake for 30 to 40 minutes longer, until the crust is golden brown all over and the bread sounds hollow when thumped on the bottom. The internal temperature should be 190°F (88°C). Let cool in the pans for at least 10 minutes, then transfer to a wire rack and let cool for at least 30 minutes longer before slicing and serving.

9 To bake rolls, preheat the oven to 400°F (204°C); steam is optional. Bake for 12 minutes, then rotate and bake for about 10 to 15 minutes longer, until the rolls are golden brown and sound hollow when thumped on the bottom (they will soften as they cool). The internal temperature should be about 190°F (88°C). Transfer to a wire rack and let cool for at least 10 minutes before serving.

Variations

Feel free to add these ingredients with the dry ingredients to create variations.

SEEDED RYE: Add 1 to 2 tablespoons (0.32 to 0.65 oz / 9 to 18 g) caraway or nigella seeds.

ONION RYE: Add 1 to 2 tablespoons (0.18 to 0.35 oz / 5 to 10 g) dried onion flakes, or use ¼ to ½ cup (1.5 to 3 oz / 42.5 to 85 g) finely diced fresh onion.

SWEDISH-STYLE LIMPA RYE: Add the grated zest of 1 orange and 1 to 2 tablespoons (0.32 to 0.65 oz / 9 to 18 g) anise seeds.

SPROUTED WHEAT PIZZA DOUGH

MAKES 5 INDIVIDUAL PIZZA CRUSTS

This dough elevates 100% whole grain pizza to the next level. Unlike most pizza doughs, it can be mixed and baked on the same day and still achieve its maximum flavor potential, thanks to the sprouted flour. However, you can also hold the dough in the refrigerator for up to three days or in the freezer for three months. Feel free to top this dough with any of your favorite cheeses and sauces, but for the best results, be sure to bake it at a high temperature.

DOUGH

INGREDIENT	VOLUME	OUNCES	GRAMS	%
sprouted whole wheat flour	5⅔ cups	24	680	100
salt	2 teaspoons	0.5	14	2.1
instant yeast	1⅝ teaspoons	0.18	5	0.7
water, at room temperature	2½ cups plus 3 tablespoons	21.5	610	90
olive oil	2 tablespoons	1	28.5	4
TOTAL		47.18	1,337.5	196.8

1 In the bowl of a stand mixer fitted with the paddle attachment, or in a large bowl, stir together the flour, salt, and yeast (on low speed if using a stand mixer). Add the water and olive oil and mix or stir until the flour is hydrated and a coarse, wet dough forms, about 1 minute.

2 Let the dough rest, uncovered, for 5 minutes. Then switch to the dough hook or use a wet spoon or wet hands and mix for 1 minute, on medium-low speed if using a stand mixer. The dough should smooth out and thicken slightly.

3 Spread about 1 teaspoon of vegetable oil or olive oil on a work surface. Using a wet or oiled bowl scraper or rubber spatula, transfer the dough to the oiled area. Lightly oil your hands, then stretch and fold the dough as shown on page 20, folding it over itself four times: once each from the top, bottom, and sides. The dough will firm up slightly but still be very soft and sticky. Cover the dough with the mixing bowl and then, at intervals of 5 minutes or up to 20 minutes, perform three additional sequences of stretching and folding. For each stretch and fold sequence, lightly oil your hands to prevent sticking. The dough will become firmer and less sticky with each stretch and fold. After the final fold it should be very tacky and supple and have a springy or bouncy quality when patted. (Note: If holding the dough overnight, put the dough in the refrigerator immediately after the final stretch and fold cycle instead of letting it rise.)

CONTINUED

4 Oil a large bowl and put the dough in the bowl. Mist the top of the dough with vegetable spray oil and cover with a lid or plastic wrap; if using plastic wrap, stretch it tightly over the bowl rather than laying it directly on the dough. Ferment the dough at room temperature for 1½ to 2 hours, until double in size. (This time can be shortened by using a warm proof box set at about 90°F / 32°C.)

5 Line a sheet pan with parchment paper or a silicone mat. Mist the surface with vegetable spray oil or lightly coat it with olive oil. Oil the work surface again, and transfer the dough to the work surface with an oiled bowl scraper or rubber spatula. Divide the dough into 5 equal pieces, each weighing about 9 ounces (255 g), with an oiled metal pastry blade or plastic bowl scraper.

6 With lightly oiled hands, form each piece into a boule as shown on pages 20 to 21. Put the dough balls on the prepared pan, spacing them evenly. Mist with vegetable spray oil, then loosely cover the pan with plastic wrap or put it in a large plastic bag. Proof for 1 to 2 hours; the dough won't double in size, but it should show signs of swelling and expansion. If you won't be making pizzas immediately, refrigerate the dough, then remove it from the refrigerator about 1½ hours before you plan to make the pizzas.

7 To shape a pizza, see page 78. Preheat the oven to the highest it will go.

8 When the crust is ready to be topped, place it on a floured peel. Be sure to use flour rather than cornmeal or semolina, as it doesn't burn as quickly in the oven. Top the pizza as desired, then slide it onto the baking stone. If you aren't using a baking stone, just put the panned pizza in the oven. While the pizza is baking, shape your next pizza.

9 Bake for about 4 minutes, then use the peel or a spatula to rotate the pizza. It will take anywhere from 5 to 7 minutes for the pizza to fully bake, depending on the oven. The edge should puff up and be a deep golden brown, perhaps even slightly charred.

10 Remove the pizza, garnish as desired, then let it cool for 1 minute before slicing and serving. Continue baking as many pizzas as you'd like (the dough will hold up to an hour out of the refrigerator.)

Variation

MULTIGRAIN SPROUTED PIZZA DOUGH: You can replace up to 20% of the sprouted whole wheat flour with an equal amount, by weight, of other sprouted or non-sprouted flours, such as rye, corn, buckwheat, or millet. Depending on the grain, you'll probably need to decrease the water by about 3 tablespoons (1.5 oz / 42.5 g).

Shaping Pizza Dough

To shape pizza dough, press the ball of dough into a flat disk using your fingertips. Slide the backs of your hands under the dough, then lift it and begin to rotate it, using your thumbs to coax the edges of the dough into a larger circle. Don't stretch the dough with the backs of your hands or your knuckles; let your thumbs and gravity do all of the work. Your hands and knuckles merely provide a platform to support the dough. (If the dough starts to shrink back, set it on the floured work surface and let it rest for a minute or two. You can move on to another dough ball, repeating the same gentle stretching.) Work from the edges only, not from the center of the dough, and continue stretching until you have a 9- to 12-inch disk. Place the shaped dough on a floured or parchment-lined peel or back of a sheet pan. Patch any holes in the dough so the sauce and other toppings don't go through the dough, then add toppings.

GLUTEN-FREE SPROUTED FLOUR PIZZA DOUGH

Because gluten-free sprouted flours generally work better in a batter than a stiff dough, they are ideal for this innovation: twice-baked gluten-free pizza crusts! After all, a pizza crust is thin, it doesn't have to hold a loaf shape, and it's best when crispy on the bottom yet moist and creamy inside. In other words, it's like a big pancake—and I have, in fact, used these crusts as pancakes, drizzling them with maple syrup rather than using savory toppings. There's no sweetener in the dough because sprouted flours are naturally sweet, and the number and variety of flours you can use is limited only by what you have in your pantry, with just one caveat: If using sprouted bean flour, include no more than 20% in your blend, as its stronger flavor tends to take over. As you become familiar with the flavors of different sprouted gluten-free flours, you can create a blend that suits your preferences. Whatever flours you use, I guarantee that this is better tasting (and better for you) than any commercial gluten-free pizza crust you can buy.

To bake the crusts, you can use any size of round glass or metal pan, but my suggestion is to use disposable aluminum pie pans. Although they make small pizzas, they do a great job of releasing the crust when properly oiled, and because they're lightweight, you can even stack and store the crusts in the pans. Plus, if you have enough of them, you can bake the entire batch of dough in one round of baking, especially if you have three or four shelves in your oven; or store them in the freezer to pull out as needed. They thaw very quickly for an instant pizza.

CONTINUED

DOUGH

INGREDIENT	VOLUME	OUNCES	GRAMS	%
sprouted gluten-free flour blend (any combination of sprouted gluten-free grain and bean flours)	about 8½ cups	28	794	97
ground sunflower seeds (optional)	¼ cup	1	28.5	3
salt	2 teaspoons	0.5	14	1.7
xanthan gum powdered or psyllium husks (optional)	2¼ teaspoons	0.25	7	0.9
instant yeast	1¼ teaspoons	0.14	4	0.5
water, lukewarm (95°F / 35°C)	5½ cups	44	1,247	152
TOTAL		73.89	2,094.5	255.1

1 In a large bowl, stir together the flour blend, sunflower seeds, salt, xanthan gum, and yeast. Add the water and stir or whisk for 30 to 60 seconds to hydrate the flour and make a thin, batter-like dough; the consistency should be similar to pancake batter (it will thicken as it sits). Scrape down the bowl with a rubber spatula and cover the bowl with plastic wrap. Ferment the dough at room temperature for 1 to 1½ hours, until it begins to bubble. If making the crusts right away, you can proceed as soon as the dough bubbles. If not, refrigerate the dough for up to 36 hours.

2 For each crust, brush a disposable aluminum pie pan or other round pan with at least ½ teaspoon of olive or vegetable oil. Ladle or pour in about ¾ cup (177ml) of the batter (more for larger pans), using enough to cover the bottom of the pan to a thickness of ¼ inch. Tilt the pan to evenly distribute the batter. Ferment at room temperature for about 1 hour, until signs of bubbling appear.

3 Preheat the oven to 350°F (177°C).

4 Put as many pans as will comfortably fit into the oven (refrigerate any others and bake them, directly from the refrigerator, after the first round of baking). Bake for 20 minutes, then rotate and bake for 10 to 20 minutes longer, until the crusts are golden brown around the edges and springy to the touch.

5 If not using disposable pie pans, transfer the baked crusts to a wire rack. You can use them immediately; or, let them cool completely, then wrap well in plastic wrap and store in the refrigerator for up to 1 week or the freezer for up to 3 months.

6 When you're ready to make pizzas, preheat the oven to 450°F (232°C). Top the crusts as you would any pizza. Bake them either in the pie pans, on sheet pans, directly on the oven racks, or on a fully heated baking stone. Bake for 6 to 8 minutes, until the toppings and cheese look done. The crust will crisp up and the edges will turn dark brown.

Why do gluten-free breads often call for xanthan gum?

Q & A

Xanthan gum, which is produced from fermented seeds, can play the role of gluten, to a limited extent, by providing stretchability. Some bakers prefer to use guar gum, but I find it can cause stomach upset for a small percentage of people. Another option is to use half guar gum and half xanthan gum; some gluten-free bakeries do it this way and believe the combination produces a stronger structure. A more recent innovation is to use powdered psyllium husks in place of xanthan gum. If making this substitution, use twice as much psyllium, by volume, as you would xanthan gum.

SPROUTED WHEAT FOCACCIA

MAKES ONE 18 BY 13-INCH PAN OF FOCACCIA; 12 SERVINGS

I may be even more well known for my focaccia recipes than I am for pizza, at least at Johnson & Wales University, where I'm asked to do focaccia demonstrations more than any other baked good. I think a key reason for this is that most Americans have never had truly great focaccia, so they experience it as a revelation when they do. Focaccia is akin to what is sometimes referred to as Sicilian-style pizza, and the following dough can be used for either. Sicilian-style pizza can be every bit as satisfying as the thin-crusted pizzas that hail from southern Italy—if you follow a few important but simple rules. Basically, success lies in a wet, sticky dough; long, slow fermentation (usually overnight); and a very hot oven. Those rules still apply to dough made with sprouted flour, with the exception of long, slow fermentation, which isn't necessary for reasons explained in this book.

Conditioning the dough overnight is certainly an option with this recipe, but sprouting the grain prior to milling flour has already accomplished the task of flavor development, so it's an unnecessary step, though it may offer convenience on bake day. Welcome to the next frontier of focaccia!

DOUGH

INGREDIENT	VOLUME	OUNCES	GRAMS	%
sprouted whole wheat flour	4¾ cups	20	567	100
salt	1¼ teaspoons	0.32	9	1.5
instant yeast	1¼ teaspoons	0.14	4	0.7
water, lukewarm (95°F / 35°C)	2¼ cups plus 1 tablespoon	18.5	524	92
olive oil	1 tablespoon	0.5	14	2.5
additional olive oil for the pan and for dimpling	about 3 tablespoons			
herb oil for topping (optional; see sidebar page 85)	about 3 tablespoons			
TOTAL		39.46	1,118	196.7

1 In the bowl of a stand mixer fitted with the paddle attachment or in a large bowl, stir together the flour, salt, and yeast (on low speed if using a stand mixer). Add the water and olive oil and mix or stir until the flour is hydrated and a coarse, wet, almost soupy dough forms, about 1 minute.

CONTINUED

NOTE: For an overnight method, you can refrigerate the dough at one of two stages—after the final stretch and fold or after panning—for later baking. If you refrigerate it after the final stretch and fold, remove the bowl from the refrigerator 4 hours before you plan to bake the focaccia, and proceed with panning and baking as described here. If you refrigerate the pan overnight, remove it from the refrigerator 3 hours before you plan to bake the focaccia, do any final dimpling necessary to fill the pan with the dough, and proof and bake as directed.

2 Let the dough rest, uncovered, for 5 minutes. Then switch to the dough hook or use a wet spoon or wet hands and mix for 1 minute, on medium-low speed if using a stand mixer. The dough should smooth out and thicken slightly, but it will still be very wet and sticky.

3 Spread about 1 teaspoon of vegetable oil or olive oil on a work surface. Using a wet or oiled bowl scraper or rubber spatula, transfer the dough to the oiled area. Lightly oil your hands, then stretch and fold the dough as shown on page 20, folding it over itself four times: once each from the top, bottom, and sides. The dough will firm up slightly but still be very soft and sticky. Cover the dough with the mixing bowl and then, at intervals of 5 minutes or up to 20 minutes, perform three additional sequences of stretching and folding. For each stretch and fold sequence, lightly oil your hands to prevent sticking. The dough will become firmer and less sticky with each stretch and fold. After the final fold it should be just slightly sticky. It will barely hold together when lifted, but it should have structure.

4 Oil a large bowl and put the dough in the bowl. Mist the top of the dough with vegetable spray oil and cover with a lid or plastic wrap; if using plastic wrap, stretch it tightly over the bowl rather than laying it directly on the dough. Ferment the dough at room temperature for 1½ to 2 hours, until double in size. (This time can be shortened by using a warm proof box set at about 90°F / 32°C.)

5 Line an 18 by 13-inch rimmed sheet pan with parchment paper or a silicone mat. Generously oil the surface, including the sides of the pan, with 1½ table-spoons (0.75 oz / 21 g) of the additional olive oil. Using an oiled bowl scraper or rubber spatula, transfer the dough to the center of the pan. Drizzle the remaining 1½ tablespoons (0.75 oz / 21 g) of additional olive oil evenly over the dough. Dip your fingertips in a bit of olive oil, then dimple the dough until it fills the pan. You may need to do this in two or three passes, allowing the dough to rest for 5 minutes between passes so it can relax enough to spread into the corners without shrinking back. If you like, drizzle the herb oil evenly over the dough. Cover the pan loosely with plastic wrap and let the dough rise at room temperature for 1 to 1½ hours, until it rises to the top of the pan. If using other toppings, add them after the dough has risen; see page 86 for ideas.

6 Position a rack in the middle of the oven and preheat the oven to 450°F (232°C).

7 Bake for 15 minutes, then rotate the pan and bake for 10 to 15 minutes longer, until the top of the focaccia is golden brown.

8 Run a metal pastry blade or metal spatula around the edges to separate the focaccia from the pan. Transfer the entire focaccia to a cutting board. If the parchment paper or silicone mat adheres to the bottom of the focaccia, carefully remove it by slightly lifting one edge of the focaccia and sliding it out after the focaccia cools for a few minutes. If any oil remains in the pan, drizzle it over the focaccia. Let cool for 5 minutes before cutting and serving.

Variations

SICILIAN-STYLE PIZZA: Bake the pan of dough without toppings after it fills the pan but before it rises, for 10 to 15 minutes, until it just starts to set and brown. You can then use this as a crust at any time, finishing it with sauce, cheese, and other toppings, then baking as directed above.

MULTIGRAIN FOCACCIA: You can replace up to 20% of the sprouted whole wheat flour with an equal amount, by weight, of other sprouted or nonsprouted flours, such as rye, corn, buckwheat, or millet. Depending on the grains, you'll probably need to decrease the amount of water by about 3 tablespoons (1.5 oz / 42.5 g).

Herb Oil

This herb oil can also be used to flavor focaccia toppings like thinly sliced tomatoes or potatoes. In addition, it's great as a dipping oil for bread or as a base for salad dressings.

2 cups (16 oz / 454 g) olive oil

2 tablespoons (0.14 oz / 4 g) dried basil

2 tablespoons (0.14 oz / 4 g) dried parsley

1 tablespoon (0.07 oz / 2 g) dried oregano

1 tablespoon (0.07 oz / 2 g) fresh rosemary leaves

1 teaspoon (0.02 oz / 0.5 g) dried thyme

2 tablespoons (0.7 oz / 22 g) granulated garlic, or 10 cloves fresh garlic, pressed and lightly sautéed in ½ cup (4 oz / 113 g) of the olive oil

1 tablespoon (about 0.5 oz / 14 g) kosher salt or coarse sea salt

¼ teaspoon (0.02 oz / 0.5 g) freshly ground black pepper

1 teaspoon (0.11 oz / 3 g) dried chile flakes (optional)

1 teaspoon (0.09 oz / 2.6 g) sweet or hot paprika (optional)

In a bowl, whisk together all the ingredients. Use immediately, or keep any extra in the refrigerator, where it will keep for a month.

Assembling a Focaccia

It may be tempting to think you can top focaccia just as you would a pizza, with everything going on top before you bake it. But this is only partially true. While a pizza may bake in 5 to 7 minutes, a focaccia, with its thicker crust, typically takes about 20 to 25 minutes to bake. Many toppings, such as cooked vegetables and tomatoes or tomato sauce, moist cheeses like feta and blue cheese, or meats like bacon, salumi, chicken, and sausage, can go on the top just prior to baking. Drier ingredients, like sun dried tomatoes or dried fruits like raisins, are best worked into the dough itself, where they will be protected from burning in the hot oven. But semi-moist cheeses, such as mozzarella, provolone, Cheddar, and Swiss, take only a few minutes to melt and caramelize, so they should be reserved and then added during the final 5 to 7 minutes of baking. Dry aged cheeses, like Parmesan, Romano, Asiago, and the like will begin to burn after only 2 to 3 minutes in the oven, so they should be held back until the focaccia looks fully baked, then added and returned to the oven for 2 additional minutes of baking, or as needed.

The general rule of thumb for how much topping to use is to keep everything in balance; too much will weigh down the dough; too many toppings will create a muddle of flavors. It's best to use a small amount of high quality, flavorful ingredients rather than to overload the dough. One or two cups of sautéed or grilled vegetables, a cup or so of cheese, ½ cup (120ml) of pizza sauce, and just enough specialty ingredients like nuts or meats to assure that every bite will contain a small amount of every topping is the key. Restraint will pay off. When using herbs, spices, and salt on the top, remember that a little goes a long way.

There are many inventive toppings that have been developed for focaccia, many of them easily found online. But the most popular versions in my classes are the following:

POTATO, BACON, PARMESAN: While the pan of focaccia dough is rising, cook up about 6 to 8 slices of bacon till crisp, then chop or crumble them into bits after they cool. Grate about 1 cup of Parmesan or other dry aged cheese and set it aside. Thinly slice any type of potato as if making potato chips, paper-thin (I use a small Kyocera ceramic slicer that I bought at Sur la Table, but there are other models available, as well as more sophisticated mandoline style slicers). It only takes one or two potatoes to make enough slices to cover the surface of a pan of focaccia. You can also use a knife but it is difficult to get the slices paper-thin. If the slices are more than ⅛ inch thick, parboil them in simmering, salted water for about 60 seconds to soften. Toss the slices in 2 table-spoons (30ml) of olive oil or, even better, herb oil (see recipe, page 85) . When the focaccia dough is fully risen and ready for baking, cover the surface with the bacon pieces and then cover the bacon with the oiled potato slices. Bake as directed, until the potatoes turn golden brown, then add the grated cheese and return to the oven and bake for 2 additional minutes, or until the cheese melts and just begins to brown. Allow the focaccia to cool for at least 10 minutes before serving.

TOMATO PESTO: Slice 6 to 8 fresh plum tomatoes about ¼ inch thick and toss with 3 tablespoons (45ml) of olive oil or, even better, herb oil (page 85). Prepare pesto using your favorite recipe, or use commercial pesto. Cover the surface of the risen focaccia with the oiled tomatoes and bake as directed. Because of the moistness of the tomatoes, the focaccia will take about 5 to 10 minutes longer to bake than a standard focaccia. When the dough under the tomatoes is golden brown and springy to the touch and the tomatoes are beginning to slightly char, the focaccia is baked. Immediately after removing it from the oven, drizzle 1 cup of pesto over the top. Let the focaccia cool for at least 10 minutes before serving.

SPROUTED WHEAT BREAKFAST FOCACCIA

MAKES ONE 18 BY 13-INCH PAN OF FOCACCIA; 12 SERVINGS

This focaccia with fruit is one of my favorite recipes in this book. Once you start eating it, it's very difficult to stop. When you first make the dough it will seem too wet, but don't overcompensate by adding more flour. It will thicken up overnight as the dried fruit plumps and absorbs some of the water. The glaze is just an option, but it will elicit encore calls. In addition to being a great breakfast bread, it can also be served as a dessert or sweet treat. Note that this is a two-day process, so plan accordingly.

DOUGH

INGREDIENT	VOLUME	OUNCES	GRAMS	%
sprouted whole wheat flour	4¾ cups	20	567	100
salt	1¼ teaspoons	0.32	9	1.6
instant yeast	2¼ teaspoons	0.25	7	1.2
water, lukewarm (95°F / 35°C)	2¾ cups plus 2 tablespoons	23	652	115
dried cranberries	about ¾ cup	5	142	25
golden raisins	about ¾ cup	5	142	25
olive oil for the proofing bowl, the pan, and topping	about 4 tablespoons			
orange or lemon glaze (optional; see sidebar)				
TOTAL		53.57	1,519	267.8

1 In the bowl of a stand mixer fitted with the paddle attachment or in a large bowl, stir together the flour, salt, and yeast (on low speed if using a stand mixer). Add the water and mix or stir until the flour is hydrated and a very wet, soupy batter forms, about 1 minute.

2 Let the dough rest, uncovered, for 5 minutes. Add the dried cranberries and raisins. Switch to the dough hook or use a wet spoon or wet hands and mix for 1 minute, on medium-low speed if using a stand mixer, until the fruit is evenly distributed. The dough should thicken slightly, but it will still be very wet, with the consistency of a thick soup. Let it rest for 5 minutes, then stir for 30 seconds.

3 Use 1 tablespoon (0.5 oz / 14 g) of the olive oil to coat a clean bowl large enough to hold the dough if it doubles in size. (It probably won't double, but it will expand and then fall.) Transfer the dough to the bowl, mist the top with vegetable spray oil, and cover the bowl with plastic wrap. Let the dough rest at room temperature for 15 minutes. Put the bowl in the refrigerator for a cold, overnight fermentation. (At this point, the dough will keep for up to 3 days.)

CONTINUED

4 Remove the dough from the refrigerator 3½ hours before you plan to bake. It will be much thicker now, though still somewhat sticky. Line an 18 by 13-inch rimmed sheet pan with parchment paper or a silicone mat. Generously oil the liner and the sides of the pan with 1½ tablespoons (0.75 oz / 21 g) of the olive oil. Using an oiled bowl scraper or rubber spatula, transfer the cold dough to the center of the pan. Drizzle the remaining 1½ tablespoons (0.75 oz / 21 g) of olive oil evenly over the dough. Dip your fingertips in a bit of olive oil, then dimple the dough until it fills the pan. You may need to do this in two or three passes, allowing the dough to rest for 5 minutes between passes so it can relax enough to spread into the corners without shrinking back. Cover the pan loosely with plastic wrap and let the dough rise at room temperature for about 3 hours, until it rises to the top of the pan.

5 Position a rack in the middle of the oven and preheat the oven to 450°F (232°C).

6 Bake for 15 minutes, then rotate the pan and bake for 15 to 20 minutes longer, until the top of the focaccia is golden brown and firm to the touch. The exposed pieces of fruit will get very dark.

7 Run a metal pastry blade or metal spatula around the edges to separate the focaccia from the pan. Transfer the entire focaccia to a cutting board. If the parchment paper or silicone mat adheres to the bottom of the focaccia, carefully remove it by slightly lifting one edge of the focaccia and sliding it out.

8 Drizzle the glaze evenly over the focaccia, then use a rubber spatula or icing spatula to spread it evenly over the top. (If you don't use the glaze, brush enough olive oil over the surface to create a shiny top.) Let the focaccia cool for at least 45 minutes, until the glaze sets up, before cutting and serving. (If you don't use the glaze, you only need to wait 10 minutes.)

Orange or Lemon Glaze

2 cups (6 oz / 170 g) confectioners' sugar, sifted

½ teaspoon (0.07 oz / 2 g) orange or lemon extract, 2 teaspoons (0.42 oz / 12 g) thawed orange juice concentrate, or 1 tablespoon (0.5 oz / 14 g) lemon juice

¼ cup to 6 tablespoons (2 to 3 oz / 56.5 to 85 g) water or milk

In a medium bowl, stir together the confectioners' sugar and orange or lemon extract. Whisk in ¼ cup (2 oz / 56.5 g) of the water or milk, adding more only if necessary to make a thick but spreadable glaze. It should be thick enough to hold a spoon upright for a few seconds. If it seems thin, add more sifted confectioners' sugar.

SPROUTED WHEAT BAGELS

MAKES 6 OR 7 BAGELS OR 12 MINI BAGELS

It seems as though everybody loves bagels, even folks who don't eat them anymore out of concerns about carbs or gluten. Perhaps creating healthier versions will allow more people to enjoy them once again. In this book you'll find two different recipes for bagels, each following different formulas and using different ingredients; both are excellent. Aside from amazing flavor, the biggest advantage of this version made with sprouted flour is that, unlike many bagel recipes, this one doesn't require an overnight method to develop optimum flavor. You can find barley malt syrup at most natural food stores and many supermarkets. If you'd like to use crystal malt, it's available at beer making supply stores or online (see Resources, page 240).

DOUGH

INGREDIENT	VOLUME	OUNCES	GRAMS	%
sprouted whole wheat flour	4¼ cups	18	510	100
salt	1¼ teaspoons	0.32	9	1.8
instant yeast	1¼ teaspoons	0.14	4	0.8
water, lukewarm (95°F / 35°C)	1¾ cups	14	397	78
barley malt syrup (see notes) or crystal malt	3½ teaspoons or 1 teaspoon	0.75 or 0.18	21.5 or 5	4.2 or 1
baking soda or honey for boiling the bagels	2 tablespoons			
cornmeal or semolina flour	about 2 tablespoons			
TOTAL		33.21 or 32.64	941.5 or 925	184.8 or 181.6

1 In the bowl of a stand mixer fitted with the paddle attachment, or in a large bowl, stir together the flour, salt, and yeast, on low speed if using a stand mixer. (If using crystal malt, add it at this point.) In a separate bowl, whisk together the water and barley malt syrup, then pour into the flour mixture. Mix or stir for 30 to 60 seconds or until the flour is hydrated and a coarse, shaggy dough forms. It will be much stiffer than any other dough in the book; this is necessary for the bagels to stand up to the boiling process without collapsing.

2 Let the dough rest, uncovered, for 5 minutes. Then switch to the dough hook and mix on low speed, or turn the dough out onto a work surface and knead, for 2 minutes. The dough should be smooth but still fairly firm and only slightly tacky.

CONTINUED

Add a bit more flour or water if necessary to achieve this texture, then mix or knead for 1 minute longer. The dough should be firm but supple, and dry and satiny rather than tacky to the touch.

3 Form the dough into a ball. Mist a large bowl with vegetable spray oil and put the dough in the bowl. Mist the top of the dough with vegetable spray oil and cover the bowl with plastic wrap. Ferment the dough at room temperature for 1½ to 2 hours, until the dough begins to swell and increases in size by about 1½ times.

4 Line a sheet pan with parchment paper or a silicone mat and mist with vegetable spray oil. Spread a bit of vegetable oil on the work surface and transfer the dough to the oiled area. Divide the dough into pieces of the desired size; I recommend 4.5 ounces (128 g), but you can make larger or smaller bagels if you prefer. Shape the bagels as instructed on page 25 and put them on the prepared pan, spacing them at least 1 inch apart. Mist the tops with vegetable spray oil and cover the pan loosely with plastic wrap.

5 Proof at room temperature for 30 to 60 minutes, until the bagels just begin to swell and rise.

6 About 20 minutes before you plan to bake the bagels, position a rack in the middle of the oven and preheat the oven to 425°F (218°C). Do a float test: Place one bagel in a small bowl of room-temperature water. If it doesn't float within 15 seconds, return it to the pan and check again every 20 minutes until a bagel passes the float test. Line a sheet pan with parchment paper or a silicone mat, mist with vegetable spray oil, and dust with cornmeal.

7 Bring 4 to 6 inches of water to a boil in a wide pot. Add the baking soda or honey to the water (both will promote deeper browning as well as add flavor) and lower the heat to maintain a simmer. Boil 2 to 4 bagels at a time for 30 seconds, then flip and boil for 30 seconds longer. Using a slotted spoon, transfer the bagels to the newly prepared baking pan, spacing them evenly, rounded side up. Garnish with selected toppings (see next page) as soon as they emerge from the water.

8 Bake for 12 minutes, then rotate the pan and bake for 8 to 12 minutes longer, until golden brown all over. If the bottoms are getting too dark during baking, slide a second pan under the first for insulation.

NOTES:

- You can substitute an equal amount of honey, agave nectar, sorghum syrup, or molasses for the malt syrup. The flavor will be slightly different with each.

- For an overnight method, instead of fermenting the dough after mixing it, immediately divide it into the desired number of pieces. Line a sheet pan with parchment paper or a silicone mat and mist with vegetable spray oil. Shape the pieces into bagels as described on page 25 and put them on the prepared pan. Mist the tops with vegetable spray oil and cover the pan with plastic wrap or a large plastic bag. Refrigerate overnight. About 1 hour before you plan to boil and bake the bagels, remove them from the refrigerator. After 1 hour, do a float test, then boil and bake as directed on page 90.

Variations

TOPPINGS: Sesame seeds and poppy seeds are the most common bagel toppings, but other options include black onion seeds (also called nigella seeds), caraway seeds, granulated garlic, dried garlic flakes (soaked in just enough water to hydrate them), coarse kosher or pretzel salt, dried onion flakes (soaked in just enough water to hydrate them), or diced fresh onion.

EVERYTHING BAGELS: Go for broke and use 1 tablespoon (about 0.18 oz / 5 g) granulated garlic or rehydrated dried garlic flakes, 1 tablespoon (0.32 oz / 9 g) poppy seeds, 1 tablespoon (0.32 oz / 9 g) sesame seeds, 1 teaspoon (about 0.16 oz / 4.5 g) coarse salt, ½ teaspoon (0.05 oz / 1.5 g) paprika or smoked paprika (sweet or hot, depending on your taste), and, optionally, 1 teaspoon (0.11 oz / 3 g) caraway or anise seeds.

CINNAMON-SUGAR BAGELS: Whisk together ½ cup (3 oz / 85 g) sugar and 2 tablespoons (0.55 oz / 15.5 g) ground cinnamon. When the bagels are just out of the oven, immediately brush the tops with melted butter, then dip into the cinnamon sugar to coat the top. As the bagels cool, the cinnamon sugar will set on the crust.

MULTIGRAIN BAGELS: You can substitute up to 20% other sprouted grain or sprouted bean flours for an equal amount of sprouted whole wheat flour to make a multigrain version. You can also substitute nonsprouted grain flours but, for best flavor, I suggest sticking with the sprouted flours.

RAISIN OR CINNAMON RAISIN BAGELS: For raisin bagels, add 1½ cups (9 oz / 255 g) raisins to the dough during the final minute of mixing or until they are evenly distributed. You may also need about 1 additional tablespoon (0.5 oz / 14 g) of water, but let the dough dictate whether or not it needs the added water. You can also add 1 teaspoon (0.09 oz / 2.6 g) ground cinnamon.

SPROUTED STRUAN BREAD

MAKES 2 LOAVES OR UP TO 24 ROLLS

In each of my bread books I include a new recipe for struan. It's my all-time favorite bread, and I keep coming up with new ways to make it because, although it's a traditional bread, there has never been a specific recipe for it other than the ones I've published. Its origins are in the Michaelmas harvest celebration of Western Scotland, where it was made only one time a year, on September 28, the eve of the feast, using whatever ingredients could be harvested. The name *struan* comes from the Gaelic *sruthan*, which means "a convergence of streams."

At Brother Juniper's Bakery this was our signature loaf, and our top-selling bread by far. I've come to think of it as a metaphor as much as a bread; the metaphor of me (and all of us, really)—yes, a convergence of streams. One of the reasons why it remains so popular is that it makes exquisite toast. For a number of years, I pretty much lived on a breakfast of two slices of buttered struan toast slathered with local blueberry or raspberry jam. It's a deeply embedded taste memory; it is my madeleine.

DOUGH

INGREDIENT	VOLUME	OUNCES	GRAMS	%
sprouted whole wheat flour	3¾ cups	16	454	87
sprouted corn flour or cornmeal	6½ tablespoons	1.6	45.5	8.7
sprouted rolled oats	⅓ cup	1.6	45.5	8.7
sprouted brown rice flour (or sprouted rye flour)	2 tablespoons plus 2 teaspoons (or 3 tablespoons plus 2 teaspoons)	0.8	22.5	4.3
salt	1½ teaspoons	0.35	10	1.9
instant yeast	5 teaspoons	0.55	15.5	2.9
brown sugar (or honey or agave nectar)	6 tablespoons (or 4½ tablespoons)	3	85	16
water, lukewarm (95°F / 35°C)	1¼ cups	10	283	54
buttermilk, lukewarm (95°F / 35°C)	¾ cup	6	170	33
cooked brown rice	⅓ cup	2	56.5	11
egg white wash	1 egg white whisked with 1 tablespoon water			
poppy or sesame seeds (optional)	2 to 3 teaspoons			
TOTAL		41.9	1,187.5	227.8

CONTINUED

1 In the bowl of a stand mixer fitted with the paddle attachment, or in a large bowl, stir together the sprouted whole wheat flour, corn flour, rolled oats, rice flour, salt, and yeast, on low speed if using a stand mixer. (If using sugar rather than honey or agave nectar, add it at this point.) In a separate bowl, stir together the water and buttermilk, then stir in the honey and cooked rice. Add the buttermilk mixture to the flour mixture and mix or stir until the flour is hydrated and a coarse, sticky dough forms, about 1 minute.

2 Let the dough rest, uncovered, for 5 minutes. Then switch to the dough hook or use a wet spoon or wet hands and mix for 2 minutes, on medium-low speed if using a stand mixer. The dough should become more cohesive, but it will still be very soft and sticky, though not as loose as a batter. (The various grains take a while to fully hydrate.) Add a bit more flour or milk if necessary to achieve this texture, but bear in mind that the dough will firm up during the stretch and fold process.

3 Spread about 1 teaspoon of vegetable oil or olive oil on a work surface. Using a wet or oiled bowl scraper or rubber spatula, transfer the dough to the oiled area. Lightly oil your hands, then stretch and fold the dough as shown on page 20, folding it over itself four times: once each from the top, bottom, and sides. The dough will firm up slightly but still be very soft and somewhat sticky. Cover the dough with the mixing bowl and then, at intervals of 5 minutes or up to 20 minutes, perform three additional sequences of stretching and folding. For each stretch and fold sequence, lightly oil your hands to prevent sticking. The dough will firm up a bit more with each stretch and fold. After the final fold it should be soft, supple, and tacky and have a springy or bouncy quality when patted.

4 Oil a large bowl and put the dough in the bowl. Mist the top of the dough with vegetable spray oil and cover with a lid or plastic wrap; if using plastic wrap, stretch it tightly over the bowl rather than laying it directly on the dough. Ferment the dough at room temperature for 1½ to 2 hours, until double in size. (This time can be shortened by using a warm proof box set at about 90°F / 32°C.)

5 Oil the work surface again. Using an oiled bowl scraper or rubber spatula, transfer the dough to the oiled area. **For pan loaves,** mist two 4½ by 8-inch loaf pans with vegetable spray oil. Divide the dough in half and shape the pieces into sandwich loaves as shown on pages 23 and 24, then put the loaves in the prepared pans. **For rolls,** line two sheet pans with parchment paper or silicone mats. Divide the dough into the desired number of pieces (24 for small dinner rolls) and shape as desired (see page 24). Put half of the rolls on each lined pan.

NOTE: You can also form this dough into 1 large or 2 smaller freestanding boules. Proof each on a sheet pan lined with parchment paper or a silicone mat, then bake as described for rolls. Large boules will take 35 to 45 minutes to bake; small boules 30 to 40 minutes.

6 Brush the tops of the dough with the egg white wash and sprinkle with poppy seeds if you wish. Mist with vegetable spray oil, then cover loosely with plastic wrap or place the pans in a large plastic bag. Proof for 1 to 1½ hours at room temperature, until the dough increases in size by 1½ times.

7 To bake pan loaves, position a rack in the middle of the oven and preheat the oven to 350°F (177°C). Bake for 20 minutes, then rotate and bake for 25 to 40 minutes longer, until the crust is golden brown on all sides and the loaves sound hollow when thumped. The internal temperature should be about 190°F (88°C).

8 To bake rolls, position two racks in the oven an equal distance apart and preheat the oven to 400°F (204°C). Bake for 10 minutes, then rotate the pans front to back and between racks. Bake for 10 to 12 minutes longer, until the crust is golden brown and the rolls sound hollow when thumped. The internal temperature should be about 190°F (88°C).

9 Transfer from the pans to a wire rack. Let loaves cool for at least 1 hour before serving. Rolls can be served after 10 minutes.

Variation

You can replace any or all of the nonwheat flours with an equal amount, by weight, of a sprouted flour multigrain blend, such as Lindley Mills Ancient Grain (see Resources, page 240), or individual flours, such as sprouted millet, quinoa, or spelt. You can also use nonsprouted flours or grains, such as conventional cornmeal or rolled oats, if you wish.

SPROUTED WHEAT SOFT ROLLS OR SANDWICH BREAD

MAKES 2 LOAVES OR UP TO 36 ROLLS

Many people find the Sprouted Whole Wheat Bread (page 63) sufficiently sweet and soft to use for sandwiches and rolls. However, sandwich loaves and dinner rolls typically include enrichments such as milk, oil or butter, and sweeteners, so I also offer this recipe, which is formulated to more closely approximate the soft, sweet texture and flavor of enriched white bread while still using 100% sprouted whole wheat flour. This kind of dough is generically referred to as milk dough because it uses milk rather than water as the liquid. If you like a little tang, go for the buttermilk option, which provides some acidity for enhanced flavor.

DOUGH

INGREDIENT	VOLUME	OUNCES	GRAMS	%
sprouted whole wheat flour	6⅔ cups	28	794	100
salt	2 teaspoons	0.5	14	1.8
instant yeast	2¼ teaspoons	0.25	7	0.9
sugar (or honey or agave nectar)	5 tablespoons (or 3 tablespoons)	2	56.5	7
milk or buttermilk, lukewarm (95°F / 35°C)	3 cups	24	680	86
vegetable oil	3 tablespoons	1.5	42.5	5.4
egg wash	1 egg whisked with 1 tablespoon water			
sesame or poppy seeds for topping (optional)				
TOTAL		56.25	1,594	201.1

1 In the bowl of a stand mixer fitted with the paddle attachment, or in a large bowl, stir together the flour, salt, and yeast (on low speed if using a stand mixer). Stir in the sugar (if using honey or agave nectar, add it to the milk in the next step). Add the milk and oil and mix or stir until the flour is hydrated and a coarse, sticky dough forms, about 1 minute.

2 Let the dough rest, uncovered, for 5 minutes. Then switch to the dough hook or use a wet spoon or wet hands and mix for 1 minute, on medium-low speed if using a stand mixer. The dough should be smooth but still very soft and sticky. Add a bit more flour or milk if necessary to achieve this texture, but bear in mind that the dough will firm up during the stretch and fold process.

3 Spread about 1 teaspoon of vegetable oil or olive oil on a work surface. Using a wet or oiled bowl scraper or a rubber spatula, transfer the dough to the oiled area. Lightly oil your hands, then stretch and fold the dough as shown on page 20, folding it over itself four times: once each from the top, bottom, and sides. The dough will firm up slightly but still be very soft and somewhat sticky. Cover the dough with the mixing bowl and then, at intervals of 5 minutes or up to 20 minutes, perform three additional sequences of stretching and folding. For each stretch and fold sequence, lightly oil your hands to prevent sticking. The dough will firm up a bit more with each stretch and fold sequence. After the final fold it should be soft, supple, and tacky and have a springy or bouncy quality when patted.

4 Oil a large bowl and put the dough in the bowl. Mist the top of the dough with vegetable spray oil and cover with a lid or plastic wrap; if using plastic wrap, stretch it tightly over the bowl rather than laying it directly on the dough. Ferment the dough at room temperature for 1½ to 2 hours, until double in size. (This time can be shortened by using a warm proof box set at about 90°F / 32°C.)

5 Oil the work surface again and use an oiled bowl scraper or rubber spatula to transfer the dough to the oiled area. **For pan loaves,** mist two 4½ by 8-inch loaf pans with vegetable spray oil. Divide the dough in half and shape the pieces into sandwich loaves as shown on pages 23 and 24, then put the shaped loaves in the prepared pans. **For rolls,** line two sheet pans with parchment paper or silicone mats. Divide the dough into the desired number of pieces and shape as desired (see page 24). Put half of the rolls on each lined pan.

6 Mist the exposed surface of the dough with vegetable spray oil. Cover loosely with plastic wrap or place the pans in a large plastic bag. Proof for 1 to 1½ hours at room temperature, until the dough increases in size by 1½ times. If making pan loaves, the dough should dome up above the pan by 1 inch or more.

7 To bake pan loaves, position a rack in the middle of the oven and preheat the oven to 350°F (177°C). Brush the tops of the loaves with the egg wash and sprinkle with sesame or poppy seeds if you wish. Bake for 20 minutes, then rotate and bake for 25 to 40 minutes longer, until the crust is golden brown on all sides and the loaves sound hollow when thumped. The internal temperature should be about 190°F (88°C).

8 To bake rolls, position two racks in the oven an equal distance apart and preheat the oven to 400°F (204°C). Brush the tops of the rolls with the egg wash and sprinkle with sesame or poppy seeds if you wish. Bake for 12 minutes, then rotate the pans front to back and between racks. Bake for 8 to 12 minutes longer, until the crust is golden brown and the rolls sound hollow when thumped. The internal temperature should be about 190°F (88°C).

9 Transfer from the pans to a wire rack. Let loaves cool for at least 1 hour before slicing and serving. Rolls can be served after 10 minutes.

SPROUTED SANDWICH RYE BREAD

MAKES 1 LARGE OR 2 SMALL LOAVES

Sandwich rye breads generally contain far less rye flour than wheat flour, mainly because the gluten content of rye is only about half that of wheat. In many commercial rye breads, the dough is reinforced with vital wheat gluten to ensure a tall, airy loaf. Another characteristic of sandwich rye bread is that sourdough starter is often used in addition to commercial yeast. It isn't the primary leavening, but it does provide some acidity and flavor and also helps control enzyme activity. Therefore, this recipe doesn't require building a final starter; rather, you can simply use a freshly rebuilt mother starter.

Sprouted rye flour isn't as easy to find as sprouted whole wheat flour, so you may need to purchase it online (see Resources, page 240). You can also use regular, nonsprouted rye flour, as long as the primary flour is sprouted wheat. Either way, this is a great bread for grilled cheese sandwiches and, of course, corned beef or pastrami sandwiches.

DOUGH

INGREDIENT	VOLUME	OUNCES	GRAMS	%
sprouted whole wheat flour	4¾ cups	20	567	80
sprouted rye flour	1¼ cups plus 3 tablespoons	5	142	20
salt	2 teaspoons	0.5	14	2
instant yeast	1⅝ teaspoons	0.18	5	0.7
toasted caraway seeds or black nigella seeds (optional; see page 101 for toasting instructions)	about 1 tablespoon	0.32	9	1.3
water, lukewarm (95°F / 35°C)	2½ cups	20	567	80
molasses	1½ tablespoons	1	28.5	4
Mother Starter (page 40), recently refreshed	⅔ cup	5	142	20
TOTAL		52	1,474.5	208

1 In the bowl of a stand mixer fitted with the paddle attachment, stir together the flours, salt, yeast, and caraway seeds (on low speed if using a stand mixer). In a separate bowl, combine the water, molasses, and mother starter and stir for about

CONTINUED

20 seconds to soften the starter. Add the starter mixture to the flour mixture and mix or stir until the flour is hydrated and a coarse, sticky dough forms, about 1 minute.

2 Let the dough rest, uncovered, for 5 minutes. Then switch to the dough hook or use a wet spoon or wet hands and mix for 1 to 2 minutes, on medium-low speed if using a stand mixer. The dough should be smooth but still slightly soft and sticky. Add a bit more flour or water if necessary to achieve this texture, but bear in mind that the dough will firm up during the stretch and fold process.

3 Spread about 1 teaspoon of vegetable oil or olive oil on a work surface. Using a wet or oiled bowl scraper or rubber spatula, transfer the dough to the oiled area. Lightly oil your hands, then stretch and fold the dough as shown on page 20, folding it over itself four times: once each from the top, bottom, and sides. The dough will firm up slightly but still be very soft and somewhat sticky. Cover the dough with the mixing bowl and then, at intervals of 5 minutes or up to 20 minutes, perform three additional sequences of stretching and folding. For each stretch and fold sequence, lightly oil your hands to prevent sticking. The dough will firm up a bit more with each stretch and fold. After the final fold it should be firm and bouncy when slapped, and only slightly tacky.

4 Oil a large bowl and put the dough in the bowl. Mist the top of the dough with vegetable spray oil and cover with a lid or plastic wrap; if using plastic wrap, stretch it tightly over the bowl rather than laying it directly on the dough. Ferment the dough at room temperature for 1½ to 2 hours, until double in size. (This time can be shortened by using a warm proof box set at about 90°F / 32°C.)

5 Oil the work surface again. Using an oiled bowl scraper, transfer the dough to the oiled area. **For a hearth loaf or 2 freestanding loaves,** prepare two bannetons or a *couche* as shown on page 26 or line an 18 by 13-inch sheet pan with parchment paper then mist with vegetable spray oil. Shape the dough into one large boule or bâtard as shown on pages 20 to 21, or divide the dough in half and shape each piece into a small boule or bâtard as shown on pages 20 to 21. Put the shaped loaves in the prepared proofing vessel(s) or on the sheet pan. **For pan loaves,** mist two 4½ by 8-inch loaf pans with vegetable spray oil. Divide the dough in half and shape the pieces into sandwich loaves as shown on pages 23 and 24, then put the shaped loaves in the prepared pans.

6 Mist the exposed surface of the dough with vegetable spray oil. Cover loosely with plastic wrap or put the shaped loaves in a large plastic bag. Proof for 1 to 1½ hours at room temperature, until the dough increases in size by 1½ times. If making pan loaves, the dough should dome up above the pan by 1 inch or more.

7 To bake 1 or 2 freestanding loaves, about 45 minutes before you plan to bake, prepare the oven for hearth baking with a baking stone and steam pan as shown on page 29, then preheat the oven to 450°F (232°C). Transfer the dough to a floured peel (or keep it on the sheet pan for baking). Score the top with 3 or 4 parallel cuts, about ½ inch deep, across the top (see page 29). (Rye bread is typically sliced straight across as opposed to diagonally, but this is really the baker's choice.) Transfer the dough to the middle shelf of the oven and, if baking hearth bread, pour about 1 cup of hot water into the steam pan. Bake for 5 minutes, then lower the temperature to 425°F (218°C). Bake for 20 minutes, then rotate and bake for 15 to 20 minutes longer, until the crust is golden brown and the bread sounds hollow when thumped on the bottom. The internal temperature should be about 195°F (91°C). Transfer to a wire rack and let cool for at least 1 hour before slicing and serving.

8 To bake pan loaves, preheat the oven to 375°F (191°C). Bake for 25 minutes, then rotate and bake for 25 to 35 minutes longer, until the crust is golden brown and the bread sounds hollow when thumped on the bottom. The internal temperature should be about 190°F (88°C). Transfer the loaves from the pans to a wire rack and let cool for at least 1 hour for before slicing and serving.

Variations

DARK SANDWICH RYE: Add 3 tablespoons (1 oz / 28.5 g) cocoa powder to the flour mixture and increase the amount of water by 1 tablespoon (0.5 oz / 14 g).

ONION RYE: Add 2 tablespoons (0.35 oz / 10 g) dried onion flakes or 1 onion, finely chopped, to the flour mixture.

Toasting Seeds and Nuts

Toast in a dry skillet over medium heat, stirring constantly, until they begin to darken and smell nutty. Immediately remove from the heat and transfer to a bowl to cool. An alternative method is to lay them out on a sheet pan and toast in a preheated oven 350°F / 177°C. Stir them every 3 minutes until they begin to darken and smell nutty. Whole nuts will take longer than chopped nuts or seeds.

GLUTEN-FREE "DO NO HARM" SPROUTED GRAIN BREAD

MAKES 1 LOAF

There are a lot of gluten-free sandwich bread recipes and products out there, but to the best of my knowledge, no one has yet marketed a bread made solely with sprouted gluten-free flour, as this one is. This recipe employs a hybrid leavening of both yeast and baking powder. It also uses xanthan gum, which provides enough structure to hold the loaf together and to create a slightly open crumb. The dough is more like a batter, which is about the only way I've found to make a moist loaf with gluten-free flour. If the dough were firm enough to be moldable, it would taste like cardboard by the time it came out of the oven. Therefore, it can't be made as a hearth loaf, but that's about the only drawback to this recipe. It's free from the most common allergens, such as dairy, eggs, nuts, and wheat. It's why I call it Do No Harm Bread. The internal texture of this bread is soft and creamy, the crust is crisp and nutty, and it tastes great, especially when toasted. To maximize the flavors and texture, toast this bread until crisp and golden brown, which may take a few plunges of the toaster. If you have a corn sensitivity, you can replace the corn with more sprouted brown rice flour or a comparable increase in the other sprouted grain or bean flours in the recipe (all of which are available online, see Resources, page 240). One final note: If you have a set of mini loaf pans, this is a good time to use them, although you can also make a full size loaf. The mini loaves take only half as long to bake and are easy to store in the freezer, which is why I like them. Don't worry if the top of the loaf flattens out during baking due to the absence of gluten; it's a very small tradeoff for the moist, creamy interior.

DOUGH

INGREDIENT	VOLUME	OUNCES	GRAMS	%
sprouted corn flour	1¾ cups	7	198	44
sprouted brown rice flour	1½ cups	7	198	44
sprouted amaranth, quinoa, black bean, garbanzo, or lentil flour	about ½ cup	2	56.5	12
flaxseeds or sesame seeds (optional)	about 4 teaspoons	0.5	14	3.1
salt	1 teaspoon	0.25	7	1.5
instant yeast	1½ teaspoons	0.16	4.5	1
baking powder	1½ teaspoons	0.28	8	1.8

INGREDIENT	VOLUME	OUNCES	GRAMS	%
xanthan gum (see page 81)	1 tablespoon	0.32	9	2
sugar or liquid stevia	2 tablespoons or ⅛ teaspoon (about 10 drops)	1 or 0.04	28.5 or 1	6.3 or 0.2
water or unsweetened nondairy milk, lukewarm (95°F / 35°C)	3 cups plus 2 tablespoons	25	709	157
TOTAL		43.51 or 42.55	1,232.5 or 1,205	272.7 or 266.6

1 In a large bowl, stir together the sprouted flours, flaxseeds, salt, yeast, xanthan gum, and sugar. (If using liquid stevia, add it with the water in the next step.) Add the water and stir for about 1 minute to make a thick, sticky batter-like dough. Cover the bowl with plastic wrap and let the dough rest at room temperature for about 1 hour, until the dough swells slightly and shows signs of fermentation. It will thicken as it sits.

2 Line the bottom of a 5 by 9-inch (or 4½ by 8-inch) loaf pan with parchment paper and generously mist the pan with vegetable spray oil (if using mini pans you do not need to line them with parchment). Transfer the dough to the prepared pan; it should be about three-quarters full. Mist the top with vegetable spray oil and pat the dough into the pan to spread it evenly and smooth the top. Cover loosely with plastic wrap and proof at room temperature for about 45 minutes, until the dough rises almost to the top of the pan (the dough has very little oven spring once baked, so it shouldn't spill over the sides of the pan).

3 Position a rack in the middle of the oven and preheat the oven to 350°F (177°C).

4 Bake for 40 minutes, then rotate and bake for 40 to 45 minutes longer. Remove the loaf from the pan and put it on a sheet pan or directly on the oven rack, then continue baking for about 10 minutes, until the top is hard when tapped, the loaf sounds hollow when thumped on the bottom, and the crust is dark golden brown (though there may be a whitish hue over some of the top crust from the long bake and dry oven). The internal temperature of the loaf should be at least 190°F (88°C).

5 Transfer to a wire rack and let cool for at least 1 hour before slicing and serving.

Can these recipes be made using standard, nonsprouted gluten-free flours, rather than the sprouted versions?

Yes, but the nutritional and digestive benefits are greater when using sprouted flour.

Q & A

SPROUTED VOLLKORNBROT

MAKES 2 LARGE LOAVES OR 6 TO 8 SMALL LOAVES

Dense, chewy German-style breads are coming into vogue, with increasing numbers of bakeries featuring their own versions under various names. This recipe is for vollkornbrot, which simply means "whole grain bread." It's a type of bread designed to be dense and packed with intense flavor and fiber, so a thin slice goes a long way. Toasted or untoasted, it's a great cocktail or appetizer bread for serving with spreads, cheeses, and pâtés.

Although vollkornbrot is usually associated with whole rye flour, there are many ways to make it. In *Peter Reinhart's Whole Grain Breads*, I offered a version that called for making a scalded mash of rye flour to heighten the enzyme activity, along with a pre-ferment. In this new version, neither of those approaches is needed, thanks to the high enzyme activity of sprouted flour. However, including some recently refreshed mother starter is an option if you'd like to add more acidic flavor (see the variation). Because there are so many ways to make this bread, you'll see that a number of the ingredients are optional. Although the cooked rye or wheat berries are among the optional ingredients, they do add a wonderful, chewy texture. If you use them, be sure to cook them thoroughly so they don't dry out during baking, especially those near the surface.

Although these breads are often made in long loaf pans and baked for a long time at low temperatures, I now prefer using mini loaf pans and making smaller loaves. The advantage of this is that the breads take far less time to bake and you can freeze the extra mini loaves for future use. This kind of dense bread is often at its most flavorful the day after baking. If storing, let the loaves cool completely before wrapping them in aluminum foil or plastic wrap.

CONTINUED

DOUGH

NOTES:

- You can use all sprouted rye flour or all sprouted whole wheat flour, or any combination of those flours, as long as the total weight is 28 ounces (793 g).

- The amount of water needed may vary depending on which optional ingredients you use. View the amount listed as a guideline and adjust as needed, following the cues in the recipe.

- To cook the rye or wheat berries, combine ½ cup (about 6.5 oz / 185 g) grain with 1½ cups (12 oz / 340 g) water in a saucepan and bring to a boil. Lower the heat, cover, and simmer until the grains are soft, about 1 hour. Drain, reserving the liquid if you'd like to use it as part of the water in the recipe. Let the grains cool completely before use. Because of the time needed for cooling, you might prefer to cook the grains a day or two ahead and keep them in the refrigerator.

INGREDIENT	VOLUME	OUNCES	GRAMS	%
sprouted rye flour	5 cups plus 2 tablespoons	18	510	64
sprouted whole wheat flour	2⅓ cups	10	283	36
sunflower seeds, lightly toasted (see page 101 for toasting instructions)	about ¼ cup	1.5	42.5	5.4
whole flaxseeds	about 3 tablespoons	1	28.5	3.6
cocoa powder (optional)	1½ tablespoons	0.5	14	1.8
salt	2 teaspoons	0.5	14	1.8
water, at room temperature (see notes)	3½ cups	28	794	100
molasses (optional)	3 tablespoons	2	56.5	7.1
instant yeast	5 teaspoons	0.55	15.5	2
cooked rye or wheat berries (optional; see notes)	1 cup	6	170	21
TOTAL		68.05	1,928	242.7

1 In the bowl of a stand mixer fitted with the paddle attachment, or in a large bowl, stir together the sprouted flour, toasted sunflower seeds, flaxseeds, cocoa powder, and salt (on low speed if using a stand mixer). In a separate bowl, whisk together the water and molasses, then stir in the yeast to dissolve it (it need not bloom or bubble). Add the molasses mixture and cooked rye berries to the flour mixture and mix or stir until the flour is hydrated and a coarse, wet dough forms. The texture will be similar to mud. Mix for 2 more minutes; if using a stand mixer, start on low speed and increase to medium for the last 15 seconds. The dough should be quite wet and just firm enough to hold its shape if squeezed. Add a bit more water or flour if necessary to achieve this texture, but bear in mind that the dough will thicken as it sits, so a wet and somewhat loose dough is better than dry and stiff. All of that said, there's a fair amount of leeway regarding the texture as long as the dough can be molded by hand.

2 Spread a bit of vegetable oil on a work surface. Using an oiled bowl scraper, transfer the dough to the oiled area. Lightly oil your hands and press the dough into a rounded mound. It won't feel like any other kind of dough, and it will have little or no gluten structure. Mist a bowl with vegetable spray oil and cover the dough with the bowl, or transfer the dough to the bowl, mist the top with vegetable spray oil, and cover the bowl with plastic wrap. Ferment at room temperature for 1 hour. The dough will hardly rise, but the yeast will begin working.

3 Generously mist two 4½ by 8-inch loaf pans or 6 to 8 mini loaf pans with vegetable spray oil or rub them with vegetable oil; if you'd like to make freestanding loaves, line a sheet pan with parchment paper or a silicone mat and mist the surface with vegetable spray oil.

4 Generously dust the work surface with flour. Transfer the dough onto the floured work surface and divide into the appropriate number of pieces. Roll each piece in the flour on the work surface until completely coated, adding more flour to the work surface if necessary. Shape each piece into a bâtard as shown on pages 20 to 21; don't worry about cracks in the surface, as these will be part of the finished look. Put the pieces in the prepared pans or on the sheet pan and cover loosely with plastic wrap. Proof at room temperature for 1 hour. Again, the dough will hardly rise.

5 About 45 minutes before you plan to bake, prepare the oven for hearth baking with a baking stone and steam pan as shown on page 29. Preheat the oven to 500°F (260°C).

6 Put the loaves in the oven and pour about 1 cup of hot water into the steam pan. Immediately lower the temperature to 375°F (191°C) for freestanding loaves or 350°F (177°C) for pan loaves. Bake for 30 minutes, then rotate and bake until the crust is hard and the loaves sound hollow when thumped on the bottom, about 30 minutes longer for mini loaves and freestanding loaves, or 45 to 50 minutes longer for large pan loaves. The internal temperature should be at least 190°F (88°C). The loaves won't rise very much in the oven and will feel very heavy and dense, but they will rise enough for the dusting of flour on the surface to create an interesting pattern.

7 Transfer from the pans to a wire rack and let cool completely before slicing and serving—at least 1 hour for small loaves, and at least 2 hours for large loaves.

Variation

To make this with natural leaven, add 7 ounces (198 g) recently refreshed Mother Starter (page 40) and an extra ¼ teaspoon (0.06 oz / 1.5 g) salt. You can decrease the amount of instant yeast by as much as half if you'd like a slightly tangier loaf. In that case, increase the rising time by 1 hour during both the first fermentation and the final proofing.

SPROUTED WHEAT CHALLAH

MAKES 1 LARGE OR 2 SMALL LOAVES

Over time, I continue to develop new variations of challah, and one of the things I've learned over the years is that challah dough, which is defined primarily by enrichment with eggs, always seems better with more yolks and fewer whites. Although egg whites are very nutritious, they have a drying effect on foods. Egg yolks, on the other hand, are rich in natural oils and lecithin and therefore help keep bread moist and give it a creamy mouth-feel. So these days I use only yolks, saving the whites for other purposes, such as meringues, egg white omelets, or as an egg white wash on breads. This dough can be made in any number of shapes (including as an alternative dough for the cinnamon buns on page 128), but braided challah is the most well-known version. There are many traditions associated with the braids, but my research hasn't yet revealed any rule governing the number of strands. The tradition that makes the most sense to me is that the braided loaf should have twelve sections, symbolizing the twelve tribes of Israel, but this is just one among many interpretations. New Year's challah (for Rosh Hashanah) is typically coiled rather than braided, symbolizing the eternal cycles of life. Note that this recipe calls for vegetable oil, rather than butter, because butter wouldn't be compatible with a meat-based meal according to kosher laws. If you aren't keeping a kosher diet, you can certainly substitute melted unsalted butter for the oil. However, even though I personally love the flavor of butter, I find that vegetable oil is actually more functional in this bread, contributing to a softer texture.

DOUGH

INGREDIENT	VOLUME	OUNCES	GRAMS	%
sprouted whole wheat flour	4¼ cups	18	510	100
salt	1¼ teaspoons	0.32	9	1.8
instant yeast	2¼ teaspoons	0.25	7	1.4
sugar (or honey or agave nectar)	3 tablespoons (or 2 tablespoons plus ¾ teaspoon)	1.5	42.5	8.3
water, lukewarm (95°F / 35°C)	1¼ cups plus 2 tablespoons	11	312	61
egg yolks, slightly beaten	5	3.75	106	21
vegetable oil	3 tablespoons	1.5	42.5	8.3
egg wash	1 egg whisked with 1 tablespoon water			
sesame or poppy seeds for topping (optional)				
TOTAL		36.32	1,029	201.8

1 In the bowl of a stand mixer fitted with the paddle attachment, or in a large bowl, stir together the flour, salt, and yeast (on low speed if using a stand mixer). Stir in the sugar (if using honey or agave nectar, add it to the water in the next step.) In a separate bowl, whisk together the water, egg yolks, and oil, then pour into the flour mixture and mix or stir until the flour is hydrated and a coarse, sticky dough forms, about 1 minute.

2 Let the dough rest, uncovered, for 5 minutes. Then switch to the dough hook or use a wet spoon or wet hands and mix for 1 to 2 minutes, on medium-low speed if using a stand mixer. The dough should be smooth but still slightly soft and sticky (however, it should not be as soft as the Sprouted Whole Wheat Bread on page 63). Add a bit more flour or water if necessary to achieve this texture, but bear in mind that the dough will firm up during the stretch and fold process.

3 Spread about 1 teaspoon of vegetable oil or olive oil on a work surface. Using a wet or oiled bowl scraper or rubber spatula, transfer the dough to the oiled area. Lightly oil your hands, then stretch and fold the dough as shown on page 20, folding it over itself four times: once each from the top, bottom, and sides. The dough will firm up slightly but still be soft and slightly sticky. Cover the dough with the mixing bowl and then, at intervals of 5 minutes or up to 20 minutes, perform three additional sequences of stretching and folding. For each stretch and fold sequence, lightly oil your hands to prevent sticking. The dough will firm up a bit more with each stretch and fold. After the final fold it should be only slightly tacky. It will be firmer than many doughs, because it must hold up to the braiding and retain the braided appearance when baked. That said, it must also be supple and extensible enough to roll out for braiding.

4 Oil a large bowl and put the dough in the bowl. Mist the top of the dough with vegetable spray oil and cover the bowl with a lid or plastic wrap; if using plastic wrap, stretch it tightly over the bowl rather than laying it directly on the dough. Ferment the dough at room temperature for 1½ to 2 hours, until double in size. (This time can be shortened by using a warm proof box set at about 90°F / 32°C.)

5 Oil the work surface again and transfer the dough to the oiled area. Divide it evenly into the desired number of pieces. The number of strands in the braid is up to you, with the main rule being that the strands should each be the same weight and be rolled out to the same length. Flatten each piece with the palms of your hands, then roll each into a cigar shape about 3 inches in length. Let rest for 2 minutes, then roll each piece into a tapered strand 10 to 12 inches in length. (If making 2 smaller loaves, cut the pieces in half but roll them out to about 8 inches in length.) Braid the strands until you get to the ends, then pinch the tips together to seal. (See sidebar on page 110 for more information.)

6 Line a sheet pan with parchment paper or a silicone mat and mist with vegetable spray oil. Transfer the braided dough to the baking pan. If making 2 smaller loaves, lay them side by side crosswise on the pan, allowing at least 2 inches between them so they

CONTINUED

won't touch when they rise. Brush the entire top and side surfaces with about half of the egg wash. Mist the top with vegetable spray oil and cover loosely with plastic wrap. Let proof for about 1 hour at room temperature. Brush with the remaining egg wash and generously sprinkle with seeds if you like. Proof for 10 to 15 minutes longer, until the dough increases in size by nearly 1½ times. (It will rise further in the oven.)

7 Position a rack in the middle of the oven and preheat the oven to 350°F (177°C).

8 Bake for 20 minutes, then rotate and bake for 10 minutes longer for small loaves, or 15 to 20 minutes longer for a large loaf, until the crust is rich golden brown and the bread sounds hollow when thumped on the bottom. The internal temperature should be about 190°F (88°C).

9 Transfer to a wire rack and let cool for at least 30 minutes before slicing and serving.

Braided Loaves

You can make braided breads with 2, 3, 4, or 5 strands—or more. The most important principle is to be sure each strand is the same weight and length. If you don't have a scale, estimate the size as closely as possible. Also keep in mind that the position numbers refer to the actual position of the strands on the counter, starting from your left, rather than to the particular strands; in other words, the number of a given strand changes as it's moved during the braiding process. To form the strands, use the same gentle rocking motion as for shaping baguettes (see page 23). For all braids, place the prettiest side up when you transfer to the baking sheet, then cover and proof.

TO SHAPE A 2-BRAID LOAF, lay 2 strands of equal weight and length on the work surface, perpendicular to one another and crossed in the center. Take both ends of the strand that's underneath and cross them over to the opposite sides. Cross the ends of the other strand in the same way. Continue crossing and alternating until you get to the ends of the strands, then pinch the tips together at each end to seal off the ends. Lay the braid on its side.

TO SHAPE A 3-BRAID LOAF, lay 3 equal strands side by side, parallel to one another. Beginning in the middle of the loaf, overlap one of the outside strands over the middle strand, then take the opposite outside strand and cross it over the new middle strand. Continue this pattern until you get to the ends of the strands, then pinch the tips together to seal. Rotate the loaf so the unbraided side is facing you, then repeat the pattern on that end.

TO SHAPE A 4-BRAID LOAF, connect 4 strands of equal weight and length at one end, spreading the other ends out with the tips facing you. From the left, number the strands 1, 2, 3, 4. Follow this pattern: 4 over 2, 1 over 3, and 2 over 3. Repeat until you get to the ends of the strands, then pinch the tips together to seal.

TO SHAPE A 5-BRAID LOAF, connect 5 strands of equal weight and length at one end, spreading the other ends out with the tips facing you. From the left, number the strands 1, 2, 3, 4, 5. Follow this pattern: 1 over 3, 2 over 3, and 5 over 2. Repeat until you get to the ends of the strands, then pinch the tips together to seal.

SPROUTED MULTIGRAIN CRACKERS

MAKES UP TO 48 CRACKERS, DEPENDING ON SIZE | **MASTER FORMULA**

Crackers are like chips: it's very hard to eat just one. If I were to go back into the baking business, it would be to make crackers, specializing in making them with sprouted flour and seed and nut flours. This recipe is versatile and allows for many variations. It calls for ground seeds (or ground nuts in one of the variations). Seed and nut flours, or meals, are increasingly available for purchase, but you can easily make your own if you have a small burr mill, spice grinder, or food processor, and it can even be ground by hand using a mortar and pestle. While a regular blender will work, it's tricky; you have to be careful not to blend for too long, as the friction can easily turn the seeds from meal into butter as their natural oils heat up. Short pulses can help prevent this problem. Food processors work well for some seeds and nuts, but not hard or tiny ones, such as flax, chia, or sesame seeds; for those, use a seed or spice grinder.

Baking powder is optional in this recipe. If you omit it, the crackers won't rise and will be more like chips. With baking powder they will rise slightly and tend to be more flaky. Both methods make excellent crackers, so you may want to try it both ways to determine your own preference. Either way, I bet you can't eat just one.

DOUGH

INGREDIENT	VOLUME	OUNCES	GRAMS	%
sprouted whole wheat flour	1 cup plus 1 tablespoon	4.5	128	32
sprouted rye flour (or sprouted corn flour or other sprouted grain flours)	1¼ cups plus 1 tablespoon (or 1 cup plus 2 tablespoons or about 1 cup plus 1 tablespoon)	4.5	128	32
ground sunflower seeds, pumpkin seeds, or flaxseeds	about 1¼ cups	5	142	36
salt	¼ teaspoon	0.06	1.5	0.3
baking powder (optional)	1½ teaspoons	0.28	8	2
water	1 cup	8	227	57
vegetable oil or melted unsalted butter	2 tablespoons	1	28.5	7.2
honey or agave nectar	3½ teaspoons	0.75	21.5	5.4
egg wash	1 egg whisked with 1 tablespoon water			
TOTAL		24.09	684.5	171.9

CONTINUED

1 In the bowl of a stand mixer fitted with the paddle attachment, or in a large bowl, stir together the flours, ground seeds, salt, and baking powder (on low speed if using a stand mixer). In a separate bowl, whisk together the water, oil, and honey, then pour into the flour mixture. Mix or stir until all the ingredients gather into a coarse ball, about 1 minute. If all of the flour isn't picked up by the dough ball, add a few drops of water.

2 Lightly dust a work surface with sprouted flour or lightly oil the work surface. Transfer the dough to the work surface and knead by hand for about 30 seconds to ensure that all the ingredients are evenly distributed and the dough holds together. It should be pliable and only slightly tacky, not sticky, with a texture similar to Play-Doh.

3 Preheat the oven to 300°F (149°C).

4 Divide the dough into 4 equal pieces. (If you don't want to bake all of the crackers at once, wrap any pieces you won't be baking in plastic wrap; they can be stored in the refrigerator for up to 1 week or in the freezer for up to 3 months.) For each piece of dough you plan to bake, line a sheet pan with parchment paper or a silicone mat.

5 Generously mist two sheets of parchment paper or waxed paper with vegetable spray oil. Transfer one piece of the dough to the center of one of the prepared pieces of parchment paper. Mist the top with vegetable spray oil, then use your hands to gently pat the dough down into a thick rectangle or oblong with a fairly even surface. Flip the other piece of parchment paper over and position the oiled side atop the dough. Using a rolling pin, very gently roll the dough out until about ⅛ inch thick. When rolling the dough, use short, gentle strokes, rather than pressing hard or making long strokes. Try to ease or coax the dough into a wider and wider circle or rectangle, always rolling from the center to the corners, and then to each of the sides. Carefully peel off the top piece of parchment paper.

6 Brush with one-fourth of the egg wash. Use a pizza cutter to cut the dough into rectangles, diamonds, or any shape you like. You can also use a small biscuit cutter, dipped in flour, to make round crackers. If so, you'll have leftover scraps that you'll need to roll out again. The crackers not need all be the same size or shape. Transfer the cut pieces to the lined pan. They can be nearly touching, as they won't spread.

CONTINUED

7 Multiple pans of crackers can be baked at the same time. Put the pans on different racks and bake for 10 minutes, then rotate the pans front to back and between racks. Bake for 10 minutes longer. Rotate the pans once more and bake for 5 to 20 minutes longer, depending on thickness, until rich golden brown and fairly dry. For a bit more browning, increase the temperature to 325°F (163°C) for the final few minutes of baking.

8 Remove from the oven and leave the crackers on the pans; they'll become more crisp as they cool. If they don't snap cleanly after cooling, return the pan to a hot oven (375°F /191°C) for a few minutes, until they dry sufficiently to snap when broken. Cool for at least 15 minutes before serving. The cooled crackers can be stored in an airtight container at room temperature for up to 8 days, or in a zip-top bag in the freezer indefinitely.

Variations

Replace any or all of the sprouted flours with an equal amount, by weight, of conventional wheat or rye flour, or any other flour, including gluten-free and ancient grain flours. Depending on which flours you use, you may have to decrease the water slightly.

While ground sunflower and pumpkin seeds are often used in the dough, you may also substitute any ground seed or nut flour, such as hemp, chia, flax, pecan, walnut, or almond.

Poppy and sesame seeds are generally the best toppings because their light flavor doesn't compete with the crackers as stronger spices, like cumin or anise, would. Flavored salt blends, such as garlic or lemon pepper, and spice rubs also work nicely, but use them with a light touch. Chopped pumpkin seeds or nuts are another possibility. For all of these options, sprinkle them over the surface after applying the egg wash.

Replace the egg wash with a flavored oil, such as Herb Oil (page 85) or perhaps a blend made with salt, smoked paprika, and herbes de Provence or other herbs to taste. Alternatively, go ahead and brush the crackers with the egg wash before baking, then brush with flavored oil as soon as they come out of the oven, then return the crackers to the oven for a few minutes to set the glaze.

CHEESE CRACKERS: Grated cheese can either be worked into the dough during kneading or sprinkled on top. In either case, use about 1 cup (3 to 4 oz / 85 to 113 g) grated cheese. Given that the baking temperature is so low, most cheeses can be sprinkled on top prior to baking. However, dry aged cheeses like Parmesan will brown more quickly than semi-moist cheeses like Cheddar, Swiss, and provolone and therefore should be sprinkled on top when you rotate the pans the first time.

GLUTEN-FREE SPROUTED GRAIN CRACKERS

MAKES ABOUT 60 CRACKERS, DEPENDING ON SIZE

There are so many ways to make crackers, and that extends to gluten-free crackers. Now, sprouted grain and sprouted bean flours open yet another new realm of possibilities. The key is to have the right balance of flour, fat, and sweetness, plus good rolling technique. The rolling method here is just one of many ways to roll out crackers, but it works especially well for gluten-free versions, which are typically difficult to transfer onto a pan without falling apart. The combination of flours in this recipe provides a starting point, but feel free to experiment with other flours as desired, as long as the total flour weight remains the same. You can also use non-sprouted flour in this recipe, but the sprouted flour offers exceptional flavor. These crackers are tender and flaky; if you prefer crisper crackers, decrease the amount of oil by half. The egg whites serve as a binder; you could use a whole egg instead for both binding and more richness from the yolk. One final note: Any of the variations of the Sprouted Multigrain Crackers recipe (page 111) will also work well with this recipe.

DOUGH

INGREDIENT	VOLUME	OUNCES	GRAMS	%
sprouted brown rice flour	1¼ cups	6	170	46
sprouted corn flour	1½ cups	6	170	46
other sprouted gluten-free flour, such as quinoa, teff, lentil, black bean, garbanzo, millet, sorghum, or amaranth	about 5 tablespoons	1	28.5	8
salt	½ teaspoon	0.12	3.5	0.9
baking powder (optional)	1½ teaspoons	0.28	8	2.2
flaxseeds or sesame seeds	about 3 tablespoons	1	28.5	8
honey (or agave nectar or sugar)	1½ tablespoons (or 2 tablespoons)	1	28.5	8
egg whites, slightly beaten	¼ cup	2	56.5	15
grape seed oil, olive oil, or melted unsalted butter	6 tablespoons	3	85	23
water	1 cup	8	227	62
egg white wash	1 egg white whisked with 1 tablespoon water			
TOTAL		28.4	805.5	219.1

CONTINUED

1 In the bowl of a stand mixer fitted with the paddle attachment, or in a large bowl, stir together the sprouted flours, salt, baking powder, and flaxseeds (on low speed if using a stand mixer). (If using sugar rather than honey or agave nectar, add it at this point.) In a separate bowl, whisk together the honey, egg whites, oil, and water, then pour into the flour mixture. Mix or stir for 1 to 2 minutes to form a thick, sticky, batter-like dough, adding a bit of flour or water if necessary to achieve this texture. The dough will thicken somewhat as it sits.

2 Generously mist two sheets of parchment paper or silicone mats with vegetable spray oil. Transfer half of the batter to the center of one of the prepared pieces of parchment paper. Mist the top with vegetable spray oil, then use your hands to gently pat the dough down into a thick rectangle or oblong with a fairly even surface. Flip the other piece of parchment paper over and position the oiled side atop the dough. Using a rolling pin, very gently roll the dough out until ⅛ to ¼ inch thick, always working from the center to the corners and then from the center to the sides and ends. Carefully peel off the top piece of parchment paper. Keeping the dough on the lower piece of parchment paper, carefully lift and transfer it to a sheet pan.

3 Position two racks in the oven an equal distance apart and preheat the oven to 300°F (149°C).

4 Roll out the remaining dough in the same way, between two sheets of parchment paper or silicone mats that have been generously misted with vegetable spray oil. Transfer the rolled dough to a second sheet pan. Brush the egg wash evenly over the dough. Use a pizza cutter to the dough into rectangles or diamonds; they need not all be the same size. Don't try to move the cut pieces to separate them; they'll snap apart after they bake.

5 Bake for 15 minutes, then rotate the pans front to back and between racks. Bake 15 minutes longer, then remove any browned crackers to a wire rack (the crackers on the edges of the pan tend to bake faster). Rotate the pans once again and bake for 10 to 15 minutes longer, depending on thickness, until rich golden brown and crisp. For a bit more browning, increase the temperature to 325°F (163°C) for the final few minutes of baking.

6 Remove from the oven and leave the crackers on the pans; they'll become more crisp as they cool. If they don't snap after cooling, return the pan to a hot oven (400°F / 204°C) for a few minutes, until they dry sufficiently to snap when broken.

7 Cool for at least 15 minutes before serving. The cooled crackers can be stored in an airtight container at room temperature for up to 8 days, or in a zip-top bag in the freezer indefinitely.

SPROUTED CORN BREAD

MAKES 8 SERVINGS

When my wife, Susan, and I had our first restaurant, Brother Juniper's Bakery and Cafe, in Forestville, California, we were well known for a few signature dishes in addition to our bread. We learned that side dishes can go a long way in making a restaurant memorable, and in our case, some of the menu items that brought people back were the coleslaw, barbecue sauce, salad dressings, and corn bread. When we later moved to the Carolinas, I learned that our corn bread was what, around here, would be called Yankee-style because it was sweet and more cakelike than Southern-style corn bread, which is simpler, drier, and designed to be served with a sweetener like molasses or honey drizzled over the top. I still prefer my Yankee-style corn bread, but now I generally make it with sprouted corn flour and sprouted whole wheat flour. Sprouted corn flour (also sold as sprouted cornmeal) retains a lot more of the corn flavor than conventional cornmeal. In fact, in the past I've suggested adding fresh or frozen corn kernels to boost the corn flavor, but with sprouted corn flour that isn't necessary. Still, it never hurts to add corn kernels for the moist pop of flavor they provide, or to sprinkle crumbled bacon over the top, as suggested in the variations below.

DOUGH

NOTE: You can vary the ratio of sprouted corn flour to sprouted wheat flour if you prefer more corn flavor. For instance, you can use 75% corn flour and only 25% wheat flour, or even 100% corn flour and no wheat flour.

INGREDIENT	VOLUME	OUNCES	GRAMS	%
sprouted corn flour	1½ cups plus 3 tablespoons	6.75	191	50
sprouted whole wheat flour	1½ cups plus 1½ tablespoons	6.75	191	50
baking powder	4 teaspoons	0.72	20.5	5.4
baking soda	½ teaspoon	0.11	3	0.8
salt	1 teaspoon	0.25	7	1.8
sugar (or honey or agave nectar)	6 tablespoons (or 4½ tablespoons)	3	85	22
buttermilk	2½ cups	20	567	148
eggs, lightly beaten	2	3.5	99	26
unsalted butter, melted	2 tablespoons	1	28.5	7.5
bacon fat or unsalted butter, melted	2 tablespoons	1	28.5	7.5
TOTAL		43.08	1,220.5	319

CONTINUED

1 Position a rack in the middle of the oven and preheat the oven to 350°F (177°C).

2 In a large bowl, stir together the flours, baking powder, baking soda, salt, and sugar (if using honey or agave nectar, add it to the buttermilk in the next step). In a separate bowl, whisk together the buttermilk, eggs, and 2 tablespoons (1 oz / 28.5 g) of melted butter, then pour into the flour mixture. Stir with a large spoon to make a smooth, pourable batter.

3 Grease a 9-inch round cake pan or 8-inch square baking pan (or a larger pan for a thinner corn bread) with either the bacon fat or the butter. Put the pan in the oven for about 2 minutes, until the bacon fat almost starts to smoke (or, if using butter, until it starts to brown). Remove the pan from the oven and pour in the batter, spreading it in an even layer.

4 Bake for 20 minutes, then rotate and bake for 15 to 20 minutes longer, until the surface is golden brown and firm and springy when poked in the center and a toothpick inserted in the center comes out clean.

5 Let cool in the pan for 20 minutes before cutting and serving.

Variations

Add up to 1¼ cups (about 6 oz / 170 g) fresh or frozen corn kernels when mixing the final batter. Alternatively, or in addition, add ½ to 1 cup (about 2.5 to 5 oz / 71 to 142 g) diced vegetables (uncooked or frozen) such as red bell peppers, onion, green onions, or even red jalapeño or Fresno chiles. Another alternative, alone or in combination with the others, is adding up to 2 cups (about 8 oz / 227 g) shredded or grated soft cheese, such as Cheddar, Monterey Jack, mozzarella, or provolone. With any of these additions, you'll probably need to bake the corn bread for about 5 minutes longer.

BACON CORN BREAD: Cook about 5 slices of bacon until crisp and let cool. (Use the bacon fat to grease the pan.) Crumble the bacon and sprinkle it over the batter before baking.

SOUTHERN-STYLE CORN BREAD: Decrease the amount of sugar or sweetener to taste. Also reduce the amount of sprouted wheat flour by half, replacing it with an equal amount of sprouted corn flour.

GLUTEN-FREE SPROUTED CORN BREAD WITH TEFF

MAKES 8 SERVINGS

Teff is probably one of the most ancient grains. This tiny grain, about the size of a poppy seed, is a nutritional powerhouse, high in iron, calcium, and protein but containing no gluten. Teff is most closely associated with Ethiopia and Eritrea, where it's the main flour used to make injera, the flat, sourdough-type bread used for scooping up wonderfully spicy dishes. I find the flavor of teff a little too strong to feature as the primary flour in a bread, but I enjoy blending it with other flours. While teff can be sprouted and used in sprout form, it's difficult to dry sprouted teff and mill it into flour because it's so small. Therefore, I use standard, nonsprouted teff flour in this delicious corn bread. All of that said, you can certainly substitute other ancient grains, as well as bean flours, for the teff in this recipe. One of my favorite variations is to replace the teff with sprouted lentil flour, which makes this bread the perfect accompaniment to hearty soups. One final note: Any of the variations of the Sprouted Corn Bread recipe (page 117) will also work well with this recipe.

DOUGH

INGREDIENT	VOLUME	OUNCES	GRAMS	%
sprouted corn flour (or cornmeal)	2¾ cups plus 1 tablespoon	11.75	333	84
teff flour (or another ancient grain or bean flour)	½ cup	2.25	64	16
baking powder	4 teaspoons	0.72	20.5	5.2
baking soda	½ teaspoon	0.11	3	0.8
salt	1 teaspoon	0.25	7	1.8
sugar (or honey or agave nectar)	6 tablespoons (or 4½ tablespoons)	3	85	21
buttermilk	2½ cups	20	567	143
eggs, slightly beaten	2	3.5	99	25
unsalted butter, melted	2 tablespoons	1	28.5	7.2
bacon fat or melted unsalted butter	2 tablespoons	1	28.5	7.2
TOTAL		43.58	1,235.5	311.2

CONTINUED

1 Position a rack in the middle of the oven and preheat the oven to 350°F (177°C).

2 In a large bowl, stir together the flours, baking powder, baking soda, salt, and sugar (if using honey or agave nectar, add it to the buttermilk in the next step). In a separate bowl, whisk together the buttermilk, eggs, and 2 tablespoons (1 oz / 28.5 g) of melted butter, then pour into the flour mixture. Stir or whisk for about 1 minute to make a smooth, pourable batter.

3 Grease a 9-inch round cake pan or 8-inch square baking pan (or a larger pan for a thinner corn bread) with either the bacon fat or the melted butter. Put the pan in the oven for about 2 minutes, until the bacon fat almost starts to smoke (or, if using butter, until it starts to brown). Remove the pan from the oven and pour in the batter, spreading it in an even layer.

4 Bake for 25 minutes, then rotate and bake for 25 minutes longer, until the surface is firm and springy when poked in the center and a toothpick inserted in the center comes out clean.

5 Let cool in the pan for 20 minutes before cutting and serving.

FLAKY SPROUTED WHEAT BISCUITS

MAKES 12 TO 24 BISCUITS

The distinguishing characteristic for a great biscuit is that it be either tender or flaky. This method for making biscuits was a big hit in *Peter Reinhart's Artisan Breads Every Day* because it produces biscuits that are both tender *and* flaky. But I didn't know about sprouted whole wheat flour back then, and this updated version is even better. Sprouted pastry flour is just beginning to become available, and if you can get your hands on some, the biscuits will be even more flaky. If not, regular sprouted whole wheat flour will be just fine.

DOUGH

NOTE: You can substitute buttermilk for the cream. If you do so, increase the quantity to 1¼ cups (10 oz / 283 g) and omit the vinegar.

INGREDIENT	VOLUME	OUNCES	GRAMS	%
whipping cream or half-and-half, cold (see note)	1 cup plus 2 tablespoons	9	255	100
white vinegar, apple cider vinegar, or lemon juice	2 tablespoons	1	28.5	11
sprouted whole wheat flour or sprouted whole wheat pastry flour	2 cups plus 2 tablespoons	9	255	100
salt	½ teaspoon	0.12	3.5	1.4
baking powder	3½ teaspoons	0.6	17	6.7
baking soda	¼ teaspoon	0.05	1.5	0.6
sugar (or honey or agave nectar)	1 tablespoon (or 2¼ teaspoons)	0.5	14	5.5
unsalted butter, cold	½ cup plus 2 tablespoons	5	142	56
TOTAL		25.27	716.5	281.2

1 In a small bowl or measuring cup, stir together the cream and vinegar. Let sit for at least 10 minutes.

2 In a large bowl or a food processor fitted with the metal blade, combine the flour, salt, baking powder, baking soda, and sugar. (If using honey or agave nectar, whisk it into the cream.) Process or stir briefly to evenly distribute the ingredients. Cut the butter into small bits and use your fingertips or use quick pulses with the food processor to break the butter into small, pea-size bits and distribute it evenly throughout the flour mixture. Work quickly to prevent the butter from softening excessively.

3 Add all the cream-vinegar mixture and stir or briefly pulse just until the flour is hydrated and a soft, wet, and shaggy dough forms. If it seems stiff or the liquid doesn't adequately hydrate the flour, drizzle in a bit more cream.

4 Generously dust a work surface with sprouted whole wheat flour and use a bowl scraper or rubber spatula to transfer the dough to the work surface. Sprinkle more flour on the top of the dough. With floured hands, gently press the dough into a rectangle or oblong about ¾ inch thick, with a long edge facing you. Use a rolling pin to gently roll out the dough, using short strokes from the center of the dough outward, sprinkling more flour under the dough if it seems to be sticking, which it is likely to do. Continue rolling to form a rectangle about ½ inch thick. Using a metal pastry blade, separate the dough from the work surface, then fold it in thirds, as if folding a letter.

5 Dust the work surface with flour again and rotate the dough 90 degrees. Once again gently roll it out into a rectangle about ½ inch thick, then fold it in thirds, like a letter. Repeat the process one more time, rotating the dough 90 degrees, rolling it out into a rectangle about ½ inch thick, and folding it in thirds. The dough should be fairly firm and smooth by this point and easy to handle. Continue to use dusting flour as needed to prevent sticking.

6 Let the dough rest for about 15 minutes. If the butter seems to be softening or smearing, put the dough on a sheet pan lined with parchment paper and misted with vegetable spray oil and refrigerate it until the butter firms up.

7 Line a sheet pan with parchment paper or a silicone mat. Spread about 1 teaspoon of vegetable oil on a work surface and transfer the dough to the oiled area. Gently roll the dough out into a square or oval just under ½ inch thick. Cut the dough with a floured biscuit cutter, metal pastry blade, or pizza cutter. A 2-inch biscuit cutter will produce 20 to 24 biscuits, but you can make them larger or smaller, and they need not all be the same size. Press any scraps back together and cut more biscuits to use up all the dough.

8 Transfer the biscuits to the prepared pan, placing them ½ inch apart. Let rest for 15 to 30 minutes to relax the gluten and allow for a more even rise. Alternatively, you can refrigerate the pan of biscuits for up to 2 days and bake them later.

9 Position a rack in the middle of the oven and preheat the oven to 500°F (260°C).

10 Put the biscuits in the oven and lower the temperature to 450°F (232°C). Bake for 8 minutes, then rotate the pan and bake for 6 to 10 minutes longer, until both the tops and bottoms of the biscuits are rich golden brown. The biscuits should rise about 1½ times in height.

11 Transfer the biscuits to a wire rack and let the biscuits cool for at least 5 minutes. Serve while warm, or reheat them later if desired.

SPROUTED WHEAT SWEET POTATO BRIOCHE

MAKES 2 LARGE LOAVES OR 24 SMALL *BRIOCHE À TÊTE*

In rich doughs, of which brioche is the poster child, the combined weight of fats, eggs, and sugar is above 25% of the weight of the flour, and that percentage can climb to as high as 90%. Rich dough is fit for special occasion breads and can also elevate pedestrian fare like hamburgers into a gourmet feast. Sometimes it serves as the foundation for a dish, such as the crust of a tart or clafoutis, or for wrapping meat, fish, and other savory foods in dough to be served *en croûte*, and this dough can be used for both of those purposes.

Brioche has a very high butter content and therefore is more highly appreciated in Europe, where there is less fear of butter than in the United States. With all the eggs and butter, it ought to be the best bread you ever tasted, and when properly made, it can be. However, in my experience, brioche is a bread that promises much but often underdelivers. This can happen if the dough isn't properly mixed or isn't adequately chilled before baking. Brioche dough should always be refrigerated overnight before baking so the butter can firm up the dough. Therefore, note that making this recipe is a two-day process, so plan accordingly. Another common problem is overbaking, which results in an overly dry final product.

A fellow instructor at Johnson & Wales University, Harry Peemoeller, developed this version to celebrate both sprouted whole wheat flour and North Carolina's most iconic vegetable: sweet potatoes. It has a creamy flavor that magnifies the buttery richness and makes beautiful classic *brioches à tête*, (*à tête* means "with heads," in reference to the little top knot that distinguishes this bread). Alternatively, it can be baked in pan loaves and used for toast, sandwiches, and fantastic French toast. Although this dough can be mixed by hand, using a stand mixer is advisable because it requires a lot of mixing to work in the butter.

CONTINUED

DOUGH

NOTES:

• Don't be alarmed by the high percentage of yeast. This is often necessary for proper rising in doughs with high amounts of fat and other enrichments. There is a type of yeast, known as osmotolerant, specially designed for both rich and acidic doughs. The most well-known brand to me is SAF-Instant Gold. If you use one of these yeasts, the fermentation times will be more reliable and the amount of yeast will remain the same. However, this recipe works fine with any type of regular instant yeast.

• To make sweet potato puree, skin a sweet potato (or yam), cut it into 4 to 6 pieces, and steam for about 15 minutes, until very soft. Mash with a fork or potato masher to make a coarse puree. Let cool to room temperature or lukewarm before using.

INGREDIENT	VOLUME	OUNCES	GRAMS	%
sprouted whole wheat flour	5 cups	21.25	602	100
brown sugar	5 tablespoons	2.5	71	12
salt	1⅝ teaspoons	0.4	11.5	1.9
instant yeast (see notes)	5 teaspoons	0.55	15.5	2.6
egg	1	1.75	50	8.3
egg yolks	3	2.25	64	11
sweet potato puree (from about 1 medium to large sweet potato; see notes)	about 1 cup plus 3 tablespoons	10.5	298	50
whole milk, at room temperature	¾ cup	6	170	28
unsalted butter, at room temperature	1¼ cups plus 1 tablespoon	10.5	298	50
egg wash	1 egg whisked with 1 tablespoon water or milk			
TOTAL		55.7	1,580	263.8

1 In the bowl of a stand mixer fitted with the paddle attachment, stir together the flour, brown sugar, salt, and yeast on low speed. Add the egg, egg yolks, sweet potato puree, and milk and mix on low speed for 1 minute, until a soft, coarse dough forms. Switch to the dough hook, increase the speed to medium-low, and mix for 3 to 4 minutes, until the dough begins to pull away from the bowl and show signs of elasticity, an indication of gluten development.

2 Cut the butter into 4 pieces. While mixing on medium-low speed, add the butter one piece at a time, waiting until each piece is fully incorporated before adding the next. The dough should be soft, tacky, and supple and should feel bouncy when patted. If it's very sticky, add a bit more flour.

3 Spread a small amount of vegetable oil on a work surface (or dust the work surface with flour) and use a bowl scraper to transfer the dough to the oiled area. With either oiled or floured hands, stretch and fold the dough as shown on page 20, folding it over itself four times: once each from the top, bottom, and sides.

4 Oil a large bowl and put the dough in the bowl. Mist the top of the dough with vegetable spray oil and cover the bowl with plastic wrap. Let the dough rest at room temperature for 30 minutes. Put the bowl in the refrigerator for at least 12 hours or overnight. (It's best to use it within 2 days because of the high yeast content.)

5 About 3 hours before you plan to bake, remove the dough from the refrigerator. It will be much more solid because the butter is cold, and therefore easy to handle and shape. Transfer the dough to an oiled or floured work surface. **For pan loaves,** mist two 4½ by 8-inch loaf pans with vegetable spray oil. Divide the dough in half and shape the pieces into sandwich loaves as shown on pages 23 and 24, then put the shaped loaves in the prepared pans. You can also divide the dough into 4 pieces and round each piece into a ball. Place two balls in each prepared pan, where they will grow into a two-part loaf with rounded domes. **For brioches à tête**, mist small brioche molds or muffin cups with vegetable spray oil. Divide the dough into the desired size. For small brioches à tête, each piece should weigh about 2 ounces (56.5 g), for a yield of about 24. To shape, roll one end of a small ball of dough into a cylindrical cone. Poke a hole in the thick end, then slip the tip of the cone through it so that a nub of dough pokes through to make a "head." Transfer the shaped dough to the oiled brioche molds.

6 Mist the tops with vegetable spray oil, cover loosely with plastic wrap, and let proof at room temperature until the dough swells and rises to fill the brioche pans or crests above the loaf pans by at least 1 inch. This will take 1½ to 2 hours for brioches à tête and up to 4 hours for loaves. Brush the tops with the egg wash, using a light touch, as the dough will be very soft and fragile after warming to room temperature.

7 Position a rack in the middle of the oven and preheat the oven to 400°F (204°C).

8 Bake for 13 to 15 minutes for brioches à tête, or 50 to 60 minutes for loaves (rotating after 30 minutes for even baking), until the crust is golden brown and firm to the touch on all sides and the bread sounds hollow when thumped on the bottom.

9 Turn out onto a wire rack. Let brioches à tête cool for at least 15 minutes before serving, and let loaves cool for at least 40 minutes before slicing and serving.

SPROUTED WHEAT CINNAMON BUNS AND SWEET ROLLS

MAKES 18 CINNAMON BUNS OR 30 SWEET ROLLS

The more I try to create healthful bread options, the more I get asked for yet another recipe for sweet cinnamon buns. It seems like, in the end, comfort food always comes out ahead. So in my cookbooks, I always offer my latest version of cinnamon buns and their even more decadent cousins, sticky buns, and everyone is happy. This time around, the recipe has the paradoxical combination of extremely good-for-you 100% sprouted whole wheat dough, filled with a generous amount of cinnamon sugar, which is not so healthful, yet so deeply satisfying. You can, of course, use sucralose substitutes like Splenda if you want to replace the sugar. But unless you're diabetic, I think this is one case where it might be okay to give yourself a pass and just use classic cinnamon sugar.

This dough is like challah in that it's enriched. However, in this case the enrichments include milk but not eggs, whereas challah is enriched with eggs but never milk. If you wish, you can also make cinnamon buns with challah dough (page 108)—or for that matter, brioche dough (page 124). The final result will be similarly satisfying no matter which dough you use. That said, for cinnamon buns and sweet rolls, this is my go-to dough.

DOUGH

INGREDIENT	VOLUME	OUNCES	GRAMS	%
milk (any kind), lukewarm (95°F / 35°C)	2¼ cups	18	510	75
instant yeast	4 teaspoons	0.44	12.5	1.8
vegetable oil	6 tablespoons	3	85	12.5
honey (or agave nectar or granulated sugar)	¼ cup (or 5 tablespoons)	2.5	71	10
sprouted whole wheat flour	5⅔ cups	24	680	100
salt	1⅝ teaspoons	0.4	11.5	1.7
sugar for filling	1 cup	8	227	
cinnamon for filling	¼ cup ground cinnamon	1.12	32	
vegetable oil or melted unsalted butter for filling	2 teaspoons	0.35	10	
Quick Fondant Glaze (see sidebar)				
TOTAL		57.81	1,639	201

CONTINUED

1 In a medium bowl, whisk together the milk and yeast. Add the oil and honey and whisk until evenly combined. Set aside for 2 to 5 minutes to activate the yeast. (The mixture need not become foamy; it just needs to show signs of bubbles. This helps the yeast to get a head start in the presence of a sweeter dough.)

2 In the bowl of a stand mixer fitted with the paddle attachment, or in a large bowl, stir together the flour and salt (on low speed if using a stand mixer). Pour in the milk mixture and mix or stir until the flour is hydrated and a coarse, sticky dough forms, about 1 minute.

3 Let the dough rest, uncovered, for 5 minutes. Then switch to the dough hook or use a wet spoon or wet hands and mix for 1 minute, on medium-low speed if using a stand mixer. The dough should be smooth but still very soft and sticky. Add a bit more flour or milk if necessary to achieve this texture, but bear in mind that the dough will firm up during the stretch and fold process.

4 Spread about 1 teaspoon of vegetable oil or olive oil on a work surface. Using a wet or oiled bowl scraper or rubber spatula, transfer the dough to the oiled area. Lightly oil your hands, then stretch and fold the dough as shown on page 20, folding it over itself four times: once each from the top, bottom, and sides. The dough will firm up slightly but still be very soft and somewhat sticky. Cover the dough with the mixing bowl and then, at intervals of 5 minutes or up to 20 minutes, perform three additional sequences of stretching and folding. For each stretch and fold sequence, lightly oil your hands to prevent sticking. The dough will firm up a bit more with each stretch and fold. After the final fold it should be soft, supple, and tacky and have a springy or bouncy quality when patted.

5 Oil a large bowl and put the dough in the bowl. Mist the top of the dough with vegetable spray oil and cover the bowl with a lid or plastic wrap; if using plastic wrap, stretch it tightly over the bowl rather than laying it directly on the dough. Ferment the dough at room temperature for 1½ to 2 hours, until double in size. (This time can be shortened by using a warm proof box set at about 90°F / 32°C.)

6 Oil the work surface again and use an oiled bowl scraper or rubber spatula to transfer the dough to the oiled area. Divide the dough in half and form each piece into a ball. Cover loosely with plastic wrap or a towel and let rest for 10 minutes to allow the gluten to relax.

7 In a small bowl, whisk together the sugar and cinnamon to make the filling. Line two sheet pans with parchment paper or silicone mats.

8 Working on the oiled work surface, use your hands or a rolling pin to gently press the dough into a rectangle measuring about 12 by 15 inches, with the long side facing you. It should be a bit over ¼ inch thick. If using a rolling pin, roll out from the center to each of the four corners, and then to the sides. If the dough sticks to the rolling pin, rub a bit of vegetable oil on the surface of the dough.

9 Rub or brush 1 teaspoon of vegetable oil or melted unsalted butter over the dough. Sprinkle up to half of the cinnamon sugar over the dough, leaving a ¼-inch bare border on all four sides. Evenly roll up the dough like a rug, from the bottom to the top, to form a tight log. Use your hands to gently squeeze and form the log so it's even across and not tapered toward the ends. Cut the log into equal-size slices at least 1 inch thick and up to 1¾ inches for very large cinnamon buns; don't cut them thinner than 1 inch, or the baked buns will be tough. Put them on one of the lined pans, spacing them at least 1 inch apart. If any cinnamon sugar falls out of the buns, scoop it up and sprinkle it over the buns. Repeat the process with the other ball of dough, or return it to the bowl, cover, and refrigerate for use the next day.

10 Mist the top of the dough with vegetable spray oil and cover loosely with plastic wrap. Proof at room temperature for 1½ to 2 hours, until nearly double in size.

11 To bake one pan of buns, position a rack in the middle of the oven; to bake two, position two racks an equal distance apart. Preheat the oven to 350°F (177°C).

12 Bake for 10 minutes, then rotate the pans (switching shelves if baking two pans) and bake for 5 to 15 minutes longer, until the tops are golden brown.

13 Let cool on the baking pan or on a wire rack for at least 5 minutes before glazing and serving. As the buns cool, the glaze will harden.

Quick Fondant Glaze

The corn syrup is optional in this recipe, but be aware that it will help keep the glaze smooth and prevent crystallization.

- **4 cups (12 oz / 340 g) confectioners' sugar, sifted**
- **2 tablespoons (1.33 oz / 37.5 g) light corn syrup (optional)**
- **1 teaspoon (0.14 oz / 4 g) vanilla, lemon, or orange extract**
- **½ to ¾ cup (4 to 6 oz / 113 to 170 g) milk (any type) or water**

In a large bowl, stir together the sugar, corn syrup, and vanilla extract. While whisking, gradually pour in the milk, adding just enough to make a thick but creamy glaze that ribbons off the end of the whisk. Adjust with more confectioners' sugar or milk as needed. You can make it thinner if you prefer to brush the glaze over the buns, or thicker for drizzling if you want it to form a design of streaks or squiggles on the top.

Variations

MULTIGRAIN: You can replace up to 20% of the sprouted whole wheat flour with an equal amount, by weight, of other sprouted flours. If you do so, decrease the amount of milk by 2 to 4 tablespoons (1 to 2 oz / 28.5 to 56.5 g).

RAISIN NUT: Before rolling the dough into a log, sprinkle about ½ cup (3 oz / 85 g) raisins and about ½ cup (2 oz / 56.5 g) coarsely chopped walnuts or pecans over the surface.

FILLED SWEET ROLLS: Instead of dividing the dough in half, divide it into about 30 pieces, each weighing about 1½ ounces (43 g). Roll up each piece into a tight ball, and distribute the balls evenly on two sheet pans that have been lined with parchment paper or silicone baking mats. Cover loosely and proof at room temperature for about 1½ hours, until they increase in size by 1½ times. Make an indentation in the top of each roll with your thumb, pressing all the way to the bottom of the dough, but not through the dough. Use your fingertips to widen the indentation until there's just a ¼-inch rim of dough surrounding it. Fill the indentation with store-bought fruit pie or Danish filling (do not use fruit preserves or jelly, which are too thin), using about 1 heaping teaspoon (0.25 oz / 7 g) per bun. The rolls will swell and close around the filling as they bake, so you need to use enough filling that it doesn't disappear. Bake and glaze as for cinnamon buns.

STICKY BUNS: There are a number of sticky bun glazes available on the Internet and in my previous books that could be used. The main thing to know is that you should use a taller pan for baking to prevent the glaze from bubbling over. I use 9-inch round cake pans and bake only 5 buns per pan so they aren't crowded as they rise and bake. Coat the bottom of the pan with a ¼-inch thickness of glaze. Sprinkle nuts, raisins, or other toppings over the glaze, then put the buns on top of the glaze. Remember that the top surface will be the bottom of the buns when they're turned out of the pan, and because it's exposed, it will brown before the side in the glaze. It's important to let the glaze fully caramelize so the side in the glaze will brown slightly. If need be, cover the pans with foil toward the end of the baking time to prevent the top from getting too brown. Wait about 5 minutes before flipping the pan over onto a platter; this will give the glaze a chance to set up somewhat so that it doesn't slide off the top of the buns. Be very careful when doing this tricky maneuver, because the glaze will be molten hot. Oven mitts are essential, and a rubber spatula will be very helpful.

SPROUTED WHEAT CROISSANTS

MAKES 10 CROISSANTS

Along with brioche, perhaps the most popular rich breads are croissants and their kissing cousins, Danish pastries. Yes, sweet indulgence! Whenever people tell me they want to open a bakery café, I tell them that if they offer nothing more than great baguettes, ciabattas, and whole grain breads, along with the best croissants in town, they'll be successful. (Of course, excellent coffee and tea are also a must.) Some bakers have tried to formulate whole wheat croissants in an effort to create a more guilt-free treat, but until recently I haven't had one that got me excited.

Enter Harry Peemoeller, who is quite well known in the artisan bread world, having represented the United States at the 2012 Coupe du Monde de la Boulangerie (aka the International Bread Championship or Bread Olympics), where Team USA won the silver medal. In addition to his wonderful brioche (on page 124), he's developed an amazing croissant recipe using sprouted whole wheat flour. In his bakeshop classroom at Johnson & Wales University, Peemoeller has the distinct advantage of having a reversible sheeter, which is kind of like a giant pasta rolling machine through which dough can travel in both directions through a set of adjustable rollers. Of course, this is something very few home bakers are likely to own—except in their dreams—so here I provide my own lamination technique. Note that this is a two-day technique, so plan accordingly.

DOUGH

INGREDIENT	VOLUME	OUNCES	GRAMS	%
milk (whole or low-fat), at room temperature	1½ cups plus 3 tablespoons	13.5	383	89
instant yeast	2¼ teaspoons	0.28	8	1.9
sugar	2 tablespoons plus 1 teaspoon	1.25	35.5	8.2
sprouted whole wheat flour	3½ cups plus 1½ tablespoons	15.2	431	100
salt	1½ teaspoons	0.35	10	2.3
unsalted butter, at room temperature	2 teaspoons	0.35	10	2.3
unsalted butter, slightly chilled but not ice-cold	1 cup plus 1½ tablespoons	8.8	250	58
egg wash (optional)	1 egg whisked with 1 tablespoon water			
TOTAL		39.73	1,127.5	261.7

CONTINUED

1 In the bowl of a stand mixer fitted with the paddle attachment, or in a large bowl, stir together the milk and yeast (on low speed if using a stand mixer). Add the sugar, flour, and salt and the 2 teaspoons of room-temperature butter. If using a stand mixer, mix on low speed about 1 minute, then switch to the dough hook and increase the speed to medium and mix for 2 to 3 minutes, until the dough is very smooth, supple, and tacky. If mixing by hand, stir with a large spoon for about 5 minutes, then briefly knead by hand until the dough is very smooth, supple, and tacky. Form the dough into a ball and return it to the bowl. Cover the bowl and let the dough rest at room temperature for 1 hour. It will rise slightly.

2 Line a sheet pan with parchment paper or a silicone mat. Mist generously with vegetable spray oil or coat lightly with vegetable oil. Spread about 1 teaspoon of vegetable oil on a work surface. Transfer the dough to the oiled area and flip it over so both sides of the dough are slightly oiled. Use your hands or a rolling pin to press or roll the dough into a rectangle about ½ inch thick, then transfer it to the prepared pan. Cover with plastic wrap and refrigerate for at least 12 hours or overnight.

3 About 1 hour before you plan to continue, remove the chilled butter from the refrigerator so it will be cool but not cold. It should be slightly pliable; 60°F (16°C) is the ideal butter temperature for lamination.

4 When ready to begin laminating, spread about 1 teaspoon of vegetable oil on the work surface, covering an area about the same size as the sheet pan, and transfer the cold dough to the oiled area. Using your hands or a rolling pin, gently form or roll it into a rectangle measuring 8½ by 14 inches.

5 Put a sheet of parchment paper or a silicone mat on the work surface and mist it with vegetable spray oil, then sprinkle about 1 tablespoon (0.26 oz / 7.5 g) of flour over the surface. Transfer the butter to the floured parchment paper. Mist the top with vegetable spray oil, then cover with plastic wrap. Working through the plastic wrap, use your hands to flatten and press the butter into a rectangle or square large enough to cover half of the dough rectangle, leaving just a ¼-inch margin; it should measure about 8 by 6¾ inches. Alternatively, use a rolling pin to tap the surface of the butter (through the plastic wrap) to achieve that same size. Lift the butter, parchment and all, onto the dough to determine whether the size is right. Once you're certain that the butter will cover half of the dough, remove the plastic wrap and, holding on to the parchment paper, invert the butter and fit it onto the dough, covering the entire left half and leaving a small, ¼-inch border around the edges. Fold the right half of the dough over the butter. Pinch the top and bottom edges together to seal the butter inside. Then use a rolling pin to gently tap or roll the dough into a larger rectangle measuring about 8 by 24 inches. Always roll in short strokes from the center of the dough outward, first to the corners and then to the sides, to ease

CONTINUED

the dough out, rather than forcing it. If the dough is sticky, dust it and the surface beneath it with flour or oil the work surface again. Once the dough is rolled out, fold it in thirds, like a letter, and pat it back into a rectangle or square with your hands. Put the dough on the prepared pan lengthwise, cover with plastic wrap, and refrigerate for 30 to 45 minutes so the butter can firm up again.

6 Once again spread about 1 teaspoon of vegetable oil on the work surface. Turn the dough 90 degrees (a one-quarter turn) on the oiled work surface, then repeat the steps above, rolling the dough out into a rectangle measuring about 24 by 8 inches, folding it in thirds, like a letter, then patting into a rectangle. Return the dough to the refrigerator for 30 to 45 minutes, then repeat the process one final time, rotating the dough, rolling it out, folding it, and patting it into a rectangle. Return the dough to the refrigerator for 1 hour.

7 Again, spread about 1 teaspoon of vegetable oil on the work surface. Place the dough on the oiled area and roll it out into an 8 by 14-inch rectangle; it should be about ½ inch thick. Return the dough to the refrigerator for 30 minutes.

8 Oil the work surface once again, or dust it lightly with flour, then transfer the dough to the work surface. Roll it out into a 10 by 24-inch rectangle; it should be about ¼ inch thick. Use a metal pastry blade or pizza cutter to cut the dough from top to bottom at 4½-inch intervals, forming 5 rectangles each measuring 10 by 4½ inches. Then, cut each rectangle diagonally into two triangles, each with a 4½-inch base.

9 Cut a ¾-inch notch in the center of each 4½-inch base. Slightly spread out the two halves of the base at the notch and roll the dough into a crescent shape. Repeat with all of the pieces. Line two sheet pans with parchment paper or silicone mats and put 5 croissants on each pan, spacing them about 2 inches apart. Brush them evenly with the egg wash if you like, then cover loosely with plastic

Q & A

Why bother with an egg wash? And why is egg wash sometimes made with egg whites and other times with whole eggs?

Both types of egg washes add to the eye appeal of baked goods, and either can help toppings adhere to the dough. Egg washes made with whole eggs tend to create a dark and glossy surface, while those made with egg whites yield a shinier, more translucent gloss. Some people like to add a pinch of salt or sugar, or sometimes milk is used instead of water, but I find that a simple version with just egg and water makes for the best all-purpose egg wash.

NOTE: You can freeze unbaked shaped croissants, either individually in zip-top freezer bags or on a covered or wrapped tray. Once they're frozen solid, they can be transferred to a larger bag. To bake them, remove from the freezer 5 to 6 hours before baking and proof at room temperature, or transfer from the freezer to the refrigerator the night before and proof at room temperature for 3 to 4 hours before baking.

wrap. Proof at room temperature for 1½ to 2 hours, until the croissants swell noticeably; they won't rise, but they will expand around the roll-up.

10 Preheat the oven to 400°F (204°C).

11 Bake one pan at a time. For each pan, bake at the initial temperature for 5 minutes, then lower the temperature to 375°F (191°C). and bake for another 13 minutes, until golden brown all over, with no white showing in the folds. If the bottoms are getting too dark during baking, slide a second pan under the first for insulation.

12 Transfer the croissants to a wire rack and let cool for at least 30 minutes before serving.

Variation

CHOCOLATE CROISSANTS: Instead of cutting the rectangles into triangles, cut them in half crosswise to make squares. Cover the bottom edge of each square with about 1 ounce (28.5 g) of semisweet or bittersweet chocolate chips or chocolate strips (batons) and roll the dough over the chocolate to form a log. Place the croissants seam side down on a lined pan, then proof and bake as directed.

CHAPTER 4
SPROUTED PULP BREADS

I've known Keith Giusto for more than twenty-five years. We first met when he dropped in at Brother Juniper's Bakery, in Santa Rosa, and introduced me to the line of flours milled by his family sixty-five miles down Highway 101 in South San Francisco, Giusto's Vita-Grain. It worked perfectly for us, and I used that flour until the day I sold the bakery. I often called Keith when I had questions about flour or dough formulations because, in addition to being trained as a cereal chemist, he was also one of the best bakers I knew. He was far ahead of many of his competitors in recognizing the coming artisan bread movement and thinking about creating the kinds of flours the new breed of bakers would want. When his family sold Giusto Mills, Keith gathered some new partners and started his own flour company, Central Milling, in Petaluma, California.

In 2010 we reconnected in Denver while attending a baking symposium, and he introduced me to his nephew Nicky, whom he'd brought in with the intent of training him to be his eventual successor. This freed Keith to focus on what he loves to do: working with growers and millers, and baking.

Three years later, I visited Central Milling and was stunned by how big the business had become. As I pulled into the parking lot, I saw four huge shipping trucks emblazoned with the Central Milling logo. Nicky, looking a little older than when I first met him in Denver, greeted me in the reception area. He gave me the grand tour, through the offices, past the break room and company pool table, and into a large, open warehouse well stocked with a variety of Central Milling flours and other baking products waiting to be loaded onto trucks and shipped.

We worked our way over to the small bakeshop lab, with scaling and molding workbenches, a Kemper spiral mixer, a proofer/retarder, custom-built wooden forms (called Parisians) for proofing loaves, and an impressive WP Matador deck oven. There were also a number of bins filled with various Central Milling flours and ingredients.

Nicky showed me a beautiful, crusty hearth loaf with a large, open crumb, laced with golden raisins, and said, "I'm working on a bread formula for the annual California Raisin Marketing Board's raisin bread competition. I'm calling it Raisin de Soleil. Just a few more tweaks and I think it will be ready to submit."

"It seems like you've gone beyond the business side, Nicky," I said. "I didn't realize you were seriously into baking too."

"I've learned a lot from Keith and, hey, what can I say? Baking is in my blood."

Nicky filled me in on other developments, including that, since we met up in Denver, Keith had gone into semiretirement and essentially put the operation in Nicky's hands. Nicky had stepped up and assimilated it all, including the craft of bread baking. He is, after all, a Giusto.

"And here's something you may not know," he told me. "Remember those sprouted Vita-Grain breads that Giusto's used to make way back when? Well, we're bringing them back."

THE ROOTS OF SPROUTED PULP BREAD

I did, in fact, have an inkling that this was happening, and this was the very reason I'd come to Petaluma—to hear more about the revival of one of the Giusto family's most iconic products: sprouted grain breads dating back to the 1940s. These weren't breads made with sprouted whole wheat flour, which didn't exist back then, but breads made in much the same way as Ezekiel Bread and Alvarado Street Bakery do it, using sprouted wheat berries and other sprouted grains, which are ground into a pulp (or mash) and then mixed with other bread ingredients, such as yeast, salt, honey, and, importantly, vital wheat gluten. The result is a dough that bakes up just like regular bread even though, amazingly, the grain is never made into flour; it goes straight from sprouts to pulp, and then to dough. In a very real way, the Giusto Vita-Grain breads were the prototype for baking with sprouted grain pulp, predating by a couple of decades Ezekiel and Alvarado Street, the two most well-known sprouted grain bakeries today. But Vita-Grain Bread was sold primarily in the San Francisco Bay Area, and in the late 1990s, it faded out of production.

But by then, others had entered the game and risen to prominence. In about 1964, Max Flores, a baker in Southern California, started Food For Life, a company that produced sprouted grain products that eventually became best known under the name Ezekiel Bread. Ezekiel followed a slow but steady growth curve and then shot up in the late 1990s, when various low-carb diet plans pointed to Ezekiel as their favorite healthy bread option. And Alvarado Street Bakery, established in 1981 in Rohnert Park, California, about halfway between Petaluma and Santa Rosa, grew from a small hippie co-op bakery to a large, successful producer of a full line of organic sprouted grain products. So, the concept of breads made from the pulp of sprouted grains can't really be considered the next frontier; it was the next frontier decades ago. (And, as Ezekiel's biblical roots in Genesis 1:29 indicate, it's really a throwback to ancient times.) But what is new and exciting is that Keith and Nicky Giusto are now making it possible for other bakeries, as well as home bakers, to get into the game by providing sprouted grain pulp.

As Nicky explained, Central Milling has begun producing sprouted pulp and freezing it in vacuum-sealed cylinders called chubs. "We can ship it overnight to anyone who wants to use it, and we can even help bakers with their dough formulation." When I asked him if anyone was using the pulp yet, he told me, "We're already shipping large quantities to bakeries, and I'm currently studying how the meat industry handles shipping. So by the time your book comes out, we should be able to ship small orders to home bakers." Of course, you can also make your own sprouted pulp (see below).

The challenge when baking with sprouted grain is that when sprouts are ground into pulp rather than being dried and milled into flour, the grain's capacity to form gluten bonds is compromised. To compensate for this, sprouted pulp doughs often contain vital wheat gluten, made by washing the starch away from flour and drying the result into a powder. For most professional bakers, vital wheat gluten is a familiar ingredient, often used to boost the stretchability of breads made with weaker flours that have a lower percentage of gluten, such as rye, low-protein wheat, or multigrain blends. However, the amount of vital wheat gluten usually used for, say, rye bread is typically between 1% to 2% of the total flour weight, whereas the amount used in commercially produced sprouted pulp breads is often closer to 10%. This produces a bread that looks and feels a lot like bread made from regular flour, and it's full of the benefits of sprouted grain as long as you can tolerate the added gluten. When

Homemade Sprouted Grain Pulp

See page 48 for instructions on how to sprout and dry grain. For sprouted pulp, instead of drying the sprouted grain, run the sprouts through a meat grinder (I use the meat grinder attachment on my KitchenAid mixer). You can also process them with a bit of water in a high-powered blender, such as a Vitamix, but it's not as effective as the grinder.

you think about it, it's a very clever way to reengineer the whole notion of bread. Imagine, bread made without flour. Ingenious!

When my wife, Susan, and I owned Brother Juniper's Bakery, just twenty minutes up Highway 101 from Alvarado Street Bakery, I became friends with some of the founders and co-op members. They even helped us get our bakery off the ground by giving us their used loaf pans so we could save money for other essentials (like flour and yeast and paying our staff!). I was (and still am) a big fan of their products and have long been impressed by how they grew their business while adhering to the tricky co-op business model in which every employee is also an owner. They've made it work, and in the process, they grew from making just a few loaves a day to well over twenty thousand.

Bakers tend to be generous by nature, probably because they know how unbelievably hard it is to operate a bakery and produce consistent goods day after day. I'm so grateful to Keith and Nicky Giusto for providing some of the following formulas, and for making sprouted grain pulp available to home bakers. As Keith told me, "I'm just glad to find people who care as much as I do about baking and who are interested in hearing about some of the things I've learned along the way." And by the way, Nicky won the grand prize in the Professional Artisan category for his magnificent Raisin de Soleil (a link to his formula is in the Resources section, page 240).

Q & A

If a recipe calls for vital wheat gluten, can I make the bread without it?

You can, but it will be denser and take longer to bake. You should also lower the oven temperature by about 10% to allow more time for the loaves to bake without burning the crust; for example, if the instructions specify 380°F (193°C), bake at 340°F (171°C) instead. You can also replace the vital wheat gluten with xanthan gum or ground psyllium husks, which are often used in gluten-free baked goods. They aren't quite as effective but will help provide some structure. If using xanthan gum, the amount should be about 0.5% of the total sprouted grain weight. So for each 10 ounces (283 g) of sprouted pulp, that would be about 0.05 ounce (1.5 g), or ½ teaspoon. For psyllium, use 1 teaspoon.

MULTIGRAIN SPROUTED WHEAT PULP BREAD

MAKES 2 LOAVES OR UP TO 24 ROLLS | **MASTER FORMULA**

Here's a master formula for sprouted pulp bread, perfected by Keith and Nicky Giusto. As you add the ingredients to the mixing bowl, you may wonder if they'll truly transform into bread. They will, and the bread will taste great! You'll also notice the method is quite different from the breads in the previous chapter, which stands to reason, since this is an entirely different product. It contains quite a bit of yeast and doesn't utilize much bulk fermentation, yet turns into delicious bread in a relatively short amount of time, especially when compared to long, slow fermentation methods of making artisan bread.

To make your own sprouted pulp, see the sidebar on page 141. The soaker calls for a nine-grain cereal blend, and you should be able to find something along these lines in local markets. However, feel free to create your own combination using sprouted grains, rye or oat flakes, coarse cornmeal, grits, or seeds such as flax, chia, or hemp—whatever you have on hand, really. While it's only a small fraction of the final loaves, it adds great texture and character. You can also use sprouted grains or flours in the soaker. As you'll see, the soaker uses only a bit of water—just enough to soften the grains and get some enzyme activity going for flavor development.

SOAKER

INGREDIENT	VOLUME	OUNCES	GRAMS	%
cracked nine-grain cereal mix or any combination of grain meals or sprouted grains	1 cup	4.5	128	100
water, at room temperature	⅓ cup	2.7	77	59
TOTAL		7.2	205	159

1 Put the nine-grain cereal in a small bowl and stir in the water. Cover with plastic wrap and leave out at room temperature for 12 hours or overnight; if your kitchen is very warm, refrigerate the soaker after a few hours.

CONTINUED

FINAL DOUGH

INGREDIENT	VOLUME	OUNCES	GRAMS	%
sprouted wheat pulp	6 cups	32	907	100
water, at room temperature	½ cup	4	113	12
vital wheat gluten	½ cup plus 1 tablespoon	3	85	9.4
instant yeast	2 tablespoons	0.66	19	2.1
salt	2 teaspoons	0.5	14	1.5
honey	1½ tablespoons	1	28.5	3.1
molasses	1½ tablespoons	1	28.5	3.1
sugar	2 tablespoons	1	28.5	3.1
vegetable oil	1 tablespoon plus 1 teaspoon	0.65	18	2
Soaker	all	7.2	205	23
TOTAL		51.01	1,446.5	159.3

1 Put all the dough ingredients in a mixing bowl or the bowl of a stand mixer fitted with the paddle attachment, in the order listed. Stir or mix, on low speed if using a stand mixer, until a coarse, thick, slightly sticky dough forms, about 3 minutes. (Once the dough forms a coarse ball, you can knead it by hand if you prefer.)

2 Let the dough rest, uncovered, for 5 to 10 minutes. Then switch to the dough hook and mix on medium speed or knead by hand for 3 to 4 minutes, until the dough is tacky but supple and feels springy when poked. The internal temperature of the dough should be about 75°F (24°C). Knead it by hand for a few seconds, then form it into a ball.

3 Mist a bowl with vegetable spray oil and put the dough in the bowl. Mist the top with vegetable spray oil, and cover the bowl with plastic wrap or a lid. Let rest at room temperature for 15 minutes. It won't rise much in that time.

4 Divide the dough in half and form each piece into a ball. Mist with vegetable spray oil and cover loosely with plastic wrap. Let rest at room temperature for 20 minutes.

5 For pan loaves, mist two 4½ by 8-inch loaf pans with vegetable spray oil. Shape the pieces into sandwich loaves as shown on pages 23 and 24, then put the shaped loaves in the prepared pans. **For hearth loaves,** line two sheet pans with parchment paper or silicone mats. Shape the pieces into boules or bâtards as shown on pages 20 to 21, then put the shaped loaves on the lined pans. **For rolls,** line two sheet pans with parchment paper or silicone mats. Divide the two dough balls into the desired number of pieces and shape as desired (see page 24). Put half of the rolls on each lined pan, spacing them at least 2 inches apart.

6 Mist the tops with vegetable spray oil and cover loosely with plastic wrap. Proof at room temperature until nearly double in size, about 1½ hours.

7 To bake pan loaves, position a rack in the middle of the oven and preheat the oven to 380°F (193°C). Bake for 25 minutes, then rotate and bake for 20 to 25 minutes longer, until the crust is golden brown and the bread sounds hollow when thumped on the bottom. The internal temperature should be at least 190°F (88°C). Turn out onto a wire rack and let cool for at least 45 minutes before slicing and serving.

8 To bake hearth loaves or rolls, position two racks in the oven an equal distance apart and prepare the oven for steaming as shown on page 29. (A baking stone isn't used.) Preheat the oven to 380°F (193°C). Put the bread in the oven and pour about 1 cup of hot water into the steam pan. Bake rolls for about 10 minutes and hearth loaves for about 20 minutes, then rotate the pans front to back and between racks. Bake for 10 to 12 minutes longer for rolls or 20 to 25 minutes longer for hearth loaves, until the crust is golden brown and the bread sounds hollow when thumped on the bottom. The internal temperature should be at least 190°F (88°C). Transfer from the pans to a wire rack. Let loaves cool for at least 1 hour before slicing and serving. Rolls can be served after 10 minutes.

SPROUTED EMMER PULP POWER BREAD

MAKES 2 LOAVES OR UP TO 24 ROLLS

I remember when Keith Giusto showed me the first version of this bread over twenty-five years ago. I was so impressed that I started making my own versions, using seed flours and plumped raisins instead of sprouted pulp. Back then, Keith told me that the original intent was to create a loaf especially designed for long-distance runners and people doing other intensive physical training. This latest version, Keith's best yet, incorporates sprouted emmer wheat, an ancient strain sometimes referred to as farro and still used in Italian cooking. (The definition of farro is debated, and in Italy, the term sometimes refers to spelt or even einkorn.) It has a sweet and nutty flavor that's wonderful in this bread, but you can certainly substitute other types of sprouted wheat pulp, including spelt, einkorn, or Kamut (aka Khorasan wheat).

As you'll see, this formula calls for making a levain. If your mother starter has been refreshed within the last three days, you can use 1 cup (6.75 oz / 191 g) of that instead. However, if the hydration of your starter is different from that in the recipe, you may need to adjust the amount of flour or water in the final dough accordingly. Also, the dough includes both sprouted pulp and standard bread flour. This combination approach can be used in many recipes, including any in this book, once you become familiar with the functionality of sprouted pulp. Note that this is a two-day process, so plan accordingly.

LEVAIN

INGREDIENT	VOLUME	OUNCES	GRAMS	%
Mother Starter (page 40)	¼ cup	1.6	45.5	46
water, at room temperature	¼ cup	2	56.5	57
unbleached bread flour	¾ cup	3.5	99	100
TOTAL		7.1	201	213

Put the mother starter in a small bowl and add the water to soften it. Break the starter up into smaller pieces, then add the flour and stir until a coarse ball of dough forms. Transfer to a work surface and knead by hand for about 30 seconds, until the starter is evenly distributed and a tacky dough forms. Mist a small bowl with vegetable spray oil and put the dough into the bowl. Mist the top of the dough with vegetable spray oil and cover the bowl with plastic wrap. Let the levain rest at room temperature for 6 to 12 hours, until double in size. If it doubles in size before you're ready to make the final dough, put it in the refrigerator.

CONTINUED

SOAKED RAISINS

INGREDIENT	VOLUME	OUNCES	GRAMS
raisins	about ⅔ cup	4	113
water, at room temperature	¾ cup	6	170

1 Put the raisins in a small bowl and pour in the water. Cover the bowl with plastic wrap and leave out at room temperature for at least 6 hours or overnight.

2 To make raisin water for the final dough, drain the raisins in a strainer set over a bowl, pressing gently to extract more liquid. This will yield more than the ¼ cup (2 oz / 56.5 g) needed for the dough. You can discard the excess or use it in something else, such as a smoothie, or you can simmer it in a saucepan until reduced to the amount needed (cool it before using), to add more raisin flavor to the bread.

FINAL DOUGH

INGREDIENT	VOLUME	OUNCES	GRAMS	%
Levain	all	7.1	201	26
water, at room temperature	1¼ cups plus 2 tablespoons	11	312	40
sprouted emmer pulp or other sprouted wheat pulp (see sidebar page 142)	2 cups	11	312	40
unbleached bread flour	3½ cups plus 1 tablespoon	16.25	461	60
vital wheat gluten	1½ tablespoons	0.5	14	1.8
instant yeast	½ teaspoon	0.05	1.5	0.2
salt	2⅜ teaspoons	0.6	17	2.2
raisin water	¼ cup	2	56.5	7.3
Soaked Raisins	about ⅔ cup	4	113	15
walnuts, coarsely chopped	½ cup plus 3 tablespoons	2.75	78	10
almonds, coarsely chopped	½ cup plus 3 tablespoons	2.75	78	10
TOTAL		58	1,644	212.5

1 Cut the levain into about 5 pieces and put it in the bowl of a stand mixer fitted with the dough hook or in a large bowl. Add the water and stir (on low speed if using a stand mixer) for a few seconds to soften the levain. Add the sprouted emmer pulp, bread flour, vital wheat gluten, yeast, salt, and raisin water. Mix on low speed or knead by hand for about 3 minutes, until a coarse dough forms.

2 Let the dough rest, uncovered, for 5 minutes. Add the raisins, walnuts, and almonds and mix on medium-low speed or knead by hand for up to 6 minutes, until the dough is tacky but supple. The raisins will break down and disappear into the dough, making it wet at first, but it will eventually firm up. Add more flour if the dough remains sticky. Form the dough into a ball. Mist a large bowl with vegetable spray oil and put the dough in the bowl. Mist the top of the dough with vegetable spray oil and cover the bowl with plastic wrap. Ferment the dough at room temperature for 1½ hours, until nearly double in size.

3 Divide the dough in half and round each piece into a ball. Mist with vegetable spray oil and cover loosely with plastic wrap. Let rest at room temperature for 30 minutes.

4 For pan loaves, mist two 4½ by 8-inch loaf pans with vegetable spray oil. Shape each piece of dough into a sandwich loaf as shown on pages 23 and 24, then put the shaped loaves in the prepared pans. **For bâtards,** line a sheet pan with parchment paper or a silicone mat. Shape each piece of dough into a bâtard as shown on pages 20 and 21. Put the shaped loaves on the lined pan, spacing them at least 3 inches apart. **For rolls,** line two sheet pans with parchment paper or silicone mats. Divide the two dough balls into the desired number of pieces and shape as desired (see page 24). Put half of the rolls on each lined pan, spacing them at least 2 inches apart.

5 Mist the tops with vegetable spray oil and cover loosely with plastic wrap. Proof at room temperature for about 1½ to 2 hours, until nearly double in size.

6 To bake pan loaves, position a rack in the middle of the oven and preheat the oven to 350°F (177°C). Bake for 20 minutes, then rotate and bake for 35 minutes longer, until the crust is golden brown and the bread sounds hollow when thumped on the bottom. The internal temperature should be at least 195°F (91°C). Turn out onto a wire rack and let cool for at least 1 hour before slicing and serving.

7 To bake bâtards or rolls, position a rack in the middle of the oven and prepare the oven for steaming as shown on page 29. (A baking stone isn't used.) Preheat the oven to 460°F (238°C). If making bâtards, score them as desired. If making rolls, bake one pan at a time, holding the second pan in the refrigerator to slow the rising if necessary. Put the bread in the oven and pour about 1 cup of hot water into the steam pan. Bake rolls for 10 minutes and bâtards for 20 minutes, then rotate and bake for 5 to 10 minutes longer for rolls or 20 to 25 minutes longer for bâtards, until the crust is golden brown and the bread sounds hollow when thumped on the bottom. The internal temperature should be at least 195°F (91°C). Transfer from the pans to a wire rack. Let bâtards cool for at least 45 minutes before slicing and serving. Rolls can be served after 10 minutes.

SPROUTED WHEAT PULP BREAD WITH SPROUTED MULTIGRAIN FLOUR

MAKES 2 LOAVES OR UP TO 24 ROLLS

So, what happens when you mix sprouted wheat pulp with sprouted grain flour? Wonderfulness! In collaboration with others, I developed this formula at the end of a Bread Baker's Guild of America workshop in Atlanta, Georgia, held at Alon's Bakery. After making everything on our workshop list, we found ourselves with leftover sprouted wheat pulp and a variety of sprouted flours from To Your Health Sprouted Flour Co. and Lindley Mills, so we created this formula on the spot. We nailed it on the first try: a balanced, flavorful, and hearty yet soft bread that worked in loaf pans or as a freestanding boule or bâtard. Yes, it does call for vital wheat gluten to achieve the ideal texture, but it can also be made without it if you prefer a less airy loaf. Because all of the flour is sprouted, there's no need to make a soaker or pre-ferment. Feel free to swap in your own favorite sprouted flours, even sprouted bean flours, such as sprouted lentil or garbanzo flour, or a mixture, such as the Lindley Ancient Grain blend.

DOUGH

INGREDIENT	VOLUME	OUNCES	GRAMS	%
sprouted wheat pulp or any variety of sprouted pulp, such as emmer, Kamut, or spelt	6 cups	32	907	80
sprouted corn flour	½ cup	2	56.5	5
sprouted brown rice or sprouted spelt flour	6½ tablespoons or ½ cup	2	56.5	5
sprouted rolled oats or sprouted oat flour	½ cup	2	56.5	5
sprouted sorghum, millet, quinoa, or amaranth flour	about ½ cup	2	56.5	5
water, at room temperature	1¼ cups plus 2 tablespoons	11	312	28
vital wheat gluten	½ cup plus 1½ teaspoons	2.8	79.5	7
instant yeast	2 tablespoons	0.66	19	1.7
salt	2 teaspoons	0.5	14	1.2
honey	1½ tablespoons	1	28.5	2.5
molasses	1½ tablespoons	1	28.5	2.5
sugar	2 tablespoons	1	28.5	2.5
vegetable oil	1 tablespoon plus 1 teaspoon	0.65	18	1.6
TOTAL		58.61	1,661	147

1 Put all the ingredients in the order listed in a mixing bowl or the bowl of a stand mixer fitted with the paddle attachment. Stir or mix, on low speed if using a stand mixer, until a coarse, thick, slightly sticky dough forms, about 3 minutes.

2 Let rest, uncovered, for 5 to 10 minutes. Then switch to the dough hook and mix on medium speed or knead by hand for 3 to 4 minutes, until the dough is tacky but supple and feels springy when poked, and its temperature is about 75°F (24°C). Knead it by hand for a few seconds, then form it into a ball.

3 Mist a bowl with vegetable spray oil and put the dough in the bowl. Mist the top with vegetable spray oil and cover the bowl with plastic wrap or a lid and let rest at room temperature for 15 minutes. It won't rise much in that time.

4 Divide the dough in half and form each piece into a ball. Mist with vegetable spray oil and cover loosely with plastic wrap. Let rest at room temperature for 20 minutes.

5 For pan loaves, mist two 4½ by 8-inch loaf pans with vegetable spray oil. Shape the pieces into sandwich loaves as shown on pages 23 and 24, then put the shaped loaves in the prepared pans. **For hearth loaves,** line two sheet pans with parchment paper or silicon mats. Shape the pieces into boules or bâtards as shown on pages 20 to 21, then put the shaped loaves on the lined pans. **For rolls,** line two sheet pans with parchment paper or silicone mats. Divide the two dough balls into the desired number of pieces and shape as desired (see page 24). Put half of the rolls on each lined pan, spacing them at least 2 inches apart.

6 Mist the tops with vegetable spray oil and cover loosely with plastic wrap. Proof at room temperature until nearly double in size, about 1½ hours.

7 To bake pan loaves, position a rack in the middle of the oven and preheat the oven to 380°F (193°C). Bake for 25 minutes, then rotate and bake for 20 to 25 minutes longer, until the crust is golden brown and the bread sounds hollow when thumped on the bottom. The internal temperature should be at least 190°F (88°C). Turn out onto a wire rack and let cool for at least 45 minutes before slicing and serving.

8 To bake hearth loaves or rolls, position two racks in the oven an equal distance apart and prepare the oven for steaming as shown on page 29. (A baking stone isn't used.) Preheat the oven to 380°F (193°C). Put the bread in the oven and pour about 1 cup of hot water into the steam pan. Bake rolls for about 10 minutes and freestanding loaves for about 20 minutes, then rotate the pans front to back and between racks. Bake for 10 to 12 minutes longer for rolls or 20 to 25 minutes longer for freestanding loaves, until the crust is golden brown and the bread sounds hollow when thumped on the bottom. The internal temperature should be at least 190°F (88°C). Transfer from the pans to a wire rack. Let loaves cool for at least 1 hour before slicing and serving. Rolls can be served after 10 minutes.

SPROUTED KAMUT PULP BAGELS

MAKES 8 BAGELS

The name Kamut is trademarked by Mack and Bob Quinn, who first started cultivating this ancient variety of wheat in the United States in the 1980s. Kamut is a strain of *Triticum turanicum*, known more generically as Khorasan wheat, as this type of wheat is believed to have originated in the Persian province of Khorasan. Whole Kamut is fairly widely available, and other brands of Khorasan wheat are now appearing in the marketplace, with Central Milling selling it in sprouted pulp form (see Resources, page 240). As with spelt, einkorn, and emmer, it is reported that some people who are sensitive to conventional wheat can better tolerate this strain.

As you'll see, this formula calls for making a small piece of whole wheat levain. If your mother starter has been recently refreshed, you can simply use an equal amount of that instead. However, if the hydration of your starter is different from that in the recipe, you may need to adjust the amount of flour or water in the final dough accordingly. You can substitute any type of sprouted wheat pulp but this Khorasan version produces a beautiful, golden bagel. Note that this is a two- to three-day process, so plan accordingly.

WHOLE WHEAT LEVAIN

INGREDIENT	VOLUME	OUNCES	GRAMS	%
Mother Starter (page 40)	1 teaspoon	0.25	7	16
water, lukewarm (95°F / 35°C)	2 tablespoons plus 1¼ teaspoons	1.2	34	80
whole wheat flour	⅓ cup	1.5	42.5	100
salt	pinch	0.02	0.5	0.1
TOTAL		2.97	84	196.1

Put the starter in a small bowl and add the water to soften it. Add the flour and salt and stir until a coarse ball of dough forms. Transfer to a work surface and knead by hand for about 30 seconds, until the starter is evenly distributed and a soft, tacky dough forms. Mist a small bowl with vegetable spray oil and put the dough in the bowl. Mist the top of the dough with vegetable spray oil and cover the bowl with plastic wrap. Let the levain rest at room temperature for 6 to 12 hours, until double in size. If it doubles in size before you're ready to make the final dough, put it in the refrigerator.

CONTINUED

FINAL DOUGH

INGREDIENT	VOLUME	OUNCES	GRAMS	%
Whole Wheat Levain	all	2.97	84	12
water	½ cup	4	113	16
sprouted Kamut (Khorasan wheat) pulp	2¾ cups	15	425	60
whole-milled whole wheat flour or sprouted whole wheat flour	2¼ cups or 2⅓ cups	10	283	40
instant yeast	¾ teaspoon	0.08	2.5	0.4
vital wheat gluten	1½ tablespoons	0.5	14	2
salt	1⅝ teaspoons	0.4	11.5	1.6
honey or barley malt syrup	3½ teaspoons	0.75	21.5	3
baking soda for boiling the bagels	about 2 tablespoons			
honey for boiling the bagels (optional)	about ¼ cup			
cornmeal or semolina flour	about 2 tablespoons			
TOTAL		33.7	954.5	135

1 Cut the levain into about 5 pieces and put it in the bowl of a stand mixer fitted with the dough hook or in a large bowl. Add the water and stir (on low speed if using a stand mixer) for a few seconds to soften the levain. Add the sprouted Kamut pulp, flour, yeast, vital wheat gluten, salt, and honey in that order. Mix on low speed or knead by hand for 4 to 5 minutes to make a firm, coarse dough.

2 Let the dough rest, uncovered, for 5 minutes. Then mix on medium-low speed or knead by hand for 3 to 4 minutes. The dough should be smooth, firm, and satiny. Form the dough into a ball and return it to the oiled bowl. Cover the bowl with plastic wrap and let the dough rest for 20 minutes.

3 Divide the dough into eight 4-ounce (113 g) pieces (you can also make larger bagels if you prefer). Form each piece into a ball. Cover with plastic wrap and let rest for 10 minutes. Line a sheet pan with parchment paper or a silicone mat and mist with vegetable spray oil.

4 Shape the pieces into bagels as described on page 25 and put them on the prepared pan, spacing them at least 1 inch apart. Mist the tops with vegetable spray oil and cover the pan loosely with plastic wrap. Proof the dough at room temperature for 30 minutes, then refrigerate for at least 12 hours or overnight.

5 Follow the instructions on page 90 for boiling and baking the bagels.

6 Transfer the baked bagels to a wire rack and let cool for at least 20 minutes before slicing and serving.

CHAPTER 5
WHOLE GRAINS AND WHOLE MILLING

Whole grain breads have long been seen as the healthier option, a source of important fiber, and therefore the most guilt-free choice. But as we dive deeper into the next frontier of bread, we enter a realm of subtle, nuanced distinctions. Putting aside controversies surrounding wheat and grains in general, a new question is whether all whole wheat flour is equal.

Craig Ponsford, one of my longtime baking heroes, believes that some serious misinformation is floating around, and that much of what we believe to be 100% whole wheat flour actually isn't. He told me that when he decided to focus on baking healthy breads with whole grain flours after an award-winning career in making classic French-style white breads, he was stunned to learn that some whole wheat flours might be as unhealthful as white flour.

As he told me, "It comes down to how the wheat is milled. I learned that most so-called whole wheat flour is actually *fractionated* flour, reconstituted during milling. As a result, the body responds to it differently than true whole wheat flour. Reconstituted whole wheat flour is not the same as whole-milled wheat flour."

My first thought was *What on earth is he talking about?* Whole wheat flour, as I understood it, meant that when the wheat kernels go into the mill, all of their components get ground into flour: 100% in, 100% out. I asked Craig about this and he explained: "You could say that if 100 pounds of wheat goes into the mill and 100 pounds of flour comes out, then yes, that's whole wheat flour. That's called 100% extraction."

That's how I understood it too, just as I understood that if only 85 pounds of flour is collected, 15 pounds of bran and germ must have been sifted out, resulting in an 85% extraction rate, which bakers refer to as high-extraction flour. And as the extraction rate lowers to between 70% and 75%, the result is white flour, containing just the endosperm of the wheat—the white, starchy part that also contains the proteins gliadin and glutenin, which eventually bond to make gluten. As for the remaining 25% to 30%, it may be sold or used as wheat bran or wheat germ or used in animal feed. And sometimes it's added back into white flour to create flours with various degrees of extraction.

"But here's what most people don't know," Craig continued. "If you run the wheat through a stone mill, or even a stainless steel roller mill, and just collected it at the end, you'll end up with a lot of large bran and germ particles, resulting in a very coarse whole wheat flour, which most bakers don't really want. So mills typically sift out the germ and bran early in the process and then run them through again, separately from the endosperm, to break them down into smaller particles. Then, usually after at least two such siftings and millings, it's added back into the flour, reconstituting it to, in theory, 100% of its original weight."

"So why is that a bad thing?" I asked.

"Once it's separated and added back, it's somehow different. Something changes, and we don't get all of the nutritional benefits. It doesn't perform the same way in baking, either, or taste as good, and it also doesn't keep as well. Although I'm not a scientist and I don't know all the intricacies, I can tell you that ever since I switched to whole-milled flour, my products have improved dramatically and no one complains about digestibility. I think these are some of the best whole grain baked products you will ever taste."

He was right about that last part, as I found out a few nights later when I stayed up with Craig during his nighttime baking stint at Ponsford's Place, the little bakery he operates as a test laboratory in San Rafael, California. Craig only bakes for the public two nights a week, Thursday and Friday (or, more accurately, Friday and Saturday mornings, from about midnight until a few hours after opening at 8 a.m.). He usually sells out of everything by midafternoon. Every few weeks, he and his girlfriend, Diana Benner, also offer a Wednesday pizza night featuring his whole wheat dough and sell hundreds of slices and many whole pies to the loyalists who know where to find Ponsford's Place.

GETTING INTO THE NITTY-GRITTY

I spent a number of days with Craig, visiting various people he arranged for me to meet. One was Joe Vanderliet, the owner of Certified Foods in Woodland, about an hour east of San Rafael in California's Central Valley. Craig told me that Joe was the person who convinced him to focus totally on whole-milled flour.

Joe is a tall, strapping Dutchman who, during his fifty-plus years in the business, has worked for some of the largest flour companies in the country, such as Archer Daniels Midland and Bay State Milling. He's continued to educate himself along the way by studying at baking and brewing schools and, over the years, his frustration at seeing so many nutrients wasted in the milling process spurred him to dedicate himself to whole-milled flour, ground primarily with stone mills rather than steel rollers. Eventually, his company established Joseph's Best as their flagship brand, and at the time of my visit, they were milling and packaging more than thirty products, including four types of whole wheat flour, two types of rye flour, nine types of rice flour, and sixteen specialty flours, such as amaranth, buckwheat, emmer, spelt, teff, quinoa, and various legume flours.

As Joe took us on a tour of the mill, where the whirr of large stone mills grinding hard red wheat into flour dominated the soundscape of the high-ceilinged facility, he was clearly adamant about not separating the endosperm from the bran and germ in the early stages of milling. He told me, "Once the kernel is broken, it can't be put back together," and went on to say that the larger companies who dominate the flour industry reconstitute their sifted flour by adding bran and maybe the germ back into it—and not necessarily the bran or germ from the same wheat kernels. "It just isn't the same, and it's definitely not as good for you," he insisted.

Prior to this trip, I'd never thought about whole wheat flour not really being whole wheat flour. And though I knew the big particles might get sifted out and then run back through the mill to break them down into finer particles before adding them back into the flour, I couldn't see much harm in that, so I asked Joe about it.

He replied, "It really depends on when it gets sifted out. The longer you can keep it all together, the better it will be." And the fact is, in order to make his fine- and medium-grind whole wheat flour, even Joe sifts out the bran and germ and regrinds them before adding them back to the same batch of flour. But as he told me, most companies have two breaks, or points where the sifting occurs, and the first one comes early on. He said, "That's where the real problem is. I always wait until the second break, and believe me, those extra seconds where all three parts of the grain stay together make a huge difference."

I whispered to Craig, "Boy, that's kind of like inside baseball."

But Craig said, "Wait until we get back to my bakery. You'll see there really is a difference."

THE GLUTEN CONNECTION

It's important to clarify a few things here. First, as I was writing this book, Certified Foods was sold to a larger company, Bay State Milling, who retained Joe and his team, and they have assured me they're committed to honoring and using Joe's methods. Second, many small regional mills already use a whole milling process, especially for their coarse flour, which is usually a straightforward, whole-milled 100% extraction with little or no sifting and reconstituting, though they may not do it with as much precision as Vanderliet. If they're using a stone mill, it's likely that they're sifting out the larger particles at some point for regrinding when making fine- or medium-grind flour. And finally, I have to add that Joe's declarations are theories. When I contacted larger mills, they either refuted or sidestepped Joe's claims and wouldn't actually tell me how they reconstitute beyond vague statements like, "Everyone has to sift and reconstitute if they want a finer flour."

But Joe and Craig are both convinced that one of the causes of increasing rates of gluten sensitivity is conventional modern milling practices. And customers often tell both of them that Joe's is the only wheat flour that doesn't give them digestive problems. To me, this makes sense intuitively, as do some of the other hypotheses floating around regarding the causes of gluten sensitivity. One is the idea that ancient strains of wheat, such as spelt, einkorn, emmer, and Kamut (aka Khorasan wheat) are tolerable for some people who are otherwise sensitive to gluten, perhaps because of the genetic makeup of these strains, or maybe because the gluten isn't as complex or strong as in more recent, crossbred strains. Another is that locally grown grains are often easier to digest because they're grown in the same soil and climate where consumers live, so their bodies are more predisposed to respond positively. In any case, I generally support practices that connect us with the things we eat.

THE LOCAL CONNECTION

Other bakers, millers, and grain visionaries have been on quests similar to Craig's and Joe's. There are far too many to profile here, so I'll cover just a few.

A prime example is Bob Klein, the visionary owner of Oliveto, a restaurant in Oakland, California. He's a proponent of a new concept that's been gaining traction recently: identity-preserved grain. A few years ago he started a venture called Community Grains, using California-grown grain to make gourmet products such as pastas and polenta. He's passionate about commissioning farmers to grow specific strains of wheat and other grains that are well suited to the local soil and climate. In addition, Community Grains whole wheat flour trumpets the value of whole milling right on the packaging. Bob, who has long been a major barometer for coming culinary trends, told me, "Whole milling, rather than reconstituted, is a real difference maker. It would be a shame to take this beautiful, distinctive, carefully grown grain and then screw it up at the mill. Plus, it's the right thing to do. And identity-preserved farming supports the local economy, allows me to work closely with local farmers, and showcases both the *terroir* and the craft."

In *Peter Reinhart's Whole Grain Breads*, I wrote about Jennifer Lapidus, a baker in Asheville, North Carolina, who was making outstanding Flemish-style *desem* breads at her Natural Bridges Bakery. Since then, she's closed the bakery and established the milling company Carolina Ground. She recently told me, "I got into milling in response to the soaring cost of wheat, artificially driven up by futures traders and other people who never even touched the wheat. So I decided to focus on locally milled flour, bought from local wheat farmers and milled for local bakers." As it turns out, other farmers and millers around the country felt the same, and now numerous local mills are making flour from locally grown grain, including Farmer Ground Mill (Trumansburg, New York), Somerset Grist Mill (Skowhegan, Maine), Camas Country Mill (Eugene, Oregon), and Fairhaven Organic Flour Mill (Burlington, Washington).

Dr. Stephen Jones, of the Washington State University Agricultural Research Center, put it this way when we spoke: "Because of the commodity system, there used to be more bakers than wheat farmers in places like Vermont, but now we're seeing a lot more small-scale farmers growing wheat that's been developed specifically for their region and soil." Among the various projects he leads is a plant breeding program in which heirloom wheat strains are crossbred with disease-resistant wheat to create strains that are well suited to particular climates and soils.

According to Jones, this can even result in superior flavor: "If you plant wheat that's designed for wet regions in an area like the coastal Pacific Northwest, it will produce chocolate, spicy, and pleasant grassy flavor tones. But if you plant that same wheat in dry regions, where so much commodity wheat is grown, it's almost flavorless." He went on to tell me about Heather Darby, at the University of Vermont, who's been working with Jack Lazor, of Butterworks Farm, to develop a Vermont farmers breeding club with the same goal as his program: developing strains of wheat appropriate for their region, climate, and soil. "The same thing is happening in many other places, and the best outcome will be that the availability of locally farmed wheat creates an infrastructure that includes millers, malters, bakers, and even livestock farmers. Essentially, it restores a local grain economy and it keeps the value where it's created."

As for Carolina Ground, Jennifer told me that she's currently whole milling 100% whole wheat bread flour, and also high-extraction (85%) flour, whole wheat and high-extraction pastry flour, and a variety of rye flours, along with lighter, lower-extraction flours for bakers who want them. She also likes to focus on milling single-variety wheats, as opposed to the blends associated with commodity flour.

When I asked Jennifer where she finds her wheat, she said, "I try to source my grain from North Carolina or nearby regions, but sometimes I have to spread the net wider to find the wheat that will yield the performance bakers need. But my mission is also to support local wheat farmers and help them find buyers for their grain, even if it isn't appropriate for bread flour. One example is Asheville's Riverbend Malt House, where they sprout and roast wheat, then send it to me for milling before it's shipped out to customers for beer making. And this past season, when growing conditions produced a less-than-ideal crop, I was thrilled that many bakers were willing to step up and accept a flour that was more challenging to work with. For example, Harry Peemoeller used it in his baking classes at Johnson & Wales University, and Lionel Vatinet used it in his breads at La Farm Bakery."

This kind of community support and networking reflects a wider national movement, and I've compiled a small list of likeminded farmers, millers, and bakers in the Resources section (page 240).

If the mission of the baker is to evoke the full potential of flavor trapped in the grain, it follows that the mission of farmers and millers is to provide the best-quality wheat, ground into the highest-quality flour, so that it can be transformed into the best possible bread. The recipes in this chapter, which feature whole-milled flours and flours made from heritage varieties of wheat, showcase these congruent missions of craft and quality.

WHOLE-MILLED LEAN DOUGH FRENCH BREAD

MAKES 1 LARGE LOAF, UP TO 4 SMALLER LOAVES, OR 6 MINI BAGUETTES

This foundational dough, developed by Craig Ponsford, can be used to make any number of shapes. It's a simple, lean dough made with a poolish and featuring 100% whole-milled wheat flour. Craig is adamant that it won't be as good if made with standard, reconstituted whole wheat flour, so see the Resources section (page 240) for online purveyors if you can't find whole-milled wheat flour locally. Be aware that the hydration ratios could vary depending on the brand of flour you use. Let the dough guide you regarding adjustments to the amount of water or flour (or, as I tell my students, let the dough dictate what it needs). That said, whole wheat flour hydrates more slowly than white flour, so try to resist the temptation to add more flour. The dough will appear too sticky at first, but it will strengthen and firm up during the stretch and fold process. Craig calls for a small amount of salt in his poolish, which is unconventional, but as he explains, it's helpful because whole wheat flour has more enzyme activity than white flour, so it can easily overferment even with only a small pinch of yeast.

POOLISH (DAY 1)

INGREDIENT	VOLUME	OUNCES	GRAMS	%
whole-milled wheat flour	1⅓ cups	6	170	100
instant yeast	pinch	0.007	0.2	0.1
salt	pinch	0.02	0.5	0.3
water, at room temperature	¾ cup	6	170	100
TOTAL		12.027	340.7	200.4

In a small bowl, stir together the flour, yeast, and salt. Add the water and stir until the flour is hydrated and a thick, batter-like dough forms, about 1 minute. Use a wet bowl scraper to scrape down the sides of the bowl. Cover the bowl with plastic wrap and let the poolish rest at room temperature for 12 hours or overnight, until it gets very bubbly and swells in size. If it gets very bubbly before you're ready to make the final dough, put it in the refrigerator. If you do so, use lukewarm water, at about 95°F (35°C), when mixing the final dough.

CONTINUED

FINAL DOUGH (DAY 2)

INGREDIENT	VOLUME	OUNCES	GRAMS	%
water, at room temperature (lukewarm if poolish was refrigerated)	1¾ cups plus 1 tablespoon	14.5	411	81
Poolish	all	12.027	340.7	67
whole-milled hard wheat flour (red or white wheat, or a blend)	4 cups	18	510	100
salt	2 teaspoons	0.5	14	2.7
instant yeast	¾ teaspoon	0.08	2.5	0.5
TOTAL		45.107	1,278.2	251.2

1 In the bowl of a stand mixer fitted with the paddle attachment, or in a large bowl, stir together the water and poolish (on low speed if using a stand mixer). Add the flour, salt, and yeast and mix or stir for 20 to 30 seconds or until the flour is hydrated and a coarse, sticky dough forms. If using a stand mixer, switch to the dough hook, using wet hands to get all the dough off the paddle. Mix, or stir with a wet spoon for 2 to 3 minutes. If the dough is difficult to stir with a spoon, turn it out onto a lightly floured work surface and knead it with floured or oiled hands. The dough should be somewhat shaggy and sticky. Fold the dough into a ball.

2 Mist a large bowl with vegetable spray oil or lightly coat it with vegetable oil. Transfer the dough to the bowl, mist the top with vegetable spray oil, and cover the bowl with plastic wrap (or leave the dough on an oiled work surface and cover with the bowl). Ferment the dough at room temperature for 30 minutes.

3 Working either in the bowl or on a lightly oiled work surface, stretch and fold the dough as shown on page 20, folding it over itself four times: once each from the top, bottom, and sides. Return the dough to the bowl, smooth side up, and cover the bowl (or again leave the dough on the work surface and cover with the bowl). Let the dough rest for 30 minutes. Repeat the process, stretching and folding, then returning the dough to the bowl (or covering it with the bowl). The dough will become smoother and more supple with each stretch and fold, and after the second stretch and fold, it will be very supple and tacky but not sticky. Ferment at room temperature for 30 to 60 minutes, until it increases in size by about 1½ times.

4 Oil the work surface or dust it with flour. Using a wet or oiled bowl scraper, transfer the dough to the oiled or dusted area. Using a metal pastry blade, divide the dough into the desired number of pieces—6 for mini baguettes or 2 to 4 for smaller loaves—or use the entire amount of dough for one large loaf. Gently form each piece into a boule, bâtard, or baguette as shown on page 20. Cover loosely with a clean towel or plastic wrap.

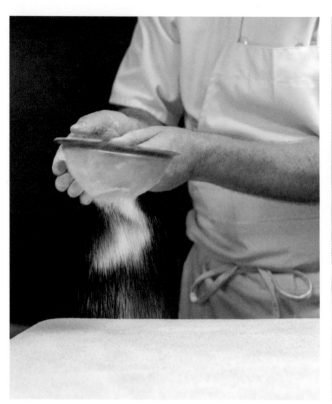

5 Mist the tops with vegetable spray oil and cover loosely with plastic wrap or a clean towel. Proof at room temperature for about 1 hour, or until the dough increases in size by 1½ times.

6 About 45 minutes before you plan to bake, prepare the oven for hearth baking with a baking stone and steam pan as shown on page 29. Preheat the oven to 500°F (260°C). About 10 minutes before baking, uncover the dough to let the surface dry a little bit.

7 Transfer the dough to a peel and score as desired. Transfer onto the baking stone and pour about 1 cup of hot water into the steam pan. Immediately lower the temperature to 450°F (232°C). Bake for 14 minutes, then rotate and bake for 10 minutes longer for mini baguettes, 15 minutes longer for small loaves, and 20 minutes longer for a large loaf, until the crust is rich golden brown and the bread sounds hollow when thumped on the bottom. The internal temperature should be at least 200°F (93°C).

8 Transfer to a wire rack and let cool for at least 30 minutes before slicing and serving.

WHOLE-MILLED WHOLE WHEAT CIABATTA

MAKES 1 LARGE CIABATTA OR 2 SMALL CIABATTAS

This wet, rustic dough is a small-scale version of the one Craig Ponsford uses at Ponsford's Place for both his ciabatta and his Wednesday night pizza events. (To use it for pizza, see the sidebar on page 171.) I also use it for focaccia. It requires a poolish pre-ferment for structure, acidity, and maximum flavor development. The dough also contains a bit of coarse whole rye flour, also known as pumpernickel flour; it adds texture and contributes to the flavor complexity. Between the poolish and the water in the final dough, the total hydration of this dough is very close to 100% water to flour, and that's one of the secrets to making whole wheat products at the quality level to which Craig aspires. It takes practice to learn to handle such wet dough, whether using oiled hands as I do or floured hands as many bakers, including Craig, prefer. You may be tempted to add more flour when mixing it to make the dough feel more "normal." Try to resist that urge, as whole-milled flour will eventually absorb a lot of water. And with the help of the three stretch and fold sequences, the dough will firm up enough to handle. Still, it may seem wetter than you're used to. This is where handling technique can make or break the final result. Especially when this dough for ciabatta is used, it must be gently cradled.

POOLISH (DAY 1)

INGREDIENT	VOLUME	OUNCES	GRAMS	%
whole-milled wheat flour	1 cup plus 2 tablespoons	5	142	100
water, at about 75°F (24°C)	½ cup plus 2 tablespoons	5	142	100
salt	pinch	0.02	0.5	0.3
instant yeast	pinch	0.007	0.2	0.1
TOTAL		10.027	284.7	200.4

In a small bowl, stir together the flour, yeast, and salt. Add the water and stir until the flour is hydrated and a thick, batter-like dough forms, about 1 minute. Use a wet bowl scraper to scrape down the sides of the bowl. Cover the bowl with plastic wrap and let the poolish rest at room temperature for 12 hours or overnight, until it gets very bubbly and swells in size. If it gets very bubbly before you're ready to make the final dough, put it in the refrigerator. If you do so, use lukewarm water, at about 95°F (35°C), when mixing the final dough.

CONTINUED

FINAL DOUGH (DAY 2)

INGREDIENT	VOLUME	OUNCES	GRAMS	%
water, at about 75°F (24°C), or 95°F (35°C) if poolish was refrigerated	1 cup plus 3 tablespoons	9.5	269	92
Poolish	all	10.027	284.7	97
whole-milled hard red winter wheat flour	2¼ cups	10	283	97
pumpernickel or coarse whole rye flour	1 tablespoon	0.3	8.5	2.9
salt	1¼ teaspoons	0.32	9	3.1
instant yeast	½ teaspoon	0.05	1.5	0.5
TOTAL		30.677	869.2	292.5

1 In the bowl of a stand mixer fitted with the paddle attachment, or in a large bowl, stir together the water and poolish (on low speed if using a stand mixer). Add the flours, salt, and yeast and mix or stir for 1 minute. Scrape down the bowl with a spatula or bowl scraper, then mix or stir for 3 minutes. If using a stand mixer, increase the speed to medium-low, and if mixing by hand, use a large spoon or your hands, dipped in water from time to time to minimize sticking, and mix for 3 minutes longer. The dough should be soft, wet, and very sticky.

2 Mist a bowl with vegetable spray oil or lightly coat it with vegetable oil. Using a wet or oiled bowl scraper, transfer the dough into the bowl. Working either in the bowl or on a lightly oiled work surface, stretch and fold the dough as shown on page 20, folding it over itself four times: once each from the top, bottom, and sides. Return the dough to the bowl, smooth side up, and cover the bowl (or again leave the dough on the work surface and cover with the bowl). Then, at intervals of 1 hour, perform two additional sequences of stretching and folding. For each stretch and fold sequence, lightly oil your hands to prevent sticking. After the final stretch and fold, cover the dough and let it rest at room temperature for 15 to 20 minutes (or up to 1 hour for more fermentation if the dough seems sluggish). The dough will become firmer with each stretch and fold. After the third stretch and fold, it will be a bit bouncy when patted but will still be soft and sticky.

3 Use the whole piece of dough for a large ciabatta, or divide it in half for 2 smaller ciabattas. Dust a sheet pan with about 3 tablespoons (0.85 oz / 24 g) of whole wheat flour or a blend of whole wheat and rye flour. With floured hands, lift, cradle, and transfer the dough pieces to the pan and gently fold each piece in thirds, like a letter, using the flour on the pan to coat the outer surface as you fold. (Alternatively, leave the pieces unfolded, coat with flour, and place them on the pan; this yields what the French would call *pain rustique*, eliminating the need to flip them over during proofing, as for ciabatta.) Roll the shaped dough in the flour to coat it again, then lay the dough seam side down on the floured pan, gently forming each piece into a slipper-like oblong or rectangle. Proof, uncovered, at room temperature for 30 minutes. Gently flip so the seam side is up, then proof for 15 to 25 minutes longer.

4 About 45 minutes before you plan to bake, prepare the oven for hearth baking with a baking stone and steam pan as shown on page 29. Preheat the oven to 550°F (288°C) or as high as it will go.

5 Just before baking, dust a peel with flour, or cover it with parchment paper and mist with vegetable spray oil. Gently transfer the shaped dough to the peel, cradling it in your hands for support and laying it seam side up. Coax the dough back into a slipper shape with floured hands. Slide the dough (and the parchment if using) onto the baking stone and pour about 1 cup of hot water into the steam pan. Lower the temperature to 400°F (204°C). Bake for 20 minutes, then rotate (if using parchment, slip it out from under the dough and discard). Bake for about 10 to 15 minutes longer for 2 small loaves or 20 to 30 minutes longer for a large loaf, until the bread sounds hollow when thumped on the bottom. The internal temperature should be at least 200°F (93°C).

6 Transfer to a wire rack and let cool for at least 30 minutes before slicing or serving.

Whole-Milled Whole Wheat Pizzas

To make individual pizzas from this dough, divide it into 3 or 4 pieces after the final stretch and fold. Gently shape each piece into a ball, as if shaping a boule, as shown on page 20. Put the balls on a floured sheet pan, mist with vegetable spray oil, and cover loosely with plastic wrap or a clean towel. Refrigerate for at least 1 hour before making the pizzas. Because the dough is so wet, it will be easier to shape when cold than when warm. But if the dough is very elastic and hard to stretch to the desired diameter of 10 to 12 inches, let it rest at room temperature for about 45 minutes so it can relax enough to stretch out. See page 78 for guidance on pizza shaping, topping, and baking.

WHOLE WHEAT CURRANT PRETZELS

MAKES 10 LARGE PRETZELS

This is my small-batch variation of Craig Ponsford's unique 100% whole wheat pretzel recipe, made with whole-milled flour. A tricky part of this recipe is using a lye dipping solution to create the distinctive dark brown sheen associated with soft pretzels, so the method also includes instructions for using a baking soda solution. Baking soda won't create the same intensity of sheen and may even leave white streaks on the dough, so if you use this method, you should also brush the tops of the pretzels with an egg white wash. Also, pretzels can lose their shape when handling and dipping. To deal with this, the method below includes a freezer trick I learned from Harry Peemoeller. This dough can also be used to make pretzel rolls, bread sticks, and any number of other shapes, and you can also make it without the soaked currants or with raisins, if you prefer.

BIGA (DAY 1)

INGREDIENT	VOLUME	OUNCES	GRAMS	%
whole-milled wheat flour	1½ cups plus 2 teaspoons	7	198	100
salt	pinch	0.02	0.5	0.3
instant yeast	pinch	0.007	0.2	0.1
water, at room temperature	½ cup plus 2 tablespoons	5	142	71
TOTAL		12.027	340.7	171.4

In a medium bowl, stir together the flour, salt, and yeast. Add the water and stir until the flour is hydrated and a coarse ball of dough forms, about 1 minute. Transfer to a lightly floured work surface and knead by hand until slightly smoother and firm, about 1 minute. Mist a clean bowl with vegetable spray oil, put the biga in the bowl, and cover the bowl with plastic wrap. Let the biga rest at room temperature for at least 12 hours or overnight, until it increases in size by 1½ to 2 times. If it approaches this size before you're ready to make the final dough, put it in the refrigerator.

CURRANTS (DAY 1)

INGREDIENT	VOLUME	OUNCES	GRAMS
currants (or raisins)	about 1 cup	6	170
water, at room temperature	¾ cup	6	170

Put the currants in a small bowl and pour in the water. Cover the bowl with plastic wrap and leave out at room temperature for at least 12 hours or overnight.

CONTINUED

FINAL DOUGH (DAY 2)

NOTE: You can also use low-fat milk or nondairy milk instead of milk powder. To do so, replace ¾ cup (6 oz / 170 g) of the water with an equal amount of milk.

INGREDIENT	VOLUME	OUNCES	GRAMS	%
whole-milled wheat flour	3¾ cups	17	482	100
salt	2 teaspoons	0.5	14	2.9
instant yeast	1 teaspoon	0.11	3	0.6
nonfat dry milk powder (see note)	4 tablespoons	0.75	21.5	4.5
brown sugar (or honey or agave nectar)	2 tablespoons (or 1½ tablespoons)	1	28.5	5.9
water, at room temperature, or 95°F (35°C) if biga was refrigerated	1½ cups plus 2 tablespoons	13	369	77
soaked currants (or raisins)	all	12	340	71
Biga	all	12.027	340.7	71
unsalted butter, at room temperature	1½ tablespoons	0.75	21.5	4.5
egg white wash (optional)	1 egg white whisked with 1 tablespoon water			
pretzel salt for topping	about 1 tablespoon or to taste			
TOTAL		57.137	1,620.2	337.4

1 In the bowl of a stand mixer fitted with the paddle attachment, or in a large bowl, stir together the flour, salt, yeast, and milk powder (on low speed if using a stand mixer). Stir in the sugar (if using honey or agave nectar, add it with the water in the next step). Add the water and currants, including their soaking water. Mix or stir for 30 to 60 seconds, until the flour is hydrated. Switch to the dough hook. Break up the biga into about 8 pieces and add it to the bowl. Mix on medium-low speed or turn out onto a floured work surface and knead for 3 minutes. Add the softened butter and mix on medium speed or knead until the dough is somewhat firm yet supple and tacky to the touch, about 1 minute. The currants will be broken into bits and dispersed throughout the dough.

2 Mist a large bowl with vegetable spray oil, put the dough in the bowl, and cover the bowl with plastic wrap. Ferment the dough at room temperature for about 1 hour.

3 Spread about 1 teaspoon of vegetable oil on the work surface and transfer the dough to the oiled area. Lightly oil your hands, then stretch and fold the dough as shown on page 20, folding it over itself four times: once each from the top, bottom,

and sides. The dough will strengthen and firm up somewhat. Return the dough to the bowl and cover the bowl with plastic wrap, or leave it on the work surface and cover it with the bowl. Ferment at room temperature for 1 to 1½ hours, until the dough increases in size by about 1½ times.

4 Spread about ½ teaspoon of vegetable oil on the work surface and transfer the dough to the oiled area. Divide the dough into 10 equal pieces, each about 5.5 ounces (156 g). (Or make a greater quantity of smaller pretzels if you prefer.) Flatten each piece and then roll it into a tight cigar-shaped cylinder 4 to 6 inches long. Cover the dough with plastic wrap or a clean towel and let it rest for 20 minutes.

5 Line two sheet pans with parchment paper or silicone mats and mist with vegetable spray oil. Use your hands to roll each piece of dough into a tapered strand 24 to 28 inches long (shorter if making smaller pretzels). If a piece resists or shrinks back, move on to the next one and return to it later. Shape each piece into a pretzel shape, then lay it on one of the prepared pans, 5 per pan. When you fill each pan, mist the top of the dough with vegetable spray oil, cover the pan with plastic wrap, and put it into the refrigerator or freezer for 1 hour to firm the dough and make the pretzels easier to handle. (The shaped pretzels can be stored in the refrigerator for up to 36 hours or in the freezer for up to 3 weeks; for long-term freezer storage, once the pretzels are frozen, transfer them to zip-top freezer bags.)

CONTINUED

6 About 1 hour before you plan to bake, remove the pretzels from the refrigerator or freezer. Bring about 2 cups (16 oz / 454 g) of water to a boil, then pour it into a stainless steel or glass bowl or pan. Add 1½ tablespoons (0.65 oz / 18 g) of lye or ¼ cup (2.5 oz / 71 g) of baking soda and whisk gently to dissolve. If using lye, be careful not to splash any on the counter or your skin, and please refer to the sidebar for tips on working with lye. Let cool.

7 Position two racks in the oven an equal distance apart and preheat the oven to 400°F (204°C). While the pretzels are still cold, remove them from the sheet pans and generously mist the pan liners with vegetable spray oil; or just line two fresh sheet pans with parchment paper or silicone mats and mist generously with vegetable spray oil. (Once dipped, in the next step, the dough will stick to parchment paper that's only lightly misted.)

8 There are two options for coating the pretzels in the lye or baking soda. The standard approach is to wear latex or other food handling gloves, and dip one pretzel at a time into the lye or baking soda solution, submerging it for 4 to 5 seconds; if the solution isn't deep enough to cover the pretzel, flip the pretzel over. Lift the pretzel out and let the solution drip back into the bowl, and then place the pretzel on one of the prepared pans; the pretzels shouldn't touch, but they won't expand much, so they can be fairly close. A new approach I learned from Craig is to use a spray bottle to mist the prepared lye solution over the tops of the pretzels as they rest on the sheet pan.

9 Sprinkle the pretzel salt over the pretzels.

10 Bake for 7 minutes, then rotate the pans front to back and between racks, and bake for 5 to 15 minutes longer, until the crust has a rich, nutlike brown color and is hard to the touch.

11 Transfer them to a wire rack immediately. The pretzels will soften slightly and be ready to eat in 5 to 10 minutes.

Variations

MULTIGRAIN PRETZELS: Replace up to 30% of the whole-milled flour, by weight, with other whole grain flours, such as barley, buckwheat, or rye (nonsprouted or sprouted). Depending on the flours you use, you may need to adjust the amount of water to achieve the textures indicated in the method.

SWEET PRETZELS: Forgo the pretzel salt and instead sprinkle coarse sugar or cinnamon sugar over the pretzels before baking.

CHEESE PRETZELS: When 5 to 7 minutes of baking time remains, sprinkle 2 tablespoons (0.5 oz / 14 g) of grated semi-moist cheese, such as Cheddar, Monterey Jack, Swiss, or mozzarella, to taste, over each pretzel. If using a hard, aged cheese, such as Parmesan, sprinkle it over the pretzels when 2 minutes of baking time remains.

Working with Lye

Lye (sodium hydroxide) is the secret ingredient that gives pretzels their unique color and taste. Bakers use a food quality lye crystal (or pellets), which is not the same as the technical grade version used in drain cleaners. It is caustic, so caution should be taken when using it. I always advise my students to wear disposable latex or food handling gloves when dipping their pretzels in lye solution to protect their hands, and then immediately discard the gloves.

The typical ratio of lye to water is between 3% to 4%. I prefer 4%, which is about 2½ tablespoons (1.25 ounces or 35 g) dissolved in 1 quart of warm or hot water. Always add the lye to the water rather than pouring the water over the lye. Use a stainless steel bowl or pot, not aluminum, which can cause a reaction. Lye is highly alkaline (about a 14 on the pH scale), much more so than baking soda, which is only 8 to 9 on the scale. If you are nervous about using lye, you can dissolve baking soda instead (use about 22% soda to water, or 14 tablespoons per quart), but it won't create the deep nut brown color of lye and can sometimes leave whitish streaks on the dough. When using a baking soda solution, I also immediately brush the pretzels with an egg white wash to get rid of the streaks. The noted food science writer Harold McGee suggests "baking" the baking soda on a dry sheet pan for 1 hour at approximately 275°F (135°C) to chemically change it through moisture evaporation from sodium bicarbonate into sodium carbonate. This increases the pH and causes it to perform more like lye (you can access his *New York Times* article for more on the subject). As a precaution, you might also want to consider wearing goggles to protect your eyes from any splashes

whenever working with lye or baking soda solutions.

There is divided opinion as to whether the dipping solution should be hot or cold. I find that the lye dissolves faster in hot or warm water, but once it's dissolved, warm or cold solutions work equally well. Work on a surface that is protected from the bleaching effects of the lye, such as ceramic tile, formica, plastic cutting boards (not wood), or stainless steel. I always line my baking pans with baking parchment and then generously mist the parchment with vegetable spray oil, and then dust the surface with either corn meal or semolina flour to prevent the pretzels sticking to the paper. Craig Ponsford, on the other hand, bakes his pretzels directly on the metal pans without any problems. While I prefer the total immersion method, dipping my pretzels into the bowl of lye solution, Craig uses a spray bottle and mists them after he pans them. He told me that the lye doesn't affect the plastic spray bottle or his sheet pans (they actually look cleaner after they come out of the oven than when they went in), but unless you have a stainless steel pan I'd go with baking parchment. The lye is completely cooked off during baking, leaving behind a shiny, rich brown crust and distinct flavor.

One final note: You can reuse lye solution over and over if you have a safe means of storing it, but I prefer to discard it and start fresh each time. You can safely pour it down your sink drain (lye is, after all, used as a drain cleaner) or down the toilet, but be careful to avoid splashing when doing so. You can easily find sources for food grade lye on the Internet, or check the Resources section (page 240) for links.

WHOLE WHEAT AND RAISIN ENGLISH MUFFINS

MAKES 6 TO 8 ENGLISH MUFFINS

This is a modified version of Craig Ponsford's hearty English muffins, which he typically makes with raisins and walnuts. The recipe calls for a small amount of applesauce in addition to soaked raisins. As the notes indicate, a bit of sweetener may be substituted for these two ingredients, but both the applesauce and the raisins help keep the English muffins soft and moist, and also add flavor. Using these enhancements is an excellent trick to incorporate into your own whole grain baking repertoire; it works well in many other bread recipes. The use of pre-ferments, in this case a biga, is one of Craig's signature techniques for capitalizing on the flavor potential in his whole grain doughs. As a bonus, it makes it possible to bake these English muffins on the same day as you mix the final dough.

English muffins are first cooked on a griddle or skillet before finishing in the oven. If you have a large griddle, you can cook and bake them all in one batch. If you only have a smaller griddle or skillet, make them in small batches, as it's important to get them into the oven as soon as they come out of the pan. After that, all you'll need is a toaster, butter, and jam!

BIGA (DAY 1)

INGREDIENT	VOLUME	OUNCES	GRAMS	%
whole-milled wheat flour	½ cup plus 3½ tablespoons	3.25	92	100
instant yeast	pinch	0.007	0.2	0.2
salt	pinch	0.02	0.5	0.5
water, at room temperature	5 tablespoons	2.5	71	76
TOTAL		5.777	163.7	176.7

In a small bowl, stir together the flour, yeast, and salt. Add the water and stir until the flour is hydrated and a coarse ball of dough forms. Transfer to a lightly oiled work surface and knead by hand until slightly smoother and firm, about 1 minute. Mist a medium bowl with vegetable spray oil and put the biga in the bowl. Mist the top with vegetable spray oil and cover the bowl with plastic wrap. Let the biga rest at room temperature for at least 12 hours or overnight, until double in size.

SOAKED RAISINS (DAY 1)

INGREDIENT	VOLUME	OUNCES	GRAMS
raisins	about 7 tablespoons	2.5	71
water, at room temperature	⅓ cup	2.7	77

Put the raisins in a small bowl and pour in the water. Cover the bowl with plastic wrap and leave out at room temperature for at least 6 hours (or overnight).

FINAL DOUGH (DAY 2)

NOTES:

• You can also use low-fat milk or nondairy milk instead of milk powder. To do so, replace ½ cup plus 2 tablespoons (5 oz / 142 g) of the water with an equal amount of milk.

• You can replace the applesauce and raisins with 1 tablespoon (0.5 oz / 14 g) sugar or 2¼ teaspoons (0.67 oz / 19 g) honey. You may need to add a bit more water to the final dough.

INGREDIENT	VOLUME	OUNCES	GRAMS	%
Biga	all	5.777	163.7	58
whole-milled wheat flour	2¼ cups	10	283	100
nonfat dry milk powder (see notes)	3½ tablespoons	0.65	18	6.4
salt	1 teaspoon	0.25	7	2.5
instant yeast	1 teaspoon	0.11	3	1.1
Soaked Raisins (see notes)	all	5.2	148	52
water, at room temperature	1 cup plus 3 tablespoons	9.5	269	95
applesauce (see notes)	1 tablespoon plus 1 teaspoon	0.65	18	6.4
unsalted butter, at room temperature	1 tablespoon	0.5	14	5
cornmeal for dipping the muffins before cooking them	about ½ cup			
TOTAL		32.637	923.7	326.4

1 Cut the biga into about 8 pieces and put it in the bowl of a stand mixer fitted with the dough hook, or in a large bowl. Add the flour, milk powder, salt, and yeast and mix or stir briefly to combine (on low speed if using a stand mixer). Strain the raisin soaking water and add it to the bowl, along with the water and applesauce. Mix or stir for about 2 to 3 minutes. Add the butter mix or stir for 2 to 3 minutes, on medium-low speed if using a stand mixer. Add the raisins and mix or stir until evenly distributed. The dough will be wet and sticky.

CONTINUED

2 Using an oiled bowl scraper or rubber spatula, transfer the dough to an oiled bowl and cover the bowl with plastic wrap. Ferment at room temperature for 40 minutes, until the dough just begins to expand. Lightly oil your hands, then stretch and fold the dough in the bowl as shown on page 20, folding it over itself four times: once each from the top, bottom, and sides. Cover and let rest for 40 minutes. Stretch and fold again, then cover the bowl and let the dough rest for 20 minutes. The dough will become tighter and firmer with each stretch and fold, but it will remain somewhat sticky.

3 Dust a work surface generously with whole wheat flour and use an oiled bowl scraper or rubber spatula to transfer the dough to the floured area. Scatter a bit of flour over the dough for easier handling. Use a metal pastry blade or plastic bowl scraper to divide the dough into 6 to 8 pieces (3.5 to 4.5 oz / 99 to 128 g each). Toss the pieces in the flour to coat them. Gently form each piece into a ball, then put it on a floured spot on the work surface, spacing the pieces at least 2 inches apart. Mist the tops with vegetable spray oil and cover loosely with plastic wrap or a clean towel. Proof at room temperature for 1 hour. The dough will swell but won't double in size.

4 Preheat the oven to 350°F (177°C). Sprinkle the cornmeal on the work surface or put it in a small bowl. Line a sheet pan with parchment or a silicone mat and mist with vegetable spray oil. Heat a griddle or large skillet over medium-low heat.

5 Dust your hands with flour. Dip and press one piece of dough in the cornmeal, turning to coat, and flatten both sides. When you've dipped enough pieces to fill your griddle, lay and press them in the hot pan about 1 inch apart and cook until a rich golden brown on the bottom, about 5 minutes. Flip and cook the other side until golden brown, about 5 minutes. Transfer to the prepared pan and bake for 8 to 10 minutes, until firm and springy to the touch. If you couldn't fit all of the muffins on the griddle in the first round, griddle the remaining muffins while the first set is baking.

Variations

FLAVORED ENGLISH MUFFINS: Omit the raisins and replace 2 tablespoons (1 oz / 28.5 g) of the water with an equal amount of amaretto, orange liqueur or other liqueur, rum, brandy, or a sweet Italian dessert wine such as vin santo or Moscato.

RAISIN NUT ENGLISH MUFFINS: Add up to 1 cup (about 4 oz / 113 g) coarsely chopped toasted walnuts or pecans when you add the raisins (see page 101 for toasting instructions).

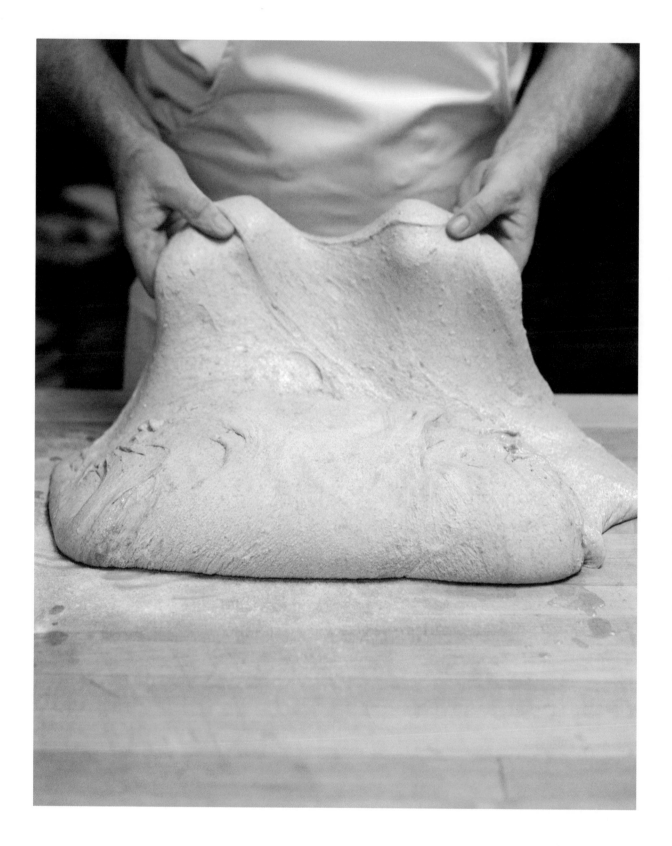

HIGH-EXTRACTION PAIN AU LEVAIN

MAKES 1 LARGE LOAF OR 2 SMALL LOAVES

This version of pain au levain, a French type of sourdough, was developed by my colleague Harry Peemoeller. Whereas classic pain au levain is usually made with just a small amount of whole grain flour, here Harry pushes the bar toward a higher-extraction flour: type 85 (meaning that 85% of the total wheat is included in the final flour, putting it somewhere between whole wheat and white flour in terms of bran and germ content). Harry, who competes in international bread competitions, works closely with Jennifer Lapidus of the milling company Carolina Ground to, as he puts it, "Test drive the flour to see what it can do." You may not be able to get the exact same flour where you live, but you might be able to find a miller in your region who's producing something similar.

The flour used to develop this recipe was made from a heritage strain of wheat known as Turkey Red, and various millers sometimes offer such flour via the Internet (see Resources, page 240). If you can't get it, blend one-third whole wheat flour with two-thirds unbleached bread flour, using the best-quality flour you can get your hands on. You can push the ratio of whole wheat flour to 50% if you prefer.

Instant yeast is optional in this recipe; including it will decrease the rising times and result in a bread that's less tangy in flavor. Also, Harry's levain is closer to a sponge-style poolish than the type of firm starter that most sourdough breads in this book use. The method here replicates the texture of his starter by building a whole wheat levain at a ratio of 1 part mother starter to 4.5 parts new flour and water. In theory, this bread could also be made with a firmer levain. Once you've mastered this recipe, feel free to use whatever type of starter you like, adjusting the final dough hydration as needed.

WHOLE WHEAT LEVAIN (DAY 1)

INGREDIENT	VOLUME	OUNCES	GRAMS	%
whole wheat flour (preferably from Turkey Red wheat; see above)	1 cup	4.5	128	100
Mother Starter (page 40)	2 tablespoons	1	28.5	22
water	½ cup plus 1 tablespoon	4.5	128	100
TOTAL		10	284.5	222

CONTINUED

In a small bowl, stir together all the ingredients for about 1 minute to evenly distribute the starter and make a smooth, sticky, batter-like dough. (The levain will thicken as it sits.) Scrape the bowl down with a wet spatula and cover with plastic wrap or a lid. Let the levain rest at room temperature for about 12 hours or overnight, until it begins to swell and bubble.

FINAL DOUGH (DAY 2)

INGREDIENT	VOLUME	OUNCES	GRAMS	%
type 85 flour (preferably from Turkey Red wheat)	2⅔ cups	12	340	92
whole wheat flour (preferably from Turkey Red wheat)	3½ tablespoons	1	28.5	8
water, at room temperature	1½ cups	12	340	92
Whole Wheat Levain	all	10	284.5	77
salt	1½ teaspoons	0.35	10	2.7
instant yeast (optional)	½ teaspoon	0.05	1.5	0.4
TOTAL		35.4	1,004.5	272.1

1 In the bowl of a stand mixer with the paddle attachment, or in a large bowl, stir together the flour, water, and levain until the flour is hydrated, the levain is evenly distributed, and a coarse, very wet dough forms, about 1 minute. Cover the bowl with plastic wrap and let the dough rest at room temperature for 30 minutes.

2 Add the salt and yeast (if using). If using a stand mixer, switch to the dough hook. Mix (on medium-low speed if using a stand mixer), stir, or knead by hand for 2 to 3 minutes, until a smooth, sticky dough forms.

3 Mist a large bowl with vegetable spray oil. Spread 1 teaspoon of oil on a work surface. Using a wet or oiled bowl scraper, transfer the dough to the oiled area. Lightly oil your hands, then stretch and fold the dough as shown on page 20, folding it over itself four times: once each from the top, bottom, and sides. Form the dough into a ball. Put it in the oiled bowl and cover the bowl with plastic wrap, or leave the dough on the work surface and cover it with the bowl. At intervals of 40 minutes, perform two additional sequences of stretching and folding. For each stretch and fold sequence, lightly oil your hands to prevent sticking. The dough will firm up a bit after each stretch and fold, but after the final fold it will still be very soft and somewhat sticky.

4 Put the dough back in the bowl and cover the bowl with plastic wrap. Ferment the dough at room temperature until it increases in size by at least 1½ times, 3 or 4 hours, or just 60 to 90 minutes if using the optional yeast.

5 Oil the work surface once again or dust it with flour. Transfer the dough to the work surface. For two smaller loaves, divide the dough in half and form each piece into a ball; otherwise leave it whole and form it into a ball. Mist the top with vegetable spray oil, cover loosely with plastic wrap or a clean towel, and let rest at room temperature for 10 to 20 minutes to relax the gluten.

6 Prepare one or two bannetons or a *couche* as shown on page 26, or line an 18 by 13-inch sheet pan with parchment paper and then mist it with vegetable spray oil. Shape the dough into one large boule or bâtard, as shown on pages 20 and 21, or divide the dough in half and shape each piece into a small boule or bâtard. Put the shaped loaves in the prepared proofing vessel(s) or on the sheet pan.

7 Loosely cover the dough with plastic wrap or a clean towel and proof at room temperature until it increases in size by 1½ times, 2 to 4 hours or just 1 to 1½ hours if using the optional yeast.

8 About 45 minutes before you bake, prepare the oven for hearth baking with a baking stone and steam pan as shown on page 29. Preheat the oven to 500°F (260°C).

9 Just before baking, dust a peel with flour. Transfer the dough to the peel and score as desired. Slide the dough onto the baking stone and pour about 1 cup of hot water into the steam pan. Lower the temperature to 470°F (243°C). Bake for 15 minutes, then rotate and bake for 15 to 25 minutes longer, until the crust is rich golden brown and the bread sounds hollow when thumped on the bottom. The internal temperature should be at least 200°F (93°C).

10 Transfer to a wire rack and let cool for at least 30 minutes before slicing and serving.

NATURALLY LEAVENED CAROLINA WHEAT HEARTH BREAD

MAKES 1 LARGE LOAF OR 2 SMALL LOAVES

This bread was created by Harry Peemoeller, winner of numerous gold medals in international baking competitions. He's been pioneering new ways to use flours made from heirloom and local varieties of wheat, and developed this recipe to showcase heritage Red Fife wheat flour from Anson Mills, of Columbia, South Carolina, developers of regional heritage grains and flours. Of course, it can also be made with other whole wheat flours, so you can make it in the spirit intended and support your own local or regional mills (or, as increasing numbers of people are doing, mill your own flour). Red Fife is a high-protein wheat, so look for something similar grown closest to home, or order Red Fife bread flour from Anson Mills (see Resources, page 240). The amount of hydration needed may vary slightly depending on the variety of wheat. This version is leavened primarily by a medium-firm levain, with only a little boost from a spike of commercial instant yeast. The resulting loaf is a seriously delicious bread with a tangy complexity created by the natural leaven and a touch of honey.

LEVAIN (DAY 1)

INGREDIENT	VOLUME	OUNCES	GRAMS	%
Mother Starter (page 40)	1 tablespoon	0.4	11.5	16
water	¼ cup plus ½ teaspoon	2.1	60	86
whole wheat flour (preferably from Red Fife wheat)	½ cup plus 1 tablespoon	2.5	70	100
TOTAL		5	141.5	202

Put the starter in a small bowl and add the water to soften it. Break the starter up into smaller pieces, then add the flour and stir until a smooth, sticky dough forms, about 1 minute. Use a rubber spatula to scrape down the sides of the bowl. Cover the bowl with plastic wrap and let the levain rest at room temperature for at least 12 hours or overnight, until it becomes bubbly and swells in size.

CONTINUED

FINAL DOUGH (DAY 2)

INGREDIENT	VOLUME	OUNCES	GRAMS	%
Levain	all	5	141.5	31
water	1½ cups plus 1 tablespoon	12.5	354	77
honey or agave nectar	1½ tablespoons	1	28.5	6.1
whole wheat flour (preferably from Red Fife wheat)	3½ cups plus 1 tablespoon	16.25	461	100
salt	1⅝ teaspoons	0.4	11.5	2.5
instant yeast	¼ teaspoon	0.03	1	0.2
TOTAL		35.18	997.5	216.8

1 Break the levain into 4 or 5 pieces and put it in the bowl of a stand mixer fitted with the dough hook or in a large bowl. Add the water and honey and stir (on low speed if using a mixer) for a few seconds to soften and break up the levain. Add the flour, salt, and yeast and mix or stir for 4 minutes. Then, if using a mixer, increase the speed to medium-low, or transfer the dough to a lightly oiled work surface and knead by hand, for 2 to 3 minutes, until a smooth, slightly sticky dough forms.

2 Oil a work surface and transfer the dough to the oiled area. Also oil a large bowl. Lightly oil your hands, then stretch and fold the dough as shown on page 20, folding it over itself four times: once each from the top, bottom, and sides. Form the dough into a ball. Put it in the oiled bowl and cover the bowl with plastic wrap, or leave the dough on the work surface and cover it with the bowl. At intervals of 40 minutes, perform two additional sequences of stretching and folding. For each stretch and fold sequence, lightly oil your hands to prevent sticking. The dough will feel stronger and less sticky after each stretch and fold, and after the final fold, it should be tacky rather than sticky.

3 Put the dough back in the bowl, cover the bowl with plastic wrap, and ferment the dough at room temperature for 1 to 1½ hours, until it nearly doubles in size.

4 Oil the work surface once again and transfer the dough to the oiled area. For two smaller loaves, divide the dough in half and form each piece into a ball; otherwise leave it whole and form it into a ball. Mist the top with vegetable spray oil, cover loosely with plastic wrap, and let rest at room temperature for 10 to 20 minutes to relax the gluten.

5 Prepare one or two bannetons or a *couche* as shown on page 26, or line an 18 by 13-inch sheet pan with parchment paper and then mist it with vegetable spray oil.

Shape the dough into one or two boules or bâtards as shown on pages 20 and 21. Put the shaped loaves in the prepared proofing vessel(s) or on the sheet pan.

6 Loosely cover with plastic wrap or a clean towel and proof at room temperature for 1½ to 2 hours, until the dough increases in size by 1½ times. (Alternatively, put the dough in the refrigerator after the first 30 minutes of proofing and bake it the next day.)

7 About 45 minutes before you plan to bake, prepare the oven for hearth baking with a baking stone and steam pan as shown on page 29. Preheat the oven to 475°F (246°C).

8 Just before baking, dust a peel with flour. Transfer the dough to the peel and score as desired. Slide the dough onto the baking stone and pour about 1 cup of hot water into the steam pan. Bake for 15 minutes, then rotate and bake for 15 to 25 minutes longer, until the crust is rich golden brown and the bread sounds hollow when thumped on the bottom. The internal temperature should be at least 200°F (93°C).

9 Transfer to a wire rack and let cool for at least 30 minutes before slicing and serving.

Variations

SEEDED CAROLINA WHEAT HEARTH BREAD: Add up to 2 cups (10 oz / 283 g) toasted sunflower seeds or pumpkin seeds to the final dough. (See page 101 for toasting instructions.)

CAROLINA WHEAT HEARTH BREAD WITH NUTS: Add up to 2 cups (8 oz / 227 g) coarsely chopped toasted nuts. (See page 101 for toasting instructions.)

Gluten-Free Breads

Not that long ago, gluten-free baking was considered to be a fairly arcane corner of the bread world. Then, in just a few short years, it became one of the most discussed and debated food issues. Dozens of new books on gluten-free baking have been published, usually with an emphasis on replacing wheat, rye, and barley—the primary sources of gluten—with flours made from rice, potatoes, cassava, quinoa, sorghum, buckwheat, and various beans. This former side street has become a vast new frontier populated with countless products, recipes, and spokespersons.

In 2012 even I chimed in, teaming with Denene Wallace to coauthor *The Joy of Gluten-Free, Sugar-Free Baking*, with a totally new take on gluten-free baking in which we offered products that were safe not only for people with gluten sensitivities (perhaps as much as 5% of the population), but also for people with diabetes and prediabetes (about 30% to 35% of the population). Denene, who has type 2 diabetes, completely weaned herself off of insulin by revamping her diet, and her approach to baked goods is reflected in that book's recipes. Basically, all starch flours are replaced with nut and seed flours, and all sugars are replaced with stevia and other alternatives.

As I've often said, when it comes to baking, flavor rules over everything else. One of the benefits of the recent interest in these lesser known grains and ingredients is that it allows us to expand our flavor horizons, escaping the confines of the monoculture farming that dominates our era. We are freeing ourselves from the monotony of reliance on just a few types of plants that are easily mass produced. From my perspective, any interest in the preservation and cultivation of plants that are less common gives us hope for diversity, along with more well-rounded nutrition. But, and here's the reality check, interest in gluten-free baking will thrive only if gluten-free products taste good.

Fortunately, we are now learning how delicious gluten-free grains can be, and we've figured out ways to make them function similarly to flours that contain gluten.

There is great debate regarding the causes of increasing sensitivity to gluten. One argument is that alterations in the genetics and protein structure of modern hybrid wheat, especially the prolific short straw dwarf variety promoted by Norman Borlaug and his many Green Revolution disciples over the past fifty years, have made mass-produced wheat less digestible. (Though it must be said that those innovations are also credited with saving countless people from death by starvation.) Other arguments focus on wheat processing, as mentioned in chapter 5, on whole-milled grains.

The jury is still out on these and other hypotheses, and it will be interesting to see what new research into this topic reveals. In the meanwhile, the good news is that the ongoing debate stimulates more diversity of thinking, more attention to our health, more variety in our diets, and more awareness of the chain of events that lead from the earth to the table, from farm to fork, or from seed to slice. Anything that makes us more aware of the bigger picture is a good thing.

Even if you aren't sensitive to gluten, I encourage you to try the following recipes. They will broaden your palate and can contribute to more well-rounded nutrition. They also break the mold in regard to baking, so they're inherently revolutionary. Plus, they all fulfill the fundamental flavor rule: that flavor rules!

GLUTEN-FREE MANY-SEED TOASTING BREAD

MAKES 1 LARGE LOAF OR 4 TO 6 MINI LOAVES

This quick bread recipe, leavened with baking powder rather than yeast, goes to show that there are many ways to make a great loaf of bread. Based on the approach Denene Wallace pioneered in our collaboration, *The Joy of Gluten-Free, Sugar-Free Baking*, it's high in fiber yet low in carbs. I like making this recipe into mini loaves, which bake up much faster than a full-size loaf. The mini loaves can be stored in the freezer, and they thaw fairly quickly at room temperature, in just 30 minutes or so. I love the variety of flavors and textures the nut and seed meals provide, but feel free to substitute other nut or seed flours for those listed, as long as the overall weight remains the same.

DOUGH

INGREDIENT	VOLUME	OUNCES	GRAMS	%
flaxseed meal	1 cup	4	113	25
pecan flour	1 cup	4	113	25
almond flour	1 cup	4	113	25
ground sesame seeds	½ cup	2	56.5	12.5
ground chia or hemp seeds	½ cup	2	56.5	12.5
sesame seeds	3 tablespoons	1	28.5	6.3
flaxseeds (optional)	3 tablespoons	1	28.5	6.3
salt	½ teaspoon	0.12	3.5	0.8
baking powder	2 tablespoons	1	28.5	6.3
xanthan gum	1½ teaspoons	0.38	11	2.4
sugar or liquid stevia (optional; see sidebar page 195)	¼ cup or ¼ teaspoon	2 or 0.05	56.5 or 1.5	12.5 or 0.3
milk (any type)	1½ cups	12	340	75
egg whites or liquid egg whites	9 or 1½ cups	11.25	319	71
TOTAL		44.75 or 42.8	1,267.5 or 1,212.5	280.6 or 268.4

1 Position a rack in the middle of the oven and preheat the oven to 375°F (191°C). Line the bottom of a 4½ by 8-inch loaf pan with parchment paper and generously mist the pan with vegetable spray oil; if making mini loaves, forgo the parchment and simply mist the pans generously with vegetable spray oil.

CONTINUED

NOTE: Baked goods made with nut and seed flour should always be stored in the refrigerator or freezer. If freezing, you might want to preslice the loaf so you can take slices out of the freezer as you need them. To maintain the freshness, store this bread in a plastic container or zip-top bag lined with a paper towel to absorb any oil that seeps out of the loaf.

2 In a large bowl, stir together the flaxseed meal, pecan flour, almond flour, ground sesame seeds, ground chia seeds, sesame seeds, flaxseeds, salt, baking powder, xanthan gum, and sugar. (If using stevia, add it to the milk in the next step.) In a separate bowl, whisk together the milk and egg whites, then pour into the flour mixture. Stir vigorously for about 2 minutes to make a thick, slightly aerated batter. Pour the batter into the prepared pan; for mini pans, fill them to about ½ inch from the top.

3 To bake a large loaf, put the bread in the oven and lower the temperature to 350°F (177°C). Bake for 45 minutes, then rotate and bake for 35 to 45 minutes longer, until the top is golden brown and springy when pressed in the center. To bake mini loaves, don't lower the oven temperature. Bake for 30 minutes, then rotate and bake for 25 to 30 minutes longer, until the top is golden brown and springy when pressed in the center.

4 Put the pan on a wire rack and let the bread cool for at least 20 minutes. Run an icing spatula or something similar around the edges to separate the bread from the pan, then transfer the bread to the rack and let cool for at least 45 minutes, until cool to the touch, before slicing and serving. (See the note for storage tips.)

Q & A

Can sprouted, gluten-free flours made from grains be substituted for the nut and seed flour in these recipes?

Yes and no. The premise of many of these recipes is to replace high-carb starch flour with nut and seed flours because they're much lower in carbohydrates and have a more favorable glycemic index. The resulting recipes are safe for both diabetics and those who are sensitive to gluten. Although it appears that sprouted flour may spike blood sugar less than its nonsprouted counterpart, it's still higher in carbs than nut and seed flours. If you have diabetes or prediabetes, I suggest a cautious approach. You can try swapping in sprouted gluten-free flours, but eat only a small amount to begin with, and test your blood sugar levels to see how your body responds.

GLUTEN-FREE HOLIDAY COOKIES

MAKES 24 COOKIES

I developed these cookies, a variation of the pecan sandies from *The Joy of Gluten-Free, Sugar-Free Baking*, for a Christmas presentation. They are a symbolic tribute to the birth of Jesus and the gifts of the magi: gold (almond flour and walnuts or pecans); frankincense (cinnamon and allspice); and myrrh (orange oil or extract). Their flavor profile is similar to classic Middle Eastern *ma'amoul* cookies. And as a bonus, they're gluten-free, making them a healthy anytime gift. Be sure to bake them until hard and golden brown, and then let them cool completely before eating; then they'll shatter and crumble in your mouth like the best flaky pie crust.

DOUGH

INGREDIENT	VOLUME	OUNCES	GRAMS	%
almond flour	2¼ cups	9	255	100
coarsely chopped walnuts or pecans	about ¾ cup	3.25	92	36
sugar	1¼ cups	10	283	111
ground cinnamon	1¾ teaspoons	0.16	4.5	1.8
ground allspice	¼ teaspoon	0.03	1	0.4
salt	¼ teaspoon	0.06	1.5	0.6
baking soda	½ teaspoon	0.11	3	1.2
unsalted butter, melted	¾ cup	6	170	67
egg, slightly beaten	1	1.75	50	20
vanilla extract	1 tablespoon	0.42	12	4.7
almond extract	2 teaspoons	0.28	8	3.1
orange extract	1 teaspoon	0.14	4	1.6
TOTAL		31.2	884	347.4

1 Position a rack in the middle of the oven and preheat the oven to 350°F (177°C). Line an 18 by 13-inch sheet pan with parchment paper or a silicone mat and mist with vegetable spray oil.

2 In the bowl of a stand mixer fitted with the paddle attachment, or in a large bowl, stir together the almond flour, walnuts, sugar, cinnamon, allspice, salt, and baking soda. In a separate bowl, whisk together the butter, egg, vanilla, almond extract, and orange extract, then pour into the flour mixture. Mix or stir, on medium-low speed if using a stand mixer for 1 minute to make a thick batter (it will thicken as it sits).

CONTINUED

3 Drop small spoonfuls of dough onto the prepared cookie sheet to make 24 cookies, spacing them evenly (they don't spread so they need be only ½ inch apart). With wet fingers, pat down the top of each cookie to make a round patty.

4 Bake for 10 minutes, then rotate and bake for 9 to 10 minutes longer, until the cookies are firm when tapped in the center and a rich golden brown. If the bottoms are getting too dark during baking, slide a second pan under the first for insulation.

5 Transfer the cookies to a wire rack and let cool for at least 10 minutes before serving.

Replacing Sugar with Stevia

Liquid stevia is an outstanding alternative sweetener because it's all natural and has no long-term side effects. If you'd like to replace the sugar in any of these recipes with liquid stevia, use about 1 teaspoon (0.25 oz / 7 g) of liquid stevia per 1 cup (8 oz / 227 g) of sugar. But because sugar (and many alternative sweeteners, like Splenda and Stevia in the Raw) also provide bulk and mass to a recipe, you must also add ¼ cup (about 1 oz / 28.5 g) of any nut flour or meal per cup of sugar (or Splenda or Stevia in the Raw) replaced with liquid stevia. If you prefer to use powdered stevia, for most brands you can replace 1 cup (8 oz / 227 g) of sugar with ½ teaspoon (0.09 oz / 2.6 g) of powdered stevia, again, adding ¼ cup (about 1 oz / 28.5 g) of nut flour or meal per cup of sugar replaced.

GLUTEN-FREE HOLIDAY BISCOTTI

MAKES 20 TO 24 SMALL BISCOTTI

Biscotti, or twice baked biscuits, are beloved because they are crisp, flaky, and have a long shelf life. They're the perfect travel companion and were probably originally developed for use on long journeys. This version is a variation of one originally published in *The Joy of Gluten-Free, Sugar-Free Baking*, embellished with holiday spices like cinnamon, powdered ginger, and allspice, which I associate with celebrations. This recipe calls for sugar but it can also be made with liquid stevia for a truly low-carb version; see the sidebar on page 195. (I now use liquid stevia almost always in place of sugar when cooking at home.)

DOUGH

INGREDIENT	VOLUME	OUNCES	GRAMS	%
walnut flour or pecan flour	1 cup	4	113	44.5
almond flour	1 cup	4	113	44.5
coconut flour	¼ cup	1	28.5	11
sugar	1 cup	8	227	89
ground cinnamon	2¼ teaspoons	0.21	6	0.4
dried ginger powder or ground allspice	½ teaspoon	0.05	1.5	0.6
salt	¼ teaspoon	0.07	2	0.8
baking powder	2 teaspoons	0.5	14	5.5
egg whites	4	5	142	56
vanilla extract	1 tablespoon	0.42	12	4.7
unsalted butter, melted	⅓ cup	2.7	77	30
coarsely chopped or slivered almonds	1½ cups	7.5	213	84
Chocolate Glaze (optional; see sidebar)				
TOTAL		33.45	949	371

1 Position a rack in the middle of the oven and preheat the oven to 375°F (191°C). Line a sheet pan with parchment paper or a silicone mat and mist with vegetable spray oil. Have a cooling rack at hand.

2 In a large bowl, stir together the flours, sugar, cinnamon, ginger, salt, and baking powder. In a separate bowl, whisk together the egg whites and vanilla. Add the butter and whisk just until blended. Pour the egg white mixture into the flour mixture and stir for about 1 minute to make a thick, moist batter similar to cookie dough.

- Use a rubber spatula to transfer the glaze into a plastic sandwich bag. Work the glaze into one corner of the bag and cut off a tiny bit of the corner. Pipe thin streaks of the glaze over the biscotti, crisscrossing it over each. (You can also drizzle the glaze off the end of a spoon or spatula in squiggles.)

- Dip one or both ends of the biscotti into the glaze to make chocolate tips, then return them to the wire rack until the glaze hardens.

- Use a pastry brush, rubber spatula, or icing spatula to spread glaze across one of the flat surfaces of each biscotti.

- If you have leftover glaze, you can apply more or cover it and refrigerate for another use. (Or just lick the bowl!)

3 Use a rubber spatula to transfer the dough to the center of the prepared pan. Mist the top with vegetable spray oil. Using wet hands or the spatula, press the dough into either one large oval about 6 inches wide and 10 to 12 inches long or two smaller ovals, each about 4 inches wide and 8 inches long; regardless of size, the dough should be about ¾ inch thick, and no thicker.

4 Bake for 12 minutes, then rotate and bake for 10 to 20 minutes longer, until the top is golden brown and the center is firm and springy to the touch.

5 Remove the pan from the oven, leaving the oven on, and let the dough rest for 1 minute to firm up slightly. While the dough is still hot, use a chef's knife or a metal pastry blade to cut the oval in half lengthwise. Then cut crosswise at ¾-inch intervals to create strips. If you let the dough cool too much, it will harden and the pieces will shatter and fall apart when sliced, so work quickly. Use a metal spatula and transfer the pieces to the wire rack, flat side down, spacing them about ½ inch apart.

6 Lower the temperature to 275°F (135°C). Put the rack of biscotti strips on a sheet pan to catch any loose crumbs and bake for 40 to 45 minutes, until all sides of the biscotti are hard to the touch.

7 Remove from the oven and let the biscotti cool on the rack until just slightly warm, then decorate with the chocolate glaze if desired. As for glazing style, you have a few options; see notes. To harden the glaze more quickly, put the biscotti in the refrigerator or freezer. Once the glaze has set, transfer the biscotti to an airtight container and store in the refrigerator for up to 2 weeks, or in the freezer for up to 6 months.

Chocolate Glaze

1 cup (6 oz / (170 g) semisweet chocolate chips

¼ cup (2 oz / 56.5 g) unsalted butter

Combine the chocolate and butter in the top of a double boiler and heat over simmering water, stirring occasionally, until melted and smooth. Alternatively, combine them in a microwave-safe bowl and microwave at medium heat. The chocolate will melt quickly in the microwave and be damaged if it overheats, so use short intervals (about 30 seconds) and stir in between. Once the chocolate is almost melted, use even shorter intervals.

CHAPTER 6
THE NEXT NEW BREAD FRONTIER

As the preceding chapters of this book amply demonstrate, the next frontier of bread is already here. Sprouted grain flours, sprouted grain pulps, whole-milled grains, regional milling, gluten-free flours, nut flours, and seed meal—all are rapidly advancing in the marketplace. In this chapter, I want to look even further ahead, where there always seems to be yet another new wave forming, even if it's too early to see it clearly or know what its impact will be. Here are some things I'm tracking on the wave beyond the current wave.

PREBIOTICS: THE NEW PROBIOTICS

A few years ago I was teaching a bread class at Reno's Nothing To It! Culinary Center when one of the attendees introduced himself. Bob Thornberg had flown in from Walhalla, North Dakota, because of something he'd read in one of my books: a reference to beer as liquid bread, and bread as solid beer. Bob was intrigued because he was in the business of fermenting grain to create highly nutritious animal feed. The notion of beer as liquid bread had triggered an idea that connected a series of dots for him, and he wanted to talk about it.

One of the breads we made during that class utilizes spent grain, a by-product of beer making, as an ingredient. It's a fun technique because so many types of beer are being made these days, and in the process, malted and roasted grains are used in a seemingly infinite number of variations. After brewing, the grain is considered spent because most of its sugars and flavors have been brewed into the wort, which is eventually transformed into beer. However, the process does leave some residual flavor in the fiber-rich husks, which are usually given or sold to livestock farmers or just discarded.

To me, this seemed like a waste, so I started experimenting with using spent grain in bread dough to bump up the flavor and fiber content. As a side benefit, this increased my bread repertoire dramatically, because I could use one master formula to create many different flavors of bread depending on the type of spent grain used; if I collected the spent grain from four different beers, I could make four different breads using the same master dough. Bob realized that what I was doing with the spent grain was essentially the same as what he was doing: creating a high-powered, nutritionally loaded food source, in his case by fermenting a blend of wheat, oats, barley, and flaxseed.

After grain is fermented, what's left behind is about 33% protein and 30% fiber, along with starches and water. Unlike humans, cows and other ruminants can make good nutritional use of that fiber because they have multichambered digestive systems with a rumen (sort of a "pre-stomach") leading to the true stomach. In the rumen, fiber is broken down by beneficial bacteria, or probiotics. Cows, then, are built for a high-fiber diet. Therefore, a fermented grain blend, served up as a wet mash snack, is a very healthful supplement to livestock feed, being full of prebiotics, material that serves as nourishment for probiotics, the good bacteria already in their guts. For twenty-five years, Bob has marketed this product under the name SweetPro, and he's received numerous testimonials about its benefits.

In Reno, Bob told me, "I've been wondering: if this is so beneficial for cows and horses, why not humans? So I started using a bit of it in my morning smoothies, and I felt great. Then, when I read what you wrote about beer being liquid bread, I started to wonder what effect the product might have on actual bread." He gave me a jar of dried SweetPro, which he now markets in its dried form as ProBiotein. "I've been having good success with it in my breads, but I'm no baker. I hope you'll try it and tell me what you think."

I promised to play around with it when I got home. My initial thought was that it probably wouldn't do much more than boost the fiber content of the bread. Then I made a couple of loaves of regular French bread adding in a small amount of the ProBiotein, just 2% of the flour weight. The crusty bread baked up as nicely as ever. The real surprise was the flavor, which was quite similar to a very tangy San Francisco sourdough bread. I made another batch using the same recipe, this time with only 1% ProBiotein, and the results were perfect! I've since tried it with other recipes, and even in breads made with sprouted flour, I achieved the same complex sourdough flavor.

When I wrote to Bob to tell him the results, he seemed pleased and told me, "I've decided to explore selling an organic version of this for human consumption. I'm setting up a separate facility since it will need to be certified as food-grade. And beyond making great bread, I think it has even bigger implications in the world of nutrition and health."

Bob and I stayed in touch over the next few years. He sent me new samples as he developed the product, and I continued to add it to bread dough whenever I wanted to add some zing to the flavor. There seemed to be just enough viable, dormant organisms in the dried grain to both enhance the fermentation of the dough and also generate sufficient lactic acid so that it acted almost like an instant sourdough starter. Many large commercial operations use sourdough powders, but I always considered it kind of like cheating. However, this stuff worked, and there was nothing in it beyond pre-fermented dried grain!

As for the nutritional and health benefits, I'll leave that explanation to Bob: "ProBiotein is full of prebiotics—fiber and other nutrients that probiotics, or beneficial gut bacteria, need to flourish. Even people who are taking probiotic supplements may not have the gut conditions to allow the good bacteria to thrive. The good bacteria in your gut love this mixture of dried, fermented grains and it helps them do what they do to keep us healthy."

Intrigued by this, I had a conversation with a nutrition researcher Craig Ponsford had introduced me to. When I asked him for his take on the seemingly rampant increase of food sensitivities, he said, "Of course, people can stop eating the things that cause reactions, but that doesn't get at the cause. I'm convinced that many of these sensitivities are indications of poor gut health, which is almost like a national epidemic. Good health starts in the gut, and I have a feeling that if people heal their gut, a lot of their sensitivities will fade away."

I think of this every time I put ProBiotein in my smoothies, sprinkle it on my food, or put it in my bread dough, and I've developed a theory of my own. Maybe there's a connection between the effect ProBiotein has on dough, turning it into an instant sourdough, and anecdotal evidence that sourdough breads in general seem to cause fewer digestive problems and reactions than commercially yeasted bread. Could it be that sourdough bread might serve as a prebiotic?

To explore this further, I spoke with Dr. Harold Dowse, who many in the bread world know as Dusty Dowse. An avid bread enthusiast, Dusty is a professor of biology, mathematics, and statistics at the University of Maine and also serves as the director of the Maine Artisan Bread Fair and on the board of the Maine Grain Alliance. One of his hypotheses is that people with celiac disease and also general gluten sensitivity may lack the enzymes or microorganisms necessary to digest gluten molecules, which are very complex and contain hundreds of amino acids. He told me, "Sourdough breads that are fermented over a long period of time and contain the right kind of bacteria seems to cut through the folds of the gluten molecule and break it down into smaller pieces."

That certainly aligns with what some sourdough advocates have long maintained. It's too soon to know whether ProBiotein does indeed provide a similar benefit when added to dough, but wouldn't it be nice if it did? I'll be tracking it, maybe for my next book . . .

PILLAGING THE POMACE PILE

Meanwhile, in Northern California, a related and highly interesting endeavor has been unfolding: a collaboration among vintners interested in making use of grape skins and grape seeds, by-products of wine making that are often discarded or composted. Craig Ponsford, who serves as a consultant on the project, set up a meeting for me with some of the principal players in this experiment, who operate under the name WholeVine Products.

WholeVine is the creation of Peggy Furth and Barbara Banke. Peggy is a cofounder of the winery Chalk Hill, and Barbara is head of Jackson Family Wines, which she helped grow into one of the world's largest and most successful wine brands in partnership with her late husband, Jess Jackson. These two wine luminaries, Peggy and Barbara, believe that the contents of the pomace pile, where "spent grapes" are discarded after wine making, can be used to make valuable and important new products. In addition to Peggy, I met Torey Arvik, director of applied and research science, and general manager Paul Novak. Over the course of the meeting, I learned that the juice in wine grapes represents about 80% of the total weight of the harvest. Once the juice is extracted, the remaining 20%, primarily skins and seeds, is typically either composted or fed to dairy cattle, or, sometimes, sent to landfills. But what if these constituents still have functional and nutritional value, like spent grain?

As it turns out, they do, and Torey Arvik showed me the results of several studies that prove this.

Paul Novak summed up WholeVine's mission well: "We want to feed more of the world, and it begins at the pomace pile."

As I was to discover, nutritional value lies not just in the seeds, which can be used to make grape seed oil, but also in the skins, which can be dried to make a kind of flour. As for the seeds after the oil has been expelled, even they need not go back to the pomace pile. They too can be dried and milled into flour. (In fact, Craig Ponsford is the person who connected WholeVine with Joe Vanderliet, who now mills their grape seed flour.) Flour made from grape skins and grape seeds? That's definitely next, new-frontier stuff.

While I loved the idea of this flour, I had to wonder how it would perform. Craig had experimented with it, and he told me, "You can't use it exclusively, in place of regular flour, but it works well as a supplemental flour. A small amount of grape seed and grape skin flour adds value." Of course, my next question was what kind of value. Enter Eric Frischkorn, chef de cuisine for Kendall-Jackson wines, which hosted our lunch meeting. In addition to being a skilled chef, Eric is a serious bread baker, and during the meeting he served us a couple of excellent breads, as well as semolina crackers and some of WholeVine's locally famous chocolate chip cookies, all containing some combination of grape seed oil, grape seed flour, and grape skin flour. I was especially impressed at how the hole structure of the breads opened up so nicely. They were equal to the products of an artisan bakery, with rich color, a moist and creamy mouthfeel, and, of course, that large, open crumb. Because the grape skin flour is used in such small proportions, its contribution to the flavor is very subtle, but it does add a lovely color and a slight undercurrent of fruitiness. The grape seed flour, on the other hand, adds a more distinctive flavor that's pleasant, and reminiscent of hemp or sunflower seeds.

Over the course of a long and lavish lunch, I learned a great deal about WholeVine, its products, and their health benefits. Much of this information is available on their website (see Resources, page 240), so here I'll just recap some of the highlights:

- Grape skin flour is naturally antimicrobial due to its malic, tartaric, ferulic, and caffeic acids, as well as phytoalexins (including resveratrol, well known for its purported antiaging effects). Grapes naturally produce these compounds to fight off microorganisms on the vine. In addition to enhancing flavor and nutrition, these compounds confer antimolding protection and give bread a longer shelf life.

- Grape skin and grape seed flours are rich in fiber, pectin, minerals, flavonols such as epicatechin (which has remarkable health benefits), and phytosterols (known to block the formation of cholesterol).

- Grape seed flour contains 30% to 50% fiber and 14% to 17% protein and is also high in calcium. Syrah seed flour has the most fiber, but the seeds of all varietals contain more fiber than a comparable amount of raspberries, broccoli, or cooked lentils. And amazingly, just 0.11 ounce (3 g) of Chardonnay seed flour has as much antioxidant capacity as 3.5 ounces (99 g) of fresh blueberries.

- Grape skin flour contains 25% to 36% dietary fiber and 7% to 13% protein, as well as calcium, iron, potassium, and nearly a full complement of amino acids.

- Both types of flour are gluten-free.

A number of studies are currently looking into the health benefits of grape seed and grape skin flours, and early results are promising. Of course, these products have a lot to commend them beyond fantastic nutrition, such as contributing interesting flavors and allowing us to make excellent use of material that was formerly discarded. So although I'm calling them the new next frontier, they are already available. I encourage you to get your hands on them and start riding the next wave!

BREAD WITH COFFEE TEA, REALLY?

Before we get to the recipes, I must introduce one final "next frontier" product: cascara seca—the dried pulp of coffee "cherries," the fruits that contain coffee beans. Cascara seca has been available for a while, but I hadn't discovered it until David Haddock, the head roaster at Boquete Mountain Coffee, in Charlotte, North Carolina, told me about it.

As David explained it, until recently, the only part of the coffee cherry thought to be valuable was the greenish bean inside, which eventually goes through a process of fermentation, drying, and roasting prior to being brewed into coffee. The dried (*seca*) fruit, which looks more like a husk (*cascara*), is usually composted or discarded (sound familiar?). But not anymore. People have figured out that cascara seca can be steeped like tea to produce a naturally sweet, translucent, dark amber brew that contains only 10% of the caffeine of coffee, but a host of beneficial antioxidants and polyphenols. As with many "discoveries," this isn't entirely new knowledge. A similar dried husk brew, called *qishr*, has long been enjoyed in Yemen, where it's sometimes steeped with cinnamon and spices, kind of like a cascara chai.

Dried coffee cherries are now also being sold as a nutritional supplement and being used as an ingredient in cosmetics because they're believed to have antiwrinkling properties—not unlike the resveratrol in grape skins and seeds. Recent studies indicate that coffee cherries have more than twice the antioxidant capacity of dark chocolate and ten times more antioxidant power than green tea, pomegranate, and açai, all currently in vogue as superfoods.

Since my conversation with David, I've been brewing cascara seca tea as an alternative to black tea or coffee—and a nice complement to my morning ProBiotein smoothie! Of course, I quickly started thinking about how it might perform in baking. After all, if other formerly discarded products like spent grain and pomace can add nutritional value to bread, why not cascara seca? So I ground up some cascara seca into a grainy powder in my little burr mill. The smell is nothing like coffee because it isn't roasted (nor is it actually coffee); it smells more like mild tobacco with subtle aromatic undertones of blueberries, rose hips, and even a hint of orange marmalade. I added a few tablespoons of the powder to a small batch of simple French bread dough and ended up with a very pretty, slightly speckled bread that looked like it had bits of vanilla bean seeds floating throughout the crumb. The flavor was subtle yet noticeable, kissed with a hint of fruited green tea flavors.

For the next batch, I brewed some cascara tea and substituted it for the water in that same recipe. This had a more dramatic influence, with the tea's brownish amber color giving the dough a light caramel color. Again, its contribution to the bread's flavor was subtle and delicate, almost floral, with a long, pleasant aftertaste. I felt like I was onto something. In a third batch, I used both the cascara tea and the steeped cascara used to make it. Ahhh, success!

As always in my books, it ultimately comes down to flavor. If an ingredient doesn't add flavor value, it will be a hard sell to convince people to use it. They might take a chance on it based on health claims, but they're unlikely to stick with it if the flavor doesn't deliver. Plus, I think the amount of cascara we could actually consume in bread would probably be negligible from a nutritional or health standpoint. Fortunately, I can assure you that it does add flavor value; the breads I've made with cascara have tasted really good. Like classic sourdough breads, they have a long finish, far longer than bread leavened only with commercial yeast, but without the sour tang. And although the health benefits of cascara are only just now being studied, I think it holds great potential. In fact, I predict that we'll be hearing a lot more about it in the coming years. Hopefully you'll already be well ahead of the wave, drinking cascara tea and using it in your breads.

SYRAH GRAPE SKIN FLOUR OLIVE BREAD

MAKES 2 LOAVES

Grape skin flour intensifies both the flavor and the color of olive bread and also helps prevent the bread from becoming stale. Here, it's a simple addition to a basic mixed-method bread, leavened with both sourdough starter and commercial yeast in the style of a French pain au levain, but it yields a totally different loaf. You can use any type of grape skin flour, but Eric Frischkorn, the Kendall-Jackson chef who created this recipe, recommends the Syrah grape skin flour called for here (available from WholeVine; see Resources, page 240) because it best complements the flavor of the olives. Note that although this version uses mostly regular bread flour and whole wheat flour, you can also make it with sprouted wheat flour instead.

DOUGH

INGREDIENT	VOLUME	OUNCES	GRAMS	%
Mother Starter (page 40), recently refreshed	½ cup	4.5	128	19
water, lukewarm (95°F / 35°C)	2 cups plus 1½ tablespoons	16.75	475	70
unbleached bread flour	4½ cups plus 1 tablespoon	20.5	581	86
whole wheat flour (preferably whole-milled)	½ cup plus 1 tablespoon	2.5	71	10
grape skin flour (preferably Syrah)	¼ cup	1	28.5	4
instant yeast	⅛ teaspoon	0.02	0.5	0.1
kalamata olives, pitted and halved	1½ cups	7.25	206	30
unbleached bread flour for the olives	1 tablespoon	0.3	8.5	1.2
salt	2 teaspoons	0.5	14	2.1
TOTAL		53.32	1,512.5	222.4

1 Break the starter into 5 or 6 pieces and put it in the bowl of a stand mixer fitted with the dough hook or in a large bowl. Add the water and stir (on low speed if using a stand mixer) for a few seconds to soften and break up the starter. Add the flours and mix or stir for about 2 minutes, until the flour is hydrated and the starter is evenly distributed. Continue mixing for about 2 minutes, until a coarse, sticky dough forms. Let the dough rest in the bowl at room temperature for 20 minutes.

2 Add the yeast and mix on medium-low speed if using a stand mixer or knead by hand for 2 to 3 minutes, until the dough is firm and slightly tacky. In a separate bowl, toss the olives with the 1 tablespoon (0.3 oz / 8.5 g) of bread flour. Add the olives to the dough and mix on low speed or knead by hand for 1 minute. Add the salt and mix or knead for 1 to 2 minutes, until the salt and olives are evenly distributed and the dough is very soft and supple and slightly sticky.

3 Oil the work surface and transfer the dough to the oiled area. Also oil a large bowl. Lightly oil your hands, then stretch and fold the dough as shown on page 20, folding it over itself four times: once each from the top, bottom, and sides. Form the dough into a ball. Put it in the oiled bowl and cover the bowl with plastic wrap, or leave the dough on the work surface and cover it with the bowl. At intervals of 45 minutes, perform two additional sequences of stretching and folding. For each stretch and fold sequence, lightly oil your hands to prevent sticking. The dough will become firmer and smoother after each stretch and fold, and after the final fold, it should be tacky and very supple and bouncy when patted.

4 Put the dough back in the bowl and cover the bowl with plastic wrap. Ferment the dough at room temperature for 30 minutes.

5 Dust two bannetons with flour and lightly dust the work surface with flour. Transfer the dough to the work surface. Divide it in half and shape into two balls. Mist the tops with vegetable spray oil and cover loosely with plastic wrap or a clean towel. Let the dough rest for 20 minutes longer.

6 Form each piece into a boule as shown on pages 20 and 21. Place the shaped loaves seam side up in the bannetons and cover loosely with plastic wrap or a clean towel. Proof at room temperature for 1½ to 3 hours, until the dough has nearly doubled in size.

7 About 45 minutes before you plan to bake, prepare the oven for hearth baking with a baking stone and steam pan as described on page 29. Preheat the oven to 450°F (232°C).

8 Just before baking, dust a peel with flour. Transfer the dough to the peel and score as desired. Slide the dough onto the baking stone and pour about 1 cup of hot water into the steam pan. Bake for 4 minutes, then lower the temperature to 425°F (218°C) and bake for 15 minutes longer, then rotate the loaves and continue baking for an additional 15 to 20 minutes, until the crust is rich golden brown and the loaves sound hollow when thumped on the bottom. The internal temperature should be at least 200°F (93°C).

9 Transfer to a wire rack and let cool for at least 30 minutes before slicing and serving.

GRAPE SKIN FLOUR RUSTIC SOURDOUGH WITH SUN-DRIED TOMATOES, ROASTED GARLIC, AND CARMODY CHEESE

MAKES 2 LARGE LOAVES

This bread showcases both grape seed oil and grape skin flour in a very inventive, fully loaded hearth bread. Eric Frischkorn, the Kendall-Jackson chef who created this recipe, recommends Chardonnay seed oil and Chardonnay grape skin flour (both available from WholeVine; see Resources, page 240) for this bread, but you can use any varietal for either. The add-ins include some interesting ingredients, including herbes de Provence and Carmody cheese. Eric sifts out the lavender from his herbes de Provence (which is kind of odd since it is the lavender that defines this blend, but it does tend to assert itself); therefore, you could use a blend of Italian herbs instead. Carmody cheese is named for a road that runs next to Bellwether Farms, one of America's finest farmstead creameries, located in Sonoma County. It's a creamy, buttery cheese similar to a rich Monterey Jack, so you could use that instead, or perhaps Fontina or even Muenster. It may seem odd to prepare the add-ins a day in advance, but overnight storage allows the cheese to become infused with the flavors of the garlic and herbs.

ADD-INS (DAY 1)

INGREDIENT	VOLUME	OUNCES	GRAMS
grape seed oil (preferably Chardonnay)	¼ cup	2	56.5
garlic cloves, peeled and quartered	about 6	1	28.5
herbes de Provence	1 tablespoon	0.07	2
Carmody cheese, cut into ½-inch pieces	1½ cups	5.75	163
sun-dried tomatoes (not oil-packed), quartered	¼ cup	1.5	42.5
water, lukewarm (95°F / 35°C)	¼ cup	2	56.5
TOTAL		12.27	347.7

1 Warm the oil in a small saucepan over low heat, add the garlic, and sauté until golden brown, 10 to 15 minutes. Drain the garlic, reserving the oil. Put the oil in a container, cover, and refrigerate. Put the garlic in a medium bowl.

2 Sift the herbes de Provence to remove the lavender, then add it to the garlic. Stir in the cheese. Cover the bowl and refrigerate.

3 Pour the water over the sun-dried tomatoes and let soak for at least 1 hour, then cover and refrigerate overnight.

CONTINUED

FINAL DOUGH (DAY 2)

INGREDIENT	VOLUME	OUNCES	GRAMS	%
Add-Ins	all	12.27	347.7	51
unbleached bread flour	4 cups plus 1 tablespoon	18.25	517	76
Mother Starter (page 40), recently refreshed	1 cup	4.5	128	19
water, at room temperature	2 cups	16	454	67
whole wheat flour	1 cup plus 1 tablespoon	4.75	135	20
grape skin flour (preferably Chardonnay)	¼ cup	1	28.5	4
instant yeast	⅛ teaspoon	0.02	0.5	0.1
salt	2 teaspoons	0.5	14	2.1
TOTAL		57.29	1,624.7	239.2

1 Remove the add-ins from the refrigerator: the oil; herbs, garlic, and cheese; and the tomatoes. Add the tomatoes (and any water that wasn't absorbed) and 2 tablespoons (0.6 oz / 1.5 g) of the bread flour to the garlic and toss until evenly distributed.

2 Break the starter into 5 or 6 pieces and put it in the bowl of a stand mixer fitted with the dough hook or in a large bowl. Add the water and stir (on low speed if using a stand mixer) for a few seconds to soften and break up the starter. Add the remaining bread flour and the whole wheat and grape skin flours and mix or stir for 2 to 3 minutes. Toward the end of the mixing time, drizzle in the oil and continue mixing until the flour is hydrated and a coarse ball of slightly sticky dough forms. Let the dough rest in the bowl, covered, at room temperature for 20 minutes.

3 Add the yeast and mix on medium-low speed or knead by hand for 2 to 3 minutes, until the dough is soft, supple, and tacky. Add the cheese mixture and mix on low speed or knead by hand for 1 minute. Add the salt and continue to mix or knead for 1 minute, until the cheese is evenly distributed. The dough should be soft, tacky or slightly sticky, and very supple.

4 Oil the work surface and transfer the dough to the oiled area. Also oil a large bowl. Lightly oil your hands, then stretch and fold the dough as shown on page 20, folding it over itself four times: once each from the top, bottom, and sides. Form the dough into a ball. Put it in the oiled bowl and cover the bowl with plastic wrap, or leave the dough on the work surface and cover it with the bowl. At intervals of 45 minutes, perform two additional sequences of stretching and folding. For each stretch and

CONTINUED

fold sequence, lightly oil your hands to prevent sticking. The dough will firm up slightly after each stretch and fold, and after the final fold, it should be very supple and bouncy when patted.

5 Put the dough back in the bowl and cover the bowl with plastic wrap. Ferment the dough at room temperature for 30 to 60 minutes, until it shows signs of rising.

6 Lightly flour a work surface. Transfer the dough to the work surface and divide it in half. Gently pat each piece into a 1-inch-thick rectangle. Cover the dough loosely with plastic wrap or a clean towel and let it rest for 20 minutes.

7 Line a sheet pan with parchment paper or a silicone mat, mist with vegetable spray oil, and, optionally, dust lightly with semolina flour or another coarse flour. Working with one piece of dough at a time, gently press to form a larger rectangle, about ½ inch thick. Fold the top edge over, bringing it to the center of the dough, then do the same with the bottom edge, bringing it to the center so it touches the edge of the top section, creating a seam. Fold the dough over the seam to make a narrower, thicker rectangle. Pinch the open sides together along the seam and the ends to seal them and tighten the surface of the dough. Gently pull both ends to make a longer rectangle about 9 to 12 inches long. Put both shaped loaves on the prepared pan. Mist with vegetable spray oil and cover loosely with plastic wrap or a clean towel. Proof at room temperature for 1½ to 3 hours, until they increase in size by at least 1½ times.

8 About 45 minutes before you plan to bake, position a rack in the middle of the oven and prepare the oven for steaming as shown on page 29. (A baking stone isn't used.) Preheat the oven to 450°F (232°C).

9 Put the pan in the oven and pour about 1 cup of hot water into the steam pan. Bake for 4 minutes, then lower the temperature to 425°F (218°C) and bake for 15 minutes. Rotate and bake for 10 to 20 minutes longer, until the crust is golden brown all over and the bread sounds hollow when thumped on the bottom. The internal temperature should be at least 195°F (91°C).

10 Transfer to a wire rack and let cool for at least 30 minutes before slicing and serving.

GLUTEN-FREE FOCACCIA

MAKES ONE 18 BY 13-INCH PAN; 8 TO 12 SERVINGS

In this focaccia, grape skin flour makes up only a small percentage of the total flour, but it makes a major contribution to both color and flavor. If you can't find quinoa flour, simple grind whole quinoa in a seed or spice mill to make your own, or use more brown rice flour or another gluten-free flour. It's also fine to substitute sprouted brown rice flour and sprouted quinoa flour for the nonsprouted versions called for here. It's also fine to use generic grape seed oil or even olive oil, though Chardonnay grape seed oil heightens flavor. This recipe was created by Eric Frischkorn, and he uses a number of interesting tricks. One is using carbonated water, which gives additional aeration to the crumb. Another is using whipped egg whites, again to provide aeration. The acidity of the vinegar helps both with flavor and with preserving some of the aeration. Plus, the high amount of yeast contributes to both flavor and rapid leavening. All in all, very innovative.

BATTER

INGREDIENT	VOLUME	OUNCES	GRAMS	%
brown rice flour	4½ cups	20	567	67
quinoa flour	1¾ cups	8	227	26.4
grape skin flour (preferably Chardonnay)	½ cup	2	56.5	6.6
xanthan gum	3 tablespoons	1	28	3.3
sugar	4 tablespoons	2	57	7
instant yeast	¼ cup	1.32	37.5	4.4
salt	4 teaspoons	1	28.5	3.4
dried basil	1 tablespoon	0.07	2	0.4
dried oregano	1 tablespoon	0.12	3.5	0.4
grape seed oil (preferably Chardonnay)	¼ cup	2	56.5	6.6
club soda or plain seltzer water	3 cups	24	680	80
white wine vinegar	2 teaspoons	0.35	10	1.2
egg whites	6	7.5	213	25
additional grape seed oil (preferably Chardonnay) for the pan and for topping	about ¼ cup			
Parmesan cheese, grated	about ½ cup			
TOTAL		69.36	1,966.5	231.7

CONTINUED

1 In the bowl of a stand mixer fitted with the paddle attachment, or in a large bowl, stir together the flours, xanthan gum, sugar, yeast, salt, basil, and oregano (on low speed if using a stand mixer). In a separate bowl, whisk the ¼ cup (2 oz / 56.5 g) of grape seed oil with the club soda and vinegar. In a third bowl, vigorously whisk the egg whites for about 1 minute to make a light to medium foam.

2 With the mixer on low speed or while mixing with a large spoon, drizzle in the egg whites and mix until fully incorporated. While continuing to mix or stir, slowly pour in the club soda mixture. Mix on medium speed or by hand for 2 minutes. Scrape down the bowl, then mix for 2 more minutes to make a thick, slightly foamy batter.

3 Line an 18 by 13-inch rimmed sheet pan with parchment paper or a silicone mat. Generously oil the surface, including the sides of the pan, with 2 tablespoons (1 oz / 28.5 g) of the grape seed oil. Pour the batter into the center of the pan. Drizzle the remaining 2 tablespoons (1 oz / 28.5 g) of oil over the batter and use a rubber spatula or icing spatula to spread the batter evenly into the pan, filling all four corners. Sprinkle the cheese over the top. Cover the pan loosely with plastic wrap and let the dough rise in a warm place (80°F / 27°C) for at least 1 hour, until nearly double in size; you can proof it in a cooler location, but it will take longer to rise.

4 Position a rack in the middle of the oven and preheat the oven to 375°F (191°C).

5 Bake for 12 minutes, then rotate the pan and bake for 12 to 18 minutes longer, until golden brown and springy to the touch when pressed in the center.

6 Let cool for at least 10 minutes before cutting and serving.

GRAPE SKIN FLOUR CRACKERS

MAKES 15 LARGE CRACKERS

This cracker recipe provides a great format for tasting the differences in flavor between grape skin flour and grape seed oil made from different grape varietals. If you prefer, feel free to use grape skin flour, grape seed oil, or both—or even grape seed flour—in any other cracker recipe. For the grape skin flour, keep the amount to 4% of the total flour weight; for grape seed flour, keep it to under 10% of the total flour weight. For grape seed oil, substitute it for some or all of the oil or other fat in the recipe, using an amount between 12% and 15% of the total flour weight. This cracker recipe is unleavened. For flakier crackers that rise a bit, add 1½ teaspoons (0.28 oz / 8 g) of baking powder when mixing the dry ingredients. The egg white wash is optional, but it will help salt and any other toppings adhere to the crackers. One final note: Feel free to substitute sprouted whole wheat flour for either the semolina flour or bread flour or both. However, you'll probably need to increase the amount of water depending on how much sprouted flour you substitute.

DOUGH

INGREDIENT	VOLUME	OUNCES	GRAMS	%
semolina flour	3⅓ cups	15	425	53
unbleached bread flour	2⅔ cups	12	340	43
grape skin flour	¼ cup	1.12	32	4
salt	1½ teaspoons	0.35	10	1.4
water, lukewarm (95°F / 35°C)	1½ cups	12	340	43
grape seed oil	½ cup	4	113	14
egg white wash (optional)	1 egg white whisked with 1 tablespoon water			
coarse salt for topping	to taste			
TOTAL		44	1,260	158.4

1 In the bowl of a stand mixer fitted with the dough hook, or in a large bowl, stir together the flours and salt (on low speed if using a stand mixer). In a separate bowl, whisk together the water and oil, then slowly pour it into the flour mixture while mixing on low speed or stirring. Mix for about 3 minutes, until the flour is hydrated and a firm, coarse ball of dough forms. Add a bit more water or flour if needed to achieve this texture. Mix or stir for about 2 or 3 more minutes, until the dough feels supple and satiny.

2 Lightly flour a work surface with either semolina flour or bread flour. Transfer the dough to the work surface and knead by hand for about 30 seconds, until the dough is a smoother and more supple ball, adjusting the flour or water as needed.

3 Mist a bowl with vegetable spray oil, put the dough in the bowl, and cover the bowl with plastic wrap. Refrigerate for at least 1 hour or up to 2 days.

4 Position two racks in the oven an equal distance apart and preheat the oven to 325°F (163°C). Line three sheet pans with parchment paper or silicone mats and mist with vegetable spray oil.

5 Divide the dough into 3 equal pieces. (If you'd like to save some of the dough to bake later, wrap the pieces in plastic wrap and refrigerate for up to a week.) Divide each piece into 5 smaller pieces of equal size; they should be just under 3 ounces (85 g) each. Shape each piece into a ball and let rest for about 5 minutes to allow the gluten to relax.

6 Dust the work surface with flour again or spread about ¼ teaspoon of vegetable oil on the work surface. Place one dough ball on the floured or oiled area and use a rolling pin to roll out the dough into a rectangle measuring about 5 by 3 inches and just under ¼ inch thick. Transfer to one of the prepared pans. Repeat, placing 5 rolled pieces of dough on each pan and spacing them evenly; they can be close because they won't spread.

7 Brush the tops with water or the egg white wash, then lightly sprinkle coarse salt over the top to taste. Use the tines of a fork to prick the surface of each cracker several times to prevent bubbling of the dough during baking.

8 Bake for 8 minutes, then rotate the pans front to back and between shelves and bake for 5 to 8 minutes longer, until the tops just begin to brown around the edges.

9 Leave the crackers on the pans and let cool for at least 10 minutes before serving. They will be soft, not hard and crisp.

Variations

CRISP CRACKERS: After rotating the pans during baking, lower the temperature to 300°F (149°C) and bake for 10 to 15 minutes longer, until the entire upper surface is golden brown.

HERB CRACKERS: After sprinkling with salt, dust the surface with any combination of herbs and spices, bearing in mind that a little goes a long way. Recommendations include basil, oregano, thyme, marjoram, rosemary, herbes de Provence, sweet paprika, cayenne, and black pepper.

CASCARA SECA LEAN BREAD

MAKES 1 VERY LARGE BOULE, 2 TO 6 SMALLER LOAVES, OR UP TO 24 ROLLS

Tea has been used for many years by many bakers and pastry chefs as a way to infuse unique, subtle flavors into their food. Here's a basic cascara-infused lean dough (aka French bread) based on the overnight method in my book *Artisan Breads Every Day*. This recipe is designed to give you a fairly neutral flavor foundation upon which to taste the contribution that cascara seca tea can add to a bread. You can use the same method of brewing to make a tea for use as the liquid in any number of other bread formulas once you get the hang of it. You can also use other teas and even brewed coffee to hydrate doughs in the same manner. But cascara seca is the new kid on the block, and one well worth getting to know. I find the flavor and long finish that it adds to bread delightful and intriguing.

DOUGH

INGREDIENT	VOLUME	OUNCES	GRAMS	%
water	2¼ cups	18	510	75
ground cascara seca	2 tablespoons	0.5	14	2.1
unbleached bread flour	5⅓ cups	24	680	100
salt	2 teaspoons	0.5	14	2.1
instant yeast	2¼ teaspoons	0.25	7	1
TOTAL		43.25	1,225	180.2

1 Bring the water to a boil. Pour it over the cascara seca and let steep for at least 15 minutes, until it cools to lukewarm (95°F / 35°C). It can then be used immediately or stored in the refrigerator for later use. If stored in the refrigerator, warm it to at least room temperature before mixing the dough.

2 In the bowl of a stand mixer fitted with the paddle attachment, or in a large bowl, stir together the flour, salt, and yeast (on low speed if using a stand mixer). Add the cascara infusion, grounds and all. Mix or stir for 2 minutes, until well blended; if mixing by hand and the spoon gets too doughy, dip it in a bowl of warm water or turn the dough out onto a lightly oiled work surface and knead by hand. The dough should be sticky and shaggy.

3 Let the dough rest, uncovered, for 5 minutes. Then switch to the dough hook and mix for 1 to 2 minutes, on medium-low speed if using a stand mixer. The dough will smooth out slightly but still be very soft and sticky.

CONTINUED

4 Mist a bowl with vegetable spray oil or lightly coat it with vegetable oil. Use a wet bowl scraper or spatula to transfer the dough to the bowl, then cover the bowl with plastic wrap (or leave the dough on the work surface and cover with the bowl). Let the dough rest for 5 minutes.

5 Oil the work surface and transfer the dough to the oiled area. Lightly oil your hands, then stretch and fold the dough as shown on page 20, folding it over itself four times: once each from the top, bottom, and sides. Cover the dough with the bowl and then, at intervals of 5 to 10 minutes, perform three additional sequences of stretching and folding. For each stretch and fold sequence, lightly oil your hands to prevent sticking. The dough will become smoother and significantly firmer with each stretch and fold. After the final fold the dough should be soft, supple, and still very tacky, but it will have a bouncy feel when patted.

6 Return the dough to the bowl, cover the bowl tightly with plastic wrap, and refrigerate for at least 12 hours or up to 4 days. The dough will double or possibly triple in size within 12 hours.

7 Remove the dough from the refrigerator about 2 hours before you plan to bake. Oil the work surface and use a wet or oiled bowl scraper to transfer the dough to the oiled area. Using a metal pastry blade, divide the dough into the desired number of pieces—2 to 6 for smaller loaves, or more for rolls—or use the entire amount of dough for one large loaf. **For one or more hearth loaves,** prepare the appropriate number of bannetons or a *couche* as shown on page 26, or line an 18 by 13-inch sheet pan with parchment paper and then mist it with vegetable spray oil. Shape each piece of dough into a boule or bâtard as shown on pages 20 and 21. Put the shaped dough in the prepared proofing vessel(s) or on the sheet pan. **For rolls,** line two sheet pans with parchment paper or silicone mats. Shape the rolls as desired (see page 24) and put half of them on each lined pan.

8 Mist the top of the dough with vegetable spray oil, then cover loosely with plastic wrap. Proof at room temperature for 1 hour. Uncover and proof for 40 to 60 minutes longer, until the dough increases in size by 1½ times. The surface will dry out slightly and the dough will spring back slowly when poked with your finger.

9 About 45 minutes before you plan to bake, prepare the oven for hearth baking with a baking stone and steam pan as described on page 29. Preheat the oven to 550°F (288°C) or as high as it will go.

10 To bake loaves, just before baking, dust a peel with flour. Transfer the dough to the peel and score as desired (see page 29). Slide the dough onto the baking stone and pour about 1 cup of hot water into the steam pan. Lower the temperature to 450°F (232°C). Bake for 10 to 12 minutes, then rotate and bake for 10 to 15 minutes longer, until the crust is hard and rich golden brown and the bread sounds hollow when thumped on the bottom. The internal temperature should be 200°F to 205°F (93°C to 96°C). Transfer to a wire rack and let cool for at least 1 hour before slicing and serving.

11 To bake rolls, bake one pan at a time. As soon as you put the pan in the oven, pour about 1 cup of hot water into the steam pan and lower the temperature to 450°F (232°C). Bake for 8 minutes, then rotate and bake for 8 to 12 minutes longer, until the crust is golden brown and the rolls sound hollow when thumped on the bottom. The internal temperature should be 200°F to 205°F (93°C to 96°C). Transfer to a wire rack and let cool for at least 10 minutes before serving.

Including Cascara Seca and ProBiotein in Dough

Cascara seca or ProBiotein can be used in any of the recipes in this book, but I suggest you make these lean versions on pages 219 and 222 first to familiarize yourself with the flavor. Steeped cascara seca (or any tea for that matter) can be substituted for water in any bread formula, and ProBiotein can be used to add a sourdough tang to any bread where you think it would be appropriate.

For cascara seca, calculate the total flour weight in the recipe and multiply by 0.02 (2%). Weigh out that amount of cascara seca, then grind it into a powder in a spice or seed grinder, coffee mill, or high-speed blender. Measure out the amount of water called for in the dough and bring it to a boil. Pour it over the cascara seca and let steep for at least 15 minutes or as long as 2 hours. When you mix the dough, use this cascara tea, including the grounds, in place of the water. When mixing, you may need to adjusting the amount of liquid or flour a bit to achieve the target texture.

For ProBiotein, calculate the total flour weight and multiply by 0.01 (1%), or 0.015 (1.5%) for a stronger tang. Add that amount of ProBiotein to the dry ingredients. Because of the process used to make this supplement, it will function in the dough like a powdered pre-ferment.

PROBIOTEIN LEAN BREAD

MAKES 1 VERY LARGE BOULE, 2 TO 6 SMALLER LOAVES, OR UP TO 24 ROLLS

The same lean dough formula on page 219 can be varied to feature ProBiotein instead of the dried coffee husks. In addition to the nutritional benefits provided by this dried spent grain powder (see page 201), it also contributes a tangy flavor and long, pleasant finish on the palate. This version calls for just 1% ProBiotein against the total flour weight, but if you prefer a sourer flavor you can double the amount. Once you determine the percentage you prefer, feel free to add ProBiotein in that same ratio to any bread dough.

DOUGH

INGREDIENT	VOLUME	OUNCES	GRAMS	%
unbleached bread flour	5⅓ cups	24	680	100
salt	2 teaspoons	0.5	14	2.1
instant yeast	2¼ teaspoons	0.25	7	1
ProBiotein	2 teaspoons	0.25	7	1
water, lukewarm (95°F / 35°C)	2¼ cups	18	510	75
TOTAL		43	1,218	179.1

1 In the bowl of a stand mixer fitted with the paddle attachment, or in a large bowl, stir together the flour, salt, yeast, and ProBiotein (on low speed if using a stand mixer). Add the water and mix or stir 2 minutes, until well blended. If mixing by hand and the spoon gets too doughy, dip it in a bowl of warm water or turn the dough out onto a lightly oiled work surface and knead it by hand. The dough should be sticky and shaggy.

2 Let the dough rest, uncovered, for 5 minutes. Then switch to the dough hook and mix or stir for 1 to 2 minutes, on medium-low speed if using a stand mixer. The dough will smooth out slightly but still be very soft and sticky.

3 Mist a bowl with vegetable spray oil or lightly coat it with vegetable oil. Use a wet bowl scraper or spatula to transfer the dough to the bowl, then cover the bowl with plastic wrap (or leave the dough on the work surface and cover with the bowl). Let the dough rest for 5 minutes.

4 Oil the work surface and transfer the dough to the oiled area. Lightly oil your hands, then stretch and fold the dough as shown on page 20, folding it over itself four times: once each from the top, bottom, and sides. Cover the dough with the bowl and then, at intervals of 5 to 10 minutes, perform three additional sequences of stretching and folding. For each stretch and fold sequence, lightly oil your hands to prevent sticking. The dough will become smoother and significantly firmer with each stretch and fold. After the final fold the dough should be soft, supple, and very tacky and bouncy when patted.

5 Return the dough to the bowl, cover the bowl tightly with plastic wrap, and refrigerate for at least 12 hours or up to 4 days. The dough will double or possibly triple in size within 12 hours.

6 Remove the dough from the refrigerator about 2 hours before you plan to bake. Oil the work surface and use a wet or oiled bowl scraper to transfer the dough to the oiled area. Using a metal pastry blade, divide the dough into the desired number of pieces—2 to 6 for smaller loaves, or more for rolls—or use the entire amount of dough for one large loaf. **For one or more hearth loaves,** prepare the appropriate number of bannetons or a *couche* as shown on page 26, or line an 18 by 13-inch sheet pan with parchment paper and then mist it with vegetable spray oil. Shape each piece of dough into a boule or bâtard as shown on pages 20 and 21. Put the shaped dough in the prepared proofing vessel(s) or on the sheet pan. **For rolls,** line two sheet pans with parchment paper or silicone mats. Shape the rolls as desired (see page 24) and put half of them on each lined pan.

7 Mist the top of the dough with vegetable spray oil, then cover loosely with plastic wrap. Proof at room temperature for 1 hour. Uncover and proof for 40 to 60 minutes longer, until the dough increases in size by 1½ times. The surface will dry out slightly and the dough will spring back slowly when poked with your finger.

8 About 45 minutes before you plan to bake, prepare the oven for hearth baking with a baking stone and steam pan as described on page 29. Preheat the oven to 550°F (288°C) or as high as it will go.

9 **To bake loaves,** just before baking, dust a peel with flour. Transfer the dough to the peel and score as desired (see page 29). Slide the dough onto the baking stone and pour about 1 cup of hot water into the steam pan. Lower the temperature to 450°F (232°C). Bake for 10 to 12 minutes, then rotate and bake for 10 to 15 minutes longer, until the crust is hard and rich golden brown and the bread sounds hollow when thumped on the bottom. The internal temperature should be 200°F to 205°F (93°C to 96°C). Transfer to a wire rack and let cool for at least 1 hour before slicing and serving.

10 **To bake rolls,** bake one pan at a time. As soon as you put the pan in the oven, pour about 1 cup of hot water into the steam pan and lower the temperature to 450°F (232°C). Bake for 8 minutes, then rotate and bake for 8 to 12 minutes longer, until the crust is golden brown and the rolls sound hollow when thumped on the bottom. The internal temperature should be 200°F to 205°F (93°C to 96°C). Transfer to a wire rack and let cool for at least 10 minutes before serving.

EPILOGUE
IS THE ROAD LESS TRAVELED THE ROAD AHEAD?

Baker Mike Pappas lives near me and has some radical ideas about natural wild yeast starters. One day Mike came to visit me and brought three loaves, along with three containers, each holding a small piece of sourdough starter. "They look alike, but each one is different," he asserted. Then he added another wrinkle, producing a small piece of Parmesan cheese, a ripe peach, and a few tablespoons of coffee beans. "I can change the flavor profile of my starters simply by using a piece of fruit, coffee beans, or cheese, almost like a magnet, to trap different strains of yeast," he said.

"Really?" I asked, skeptical but intrigued.

Mike had me uncover each of the starters in turn and take a whiff. Sure enough, each had a slightly different aroma. I figured he must have submerged those foods in the starters, but his actual method more than defied that expectation. Here's how he explained it: "All I do is leave one of these on the top of the bowl when I first make my starter, and, well, something happens. Each seems to draw different strains of wild yeast or bacteria to the flour mixture, resulting in different flavors even though these ingredients never actually touch the dough." He told me he'd noticed that coffee beans, for example, draw microorganisms that produce a robust, deeper flavor, whereas those drawn to pears or stone fruits create flavors and aromas that tend to be more floral or smooth and less acidic.

Then we tasted the breads, and I was surprised at how different each one was, and also impressed by how great each one tasted.

During subsequent meetings, Mike explained more of his bread philosophy and theories, some of which seem highly speculative, but they do follow an intuitive logic. He told me, "My goal from the start has been to create breads with excellent crumb and crust, great flavor, and also long shelf life. I'm looking for an A-plus crust, not only when the bread first comes out of the oven, but also after three or four days, if the bread is properly stored. I think the highest-quality gluten bonds are formed when the dough molecules first touch. That's why resting the dough is so important

Q & A

Could a juicer be used to make the fruit waters?

Yes, but Mike Pappas doesn't think the liquid would be as "pure," which is why he still does it by hand (squeezing the fruit through a porous cloth).

Will the recipe work if I use only apple or only peach or only pear water?

Yes, but that's not the point. This is a bread method that symbolizes the depths of the bread quest. It doesn't just push the envelope, it shatters the envelope!

Why use bottled spring water?

It's all about controlling the flavor and purity of the final result. However, you can use flitered water if necesary.

Can I use my own mother starter instead of Mike's "trap" starters?

If you have any seed culture, sponge starter, or mother starter left over from the other recipes in this book, they could certainly be used in this chapter too. Would a different "trap" produce a noticeably different flavor? Mike Pappas definitely thinks so. Does anyone need to go through all these steps to make great bread? No, but it's all part of the discovery process.

to my method. It minimizes mixing, which typically overorganizes the gluten. It preserves the initial, high-quality bonds and, in the end, releases more flavor."

During the past few years, there's been a lot of interest in short, gentle mixing methods, including so-called no-knead mixing. But this was the first time I'd talked with someone who had hypotheses about why that method makes a difference. But mixing is only one part of Mike's overall methodology. He also believes strongly in what I'll call "limited use" natural starters, which is why he developed his wild yeast "traps." Mike believes that to achieve the purest flavor, it's best to make a sourdough culture that finishes its life after a single round of baking.

As he explained it, "The longer we perpetuate a starter, the more susceptible it becomes to elements we can't control—other yeasts and bacteria that will affect the results, including the structure-building ability of the flour bonds. An older starter that has gone through many feedings and rebuildings may make fine bread, but there's an aging process that can introduce properties that aren't beneficial. I don't want this element of risk if I'm going for a very specific flavor and structure."

When I asked him if it's possible to make his breads with a long-term, perpetuated starter, he said, "Of course, but there will always be a measure of biological process within the starter's culture that, while natural to the starter, is unnecessary for baking the bread."

I took this to mean that Mike's goal is to engage in a process that's as uncorrupted as possible while still working with natural wild yeast leaven. Every baker is, of necessity, a control freak; this is just a more extreme version. You may wonder whether it's necessary to exert this much control when, as so many artisan bakers have shown, it's possible to make consistently great bread with a perpetuated starter that's well maintained. For example, Boudin Bakery in San Francisco has been using the same starter, refreshed day after day, for over 160 years, and no one is complaining.

Still, what Mike is doing, as he pushes the envelope of all the artisan techniques that we've discussed in this and other books to the outer edges of obsessiveness, reminds me of a similar approach in the world of beer (aka liquid bread), in the niche known as extreme brewing. As that niche amply demonstrates, willingness to ask what-if questions and boldly follow intuitive hunches can have extraordinary (and sometimes also negative) results. I think it's exciting that Mike and others like him are testing the limits in the bread world in a similar fashion. I encourage you to consider taking at least a brief ride on this next, next new wave in the bread revolution. Who knows where it will take you, but you're bound to expand your horizons considerably in the process.

FRAGRANT PEACH, APPLE, AND PEAR BREAD WITH "PEACH TRAP" STARTER

MAKES 2 LOAVES

This formula showcases Mike Pappas's "peach trap" method, along with the use of apple, peach, and pear water to draw in particular microorganisms and fine-tune the flavor of the final bread. As you'll see, it's a complex and lengthy process (at least four days) and asks a lot from the baker, including hand squeezing not just one but three "fruit waters." Given all that, you may wonder whether it's worth the effort. There's only one way to find out!

You may also quite reasonably ask whether, after all of the work of making the starter for this bread, it would be okay to perpetuate the starter rather than using it up? You can certainly perpetuate the starter to shortcut some of the preliminary steps next time you make the bread. In many ways, it's like the seed culture method described on page 35. Although Mike likes to start each batch of bread with a new culture in his quest for purity of flavor, most of us would be thrilled with loaves made from the original's refreshed progeny, batch after batch. You'll have to try it for yourself to see if you agree with his assessment.

Because this bread requires such a lengthy and unusual process, I'll reiterate my usual advice: The predicted time schedule for the various starters and stages is approximate and depends on the ambient temperature and other conditions in your kitchen. Adjust the times as needed, using the visual prompts and fermentation indicators as a guideline.

SEED CULTURE (DAY 1)

INGREDIENT	VOLUME	OUNCES	GRAMS	%
large peach	1			
peach water	6 tablespoons	3	85	150
whole wheat flour	7 tablespoons	2	56.5	100
overly ripe peach	1			
TOTAL		5	141.5	250

Line a fine-mesh sieve with cheesecloth and place it over a bowl. Grate the peach into the lined sieve, and lift the cheesecloth to make a pouch. Squeeze the pouch directly over the sieve to extract as much peach juice as possible into the bowl.

CONTINUED

Put 6 tablespoons (3 oz / 85 g) of the liquid in a small bowl. (Discard, or eat, the pulp; if any liquid remains, store it in a covered container in the refrigerator and use it in the Firm Starter on Day 3.) Add the flour and stir to make a smooth, wet dough. Cover about three-quarters of the bowl tightly with plastic wrap and set the overly ripe peach on top of the plastic. Let rest at room temperature for 48 hours.

SPONGE STARTER (DAY 3)

INGREDIENT	VOLUME	OUNCES	GRAMS	%
large apple	1			
apple water	¼ cup	2	56.5	99
whole wheat flour	3½ tablespoons	1	28.5	50
whole rye flour	3½ tablespoons	1	28.5	50
Seed Culture	1½ tablespoons	0.5	14	15
TOTAL		4.5	127.5	214

Line a fine-mesh sieve with cheesecloth and place it over a bowl. Grate the apple over the lined sieve, and lift the cheesecloth to make a pouch. Squeeze the pouch directly over the sieve to extract as much apple juice as possible into the bowl. Put ¼ cup (2 oz / 56.5 g) of the juice in a small bowl (discard the pulp and drink, save, or discard any remaining juice). Add the flours and the seed culture and stir to make a wet, sponge-like batter. Cover the bowl with plastic wrap and ferment at room temperature for 24 hours. The starter should show signs of bubbling the next day.

FIRM STARTER (DAY 3)

INGREDIENT	VOLUME	OUNCES	GRAMS	%
leftover peach water from Day 1	¼ cup	2	56.5	67
Seed Culture	2 tablespoons	0.75	21.5	17
whole wheat flour	⅓ cup	1.5	42.5	50
whole rye flour	⅓ cup	1.5	42.5	50
TOTAL		5.75	163	184

If you don't have enough leftover peach water from Day 1, make more using the same method. In a medium bowl, stir together all the ingredients to make a firm ball of dough. Transfer to a work surface and knead for about 30 seconds to evenly distribute all the ingredients. Return the dough to the bowl, cover the bowl with plastic wrap, and ferment at room temperature for 24 hours. The starter should swell slightly by the next day.

FINAL DOUGH (DAY 4)

INGREDIENT	VOLUME	OUNCES	GRAMS	%
apples	2			
pears	2			
apple water	¾ cup	6	170	19
pear water	¾ cup	6	170	19
bottled spring water	1¼ cups plus 2½ tablespoons	11.25	319	35
Sponge Starter	½ cup	3.2	91	10
Firm Starter	½ cup	3.2	91	10
unbleached bread flour	3½ cups	16	454	50
whole wheat flour	2¾ cups plus 2 tablespoons	13	369	40.6
whole rye flour	⅔ cup	3	85	9.4
salt	1 tablespoon	0.75	21.5	2.4
TOTAL		62.4	1,770.5	195.4

1 Line a fine-mesh sieve with cheesecloth and place it over a bowl. Grate the apples over the sieve, and lift the cheesecloth to make a pouch. Squeeze the pouch over the sieve and bowl to extract as much liquid as possible. Put ¾ cup (6 oz / 170 g) of the juice in a large bowl (discard the pulp and drink, save, or discard any remaining juice). Follow the same procedure with the pears, then add ¾ cup (6 oz / 170 g) of the pear juice to the bowl. Add the water and both starters. Stir for about 15 seconds, just long enough to distribute the starters. Add the flours and stir for about 1 minute, until the flour is hydrated and a coarse, shaggy dough forms. Cover the bowl with plastic wrap and let the dough rest for 1 hour and 45 minutes.

2 Oil a work surface and transfer the dough to the oiled area. Sprinkle half of the salt over the dough, then stretch and fold the dough as shown on page 20, folding it over itself four times: once each from the top, bottom, and sides. Sprinkle the remaining salt over the dough and perform two more sequences of stretching and folding without allowing the dough to rest between sequences. Return the dough to the bowl and cover the bowl with plastic wrap, or leave the dough on the work surface and cover it with the bowl. Then, at 1-hour intervals, perform two additional sequences of stretching and folding. The dough should be supple and tacky, with a bouncy quality when patted. After the final fold, cover the dough and let it rest at room temperature for 1 hour.

CONTINUED

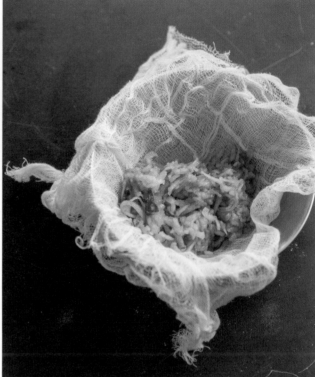

3 Prepare two bannetons or a *couche* as described on page 26. Divide the dough in half and shape each piece into a boule or bâtard as shown on pages 20 and 21. Put the shaped loaves in the prepared proofing vessels. Proof at room temperature for about 5 hours, until the loaves have increased in size by more than 1½ times but haven't doubled in size.

4 About 45 minutes before you plan to bake, prepare the oven for hearth baking with a baking stone and steam pan as shown on page 29. Preheat the oven to 435°F (224°C).

5 Just before baking, dust a peel with flour. Transfer the loaves to the peel and score as desired (see page 29). Slide the loaves onto the baking stone and pour about 1 cup of hot water into the steam pan.

6 Bake for 25 minutes, then rotate and bake for about 25 minutes longer, until the crust is golden brown and the bread sounds hollow when thumped on the bottom. The internal temperature should be at least 200°F (93°C).

7 Transfer to a wire rack and let cool for at least 30 minutes before slicing and serving, but note that the subtle flavor nuances can be more easily discerned after the bread cools completely, about 2 hours.

SEEDED MULTIGRAIN HEARTH BREAD WITH "PARMESAN TRAP" STARTER

MAKES 2 LOAVES

Like all of Mike Pappas's breads, this one involves a lot of steps and requires pretty much an all-day commitment on the final day. But if you're reading this, you must be intrigued. And, like Mike, you probably feel that the discovery process is as satisfying as the bread itself—which is delicious, by the way, with a complex nutty flavor and just a hint of umami from the cheese. Despite how much is going on in this loaf, in the end it's about simple, pure flavor evoked from fermented grain. Mike's mantra, which he told me was inspired by Steve Jobs, is "Traveling into the depths of complexity will allow us to offer our findings with grace and simplicity." That's certainly reflected in this bread.

If you don't have all the ingredients required for the seed and coating mixture, feel free to substitute other ingredients, such as sesame or poppy seeds, as long as the flavors are compatible. Also, be aware that potato flour is not the same as potato starch.

Because this bread requires such a lengthy and unusual process, I'll reiterate my usual advice: The predicted time schedule for the various starters and stages is approximate and depends on the ambient temperature and other conditions in your kitchen. Adjust the times as needed, using the visual prompts and fermentation indicators as a guideline.

SEED CULTURE (DAY 1)

INGREDIENT	VOLUME	OUNCES	GRAMS	%
apple	1			
apple water	6 tablespoons	3	85	100
whole wheat flour	⅔ cup	3	85	100
rind of Parmesan or other hard, aged cheese (whole, not grated)	about matchbook size			
TOTAL		6	170	200

Line a fine-mesh sieve with cheesecloth and place it over a bowl. Grate the apple over the lined sieve, and lift the cheesecloth to make a pouch. Squeeze the pouch directly over the sieve to extract as much juice as possible through the sieve into the bowl. Put 6 tablespoons (3 oz / 85 g) of the juice in a small bowl. (Discard, or eat, the pulp; if any juice remains, store it in a covered container in the refrigerator and use it in the Firm Starter on Day 3.) Add the flour and stir to make a smooth,

CONTINUED

wet dough. Cover about three-quarters of the bowl tightly with plastic wrap and set the cheese rind on top of the plastic. Let rest at room temperature for 48 hours.

SPONGE STARTER (DAY 3)

INGREDIENT	VOLUME	OUNCES	GRAMS	%
apple	1			
apple water	¼ cup	2	56.5	99
whole wheat flour	3½ tablespoons	1	28.5	50
whole rye flour	3½ tablespoons	1	28.5	50
Seed Culture	1½ tablespoons	0.5	14	25
TOTAL		4.5	127.5	224

Grate the apple and make apple water again using the method in the Day 1 Seed Culture. Put ¼ cup (2 oz / 56.5 g) of the liquid in a small bowl. Discard the pulp but reserve any remaining juice for use in the Firm Starter, below. Add the flours and seed culture and stir to make a wet, sponge-like batter. Cover the bowl with plastic wrap and ferment at room temperature for 24 hours. The starter should show signs of bubbling the next day.

FIRM STARTER (DAY 3)

INGREDIENT	VOLUME	OUNCES	GRAMS	%
leftover apple water	¼ cup	2	56.5	66
Seed Culture	1½ tablespoons	0.5	14	16
whole wheat flour	⅓ cup	1.5	42.5	50
whole rye flour	⅓ cup	1.5	42.5	50
TOTAL		5.5	155.5	182

If you don't have enough leftover apple water from Day 1 and the sponge above, make more using the same method. (If any juice remains, store it in a covered container in the refrigerator and use it in the final dough.) In a medium bowl, stir together all the ingredients to make a firm ball of dough. Transfer to a work surface and knead for about 30 seconds to evenly distribute all the ingredients. Return the starter to the bowl, cover the bowl with plastic wrap, and ferment at room temperature for 24 hours. The starter should swell slightly by the next day.

SEED AND COATING MIXTURE (DAY 4)

INGREDIENT	VOLUME	OUNCES	GRAMS
sunflower seeds, toasted (see page 101 for toasting instructions)	about 6 tablespoons	2	56.5
flaxseeds	about 6 tablespoons	2	56.5
millet	about 6 tablespoons	2	56.5
chia seeds	about 6 tablespoons	2	56.5
wheat bran	1 cup	4	113
rolled oats	½ cup	3	85
TOTAL		15	424

Put the sunflower seeds, flaxseeds, millet, chia seeds, and bran in a medium bowl and stir until evenly combined. Transfer one-quarter of the mixture to a separate bowl and stir in the rolled oats.

FINAL DOUGH (DAY 4)

INGREDIENT	VOLUME	OUNCES	GRAMS	%
apples	2			
apple water	1¼ cups plus 2½ tablespoons	11.25	319	35
bottled spring water	1¼ cups plus 2½ tablespoons	11.25	319	35
Sponge Starter	½ cup	3.2	91	9.9
Firm Starter	½ cup	3.2	91	9.9
Parmesan or other hard, aged cheese, grated	about 2 tablespoons	0.5	14	1.5
unbleached bread flour	3½ cups	16	454	50
whole wheat flour	2¾ cups plus 2 tablespoons	13	369	40
whole rye flour	½ cup	2.25	64	7
potato flour	3 tablespoons	1	28.5	3
salt	1 tablespoon	0.75	21.5	2.3
Seed and Coating Mixture	all	15	424	46.3
TOTAL		77.4	2,195	239.9

CONTINUED

1 Grate the apples and make apple water, again using the same method. Put 1¼ cups plus 2½ tablespoons (11.25 oz / 319 g) of the juice in a large bowl (discard the pulp and drink, save, or discard any remaining juice). Add the water, both starters, and the cheese. Stir for about 15 seconds, just long enough to distribute the starters. Add the flours and stir for about 1 minute, until the flour is hydrated and a coarse, shaggy dough forms. Cover the bowl with plastic wrap and let the dough rest for 1 hour and 45 minutes.

2 Oil a work surface and transfer the dough to the oiled area. Sprinkle half of the salt and half of the seed mixture without the rolled oats over the dough. Stretch and fold the dough as shown on page 20, folding it over itself four times: once each from the top, bottom, and sides. Sprinkle the remaining salt and seeds over the dough and perform two more sequences of stretching and folding without allowing the dough to rest between sequences. Return the dough to the bowl and cover with plastic wrap, or leave the dough on the work surface and cover it with the bowl. Then, at 1-hour intervals, perform two additional sequences of stretching and folding. The dough will be supple and tacky, with a bouncy quality when patted. After the final fold, cover the dough and let it rest at room temperature for 1 hour.

3 Prepare two bannetons or a *couche* as shown on page 26. Divide the dough in half and shape each piece into a boule as shown on pages 20 and 21. Brush the top and sides of each ball with water, then roll the brushed surface in the rolled oat mixture to coat. Put the dough in the prepared proofing vessels, top (seeded) side down. Proof at room temperature for about 5 hours, until the dough increases in size by 1½ times.

4 About 45 minutes before you bake, prepare the oven for hearth baking with a baking stone and steam pan as shown on page 29. Preheat the oven to 420°F (216°C).

5 Just before baking, dust a peel with flour. Transfer the loaves to the peel and score as desired (see page 29). Slide the loaves onto the baking stone and pour about 1 cup of hot water into the steam pan.

6 Bake for 25 minutes, then rotate and bake for about 25 minutes longer, until the crust is golden brown and the bread sounds hollow when thumped on the bottom. The internal temperature should be at least 200°F (93°C).

7 Transfer to a wire rack and let cool for at least 30 minutes before slicing and serving, but note that the subtle flavor nuances can be more easily discerned after the bread cools completely, about 2 hours.

MOZZARELLA, MILK, AND PEAR BREAD WITH "COFFEE-BEAN TRAP" STARTER

MAKES 2 LOAVES

This formula uses coffee beans as the "yeast trap" with pear water to evoke a slightly more robust flavor than the "peach trap" and "Parmesan trap" create. The flavor differences are subtle, but this process is all about possibilities and what-ifs. This bread has the wonderful addition of mozzarella cheese and milk, softening the texture to create a different kind of hearth bread from the ones to which we are accustomed, with a softer, rounder flavor followed by the long finish provided by the natural leaven with its own pear and coffee influence. Whether or not you ever make this bread, I think you'll get excited just reading about it. (But then, I do hope you'll make it.)

SEED CULTURE (DAY 1)

INGREDIENT	VOLUME	OUNCES	GRAMS	%
pear	1			
pear water	6 tablespoons	3	85	100
whole wheat flour	⅔ cup	3	85	100
whole coffee beans (any roast)	about 3 tablespoons			
TOTAL		6	170	200

Line a fine-mesh sieve with cheesecloth and place it over a bowl. Grate the pear over the lined sieve, and lift the cheesecloth to make a pouch. Squeeze the pouch directly over the sieve to extract as much pear juice as possible into the bowl. Put 6 tablespoons (3 oz / 85 g) of the juice in a small bowl. (Discard the pulp; if any juice remains, store it in a covered container in the refrigerator and use it in the Firm Starter on Day 3.) Add the flour and stir to make a smooth, wet dough. Cover about three-quarters of the bowl tightly with plastic wrap. Put the coffee beans in a small plastic container and set it on top of the plastic. Let rest at room temperature for 48 hours.

SPONGE STARTER (DAY 3)

INGREDIENT	VOLUME	OUNCES	GRAMS	%
pear	1			
pear water	¼ cup	2	56.5	99
whole wheat flour	3½ tablespoons	1	28.5	50
whole rye flour	3½ tablespoons	1	28.5	50
Seed Culture	1½ tablespoons	0.5	14	25
TOTAL		4.5	127.5	224

CONTINUED

Grate the pear and make pear water again using the method in the Day 1 Seed Culture. Put ¼ cup (2 oz / 56.5 g) of the juice in a small bowl. (Discard the pulp but reserve any remaining juice for use in the Firm Starter, below.) Add the flours and seed culture and stir to make a wet, sponge-like batter. Cover the bowl with plastic wrap and ferment at room temperature for 24 hours. The starter should show signs of bubbling the next day.

FIRM STARTER (DAY 3)

INGREDIENT	VOLUME	OUNCES	GRAMS	%
leftover pear water	¼ cup	2	56.5	66
Seed Culture	1½ tablespoons	0.5	14	16
whole wheat flour	⅓ cup	1.5	42.5	50
whole rye flour	⅓ cup	1.5	42.5	50
TOTAL		5.5	155.5	182

If you don't have enough leftover pear water from Day 1 and the sponge above, make more using the same method. (However, you will probably have enough. If any liquid remains, store it in a covered container in the refrigerator and use it in the final dough.) In a medium bowl, stir together all the ingredients to make a firm ball of dough. Transfer to a work surface and knead for about 30 seconds to evenly distribute all the ingredients. Return the starter to the bowl, cover the bowl with plastic wrap, and ferment at room temperature for 24 hours. The dough should swell slightly by the next day.

FINAL DOUGH (DAY 4)

INGREDIENT	VOLUME	OUNCES	GRAMS	%
pears	2			
pear water	½ cup plus 3 tablespoons	5.65	160	18
bottled spring water	1 cup plus 6½ tablespoons	11.25	319	35
milk (whole or low-fat)	½ cup plus 3 tablespoons	5.65	160	18
Sponge Starter	½ cup	3.2	91	10
Firm Starter	½ cup	3.2	91	10
unbleached bread flour	7 cups	32	907	100
mozzarella cheese, grated	about 3 cups	13	369	41
salt	1 tablespoon	0.75	21.5	2.4
TOTAL		74.7	2,118.5	234.4

1 Grate the pears and make pear water again using the same method. Put ½ cup plus 3 tablespoons (5.65 oz / 160 g) of the pear water in a large bowl (save, drink, or discard any remaining juice). Add the water, milk, and both starters and stir for about 15 seconds, just long enough to distribute the starters. Add the flour and cheese and stir for about 1 minute, until the flour is hydrated, the cheese is evenly distributed, and a coarse, shaggy dough forms. Cover the bowl with plastic wrap and let the dough rest for 1 hour and 45 minutes.

2 Oil a work surface and transfer the dough to the oiled area. Sprinkle half of the salt over the dough, then stretch and fold the dough as shown on page 20, folding it over itself four times: once each from the top, bottom, and sides. Sprinkle the remaining salt over the dough and perform two more sequences of stretching and folding without allowing the dough to rest between sequences. Return the dough to the bowl and cover with plastic wrap, or leave the dough on the work surface and cover it with the bowl. Then, at 1-hour intervals, perform two additional sequences of stretching and folding. The dough will be supple and tacky, with a bouncy quality when patted. After the final fold, cover the dough and let it rest at room temperature for 1 hour.

3 Prepare two bannetons or a *couche* as shown on page 26. Divide the dough in half and shape each piece into a boule or bâtard as shown on pages 20 and 21. Put the shaped loaves in the prepared proofing vessels. Proof at room temperature for about 5 hours, until the loaves have increased in size by 1½ times.

4 About 45 minutes before you plan to bake, prepare the oven for hearth baking with a baking stone and steam pan as described on page 29. Preheat the oven to 420°F (216°C).

5 Just before baking, dust a peel with flour. Transfer the loaves to the peel and score as desired. Slide the loaves onto the baking stone and pour about 1 cup of hot water into the steam pan.

6 Bake for 25 minutes, then rotate and bake for about 25 minutes longer, until the crust is golden brown and the bread sounds hollow when thumped on the bottom. The internal temperature should be at least 200°F (93°C).

7 Transfer to a wire rack and let cool for at least 30 minutes before serving, but note that the subtle flavor nuances can be more easily discerned after the bread cools completely, about 2 hours.

RESOURCES

Because this is such a new and open frontier, the amount of tools, ingredients, and general information is on an accelerating upward trajectory. What is printed here may well be out of date before this book ever hits the shelves, but at least it will provide you with some resources to get started.

I've organized these resources into three categories: articles, books, and links; ingredients; and tools. Given the ever-expanding state of the Internet and the dynamic nature of commerce, I make no promises that these links are still neither viable nor exhaustive, but they have proven useful to me as I explored the depths of the current bread revolution. I will post these and ongoing updates on my Facebook page.

ARTICLES, BOOKS, AND LINKS

THE BREAD BAKERS GUILD OF AMERICA
Every serious bread baker should be a member. The quarterly newsletters and technical reports are worth the price of admission, as is access to the many workshops and classes.
bbga.org

FLOUR POWER: A GUIDE TO MODERN HOME GRAIN MILLING BY MARLEETA F. BASEY (JERMAR PRESS)
An excellent reference for anyone interested in home milling.

IN SEARCH OF THE PERFECT LOAF BY SAMUEL FROMARTZ (VIKING)
A well-written memoir and survey of some of the newest findings in bread science and technique.

THE FRESH LOAF
A wonderful website with helpful information on home milling:
thefreshloaf.com/node/24640/home-milling

"FOR OLD-FASHIONED FLAVOR, BAKE THE BAKING SODA" BY HAROLD MCGEE (NEW YORK TIMES)
Harold McGee's article on how to make baking soda perform like lye for pretzels (see page 177):
nytimes.com/2010/09/15/dining/15curious.html

NICKY GIUSTO'S AWARD WINNING RAISIN BREAD RECIPE
(*Raisin de Soleil*, see page 142):
calraisins.org/recipe/raisin-de-soleil-grape-of-the-sun

"NUTRITIONAL IMPROVEMENT OF CEREALS BY SPROUTING" BY J.K. CHAUAN AND S.S. KADAM (CRITICAL REVIEWS IN FOOD SCIENCE AND NUTRITION)
This article from 1989 shows evidence that "sprouting of grains for a limited period causes increased activities of hydrolytic enzymes, improvement in the contents of certain essential amino acids, total sugars, and B-group vitamins, and a decrease in dry matter, starch, and antinutrients. The digestibility of storage proteins and starch are improved due to their partial hydrolysis during sprouting."
ncbi.nlm.nih.gov/pubmed/2692609

The following links all lead to articles on the health benefits of sprouted grains:

onegreenplanet.org/vegan-health/sprouted-grains-are-they-a-healthy-choice onegreenplanet.org/vegan-health/flour-power-10-reasons-you-should-bake-with-sprouted-whole-grain-flour

onegreenplanet.org/natural-health/is-going-grain-free-better-for-your-health

"WHEAT BELLY—AN ANALYSIS OF SELECTED STATEMENTS AND BASIC THESES FROM THE BOOK" BY JULIE JONES (CEREAL FOODS WORLD)
The most widely cited refutation of the book *Wheat Belly* by Dr. William Davis:
aaccnet.org/publications/plexus/cfw/pastissues/2012/OpenDocuments/CFW-57-4-0177.pdf

Other articles that rebut the *Wheat Belly* claims:

thebestgrains.com/wheat-is-not-unhealthy-a-rebuttal-to-recent-claims

forksoverknives.com/the-smoke-and-mirrors-behind-wheat-belly-and-grain-brain

Also, go to the Whole Grains Council website for all current news on the subject: wholegrainscouncil.org

INGREDIENTS

Sprouted Flour
In this book we focused primarily on two millers, Lindley Mills and To Your Health Sprouted Flour Co., but there are other producers and, most likely, new names will continue to join this list. The websites below also provide incredibly useful information:

ANITA'S ORGANIC MILL
anitasorganic.com
(604) 823-5547

ARROWHEAD MILLS
arrowheadmills.com
(800) 434-4246

ESSENTIAL EATING SPROUTED FOODS
essentialeating.com

LINDLEY MILLS
LindleyMillsInc.com
(336) 376-6190

ONE DEGREE ORGANIC FOODS
onedegreeorganics.com

SHILOH FARMS
shilohfarms.com

TO YOUR HEALTH SPROUTED FLOUR
healthyflour.com
(877) 401-6837

Sprouted Pulp (mash)
Sprouted pulp is the key ingredient in Ezekiel and Alvarado Street breads. You can either make it yourself (see page 141) or it is now available in many varieties of grain to both professional and home bakers from Central Milling. Their grain mills are located in Logan, Utah, but the office headquarters is in Petaluma, California. Write to them at flour@centralmilling.com or call (707) 778-1073. The following website lists all their products: centralmilling.com

Food Grade Lye (Sodium Hydroxide)
There are many sources on the Internet, including Amazon.com and essentialdepot.com.

Cascara Seca (dried coffee cherry husks, aka coffee flour, see page 204)
This product is now increasingly available from many sources, but the two I personally know are:

BOQUETE MOUNTAIN COFFEE
boquetemountaincoffee.com
(704) 243-8900

COFFEE FLOUR™
coffeeflour.com

Community Grains (see page 161)
Identity preserved whole grain products.
Their website is communitygrains.com.

Grape Seed and Grape Skin Flour (see page 202)
This promises to become a growth industry as more and more wineries learn how to recycle their seeds and skins into healthful, functional products. For now, however, there is one company leading the charge:

WHOLE VINE PRODUCTS
wholevine.com

ProBiotein (prebiotic fiber and protein supplement, see page 201)
probiotein.com

Whole Milled and Regional Flour Mills

There are many more than what's listed here, with new ones opening all the time, so use this list as a starting point and seek out mills closer to where to you live:

ANSON MILLS (RED FIFE, ETC.)
Columbia, South Carolina
ansonmills.com

BOB'S RED MILL (POTATO FLOUR, ETC.)
Portland, Oregon
bobsredmill.com

CAMAS COUNTRY MILL
Alvadore, Oregon
camascountrymill.com

CAROLINA GROUND
Asheville, North Carolina
carolinaground.com

CENTRAL MILLING
Petaluma, California
centralmilling.com

CERTIFIED FOODS, INC (BAY STATE MILLING)
Woodland, California
certifiedfoods.com

FAIRHAVEN ORGANIC FLOUR MILL
Bellingham, Washington
fairhavenflour.com

FARMER GROUND FLOUR
Trumansburg, New York
farmergroundflour.squarespace.com

HEARTLAND MILL
Marienthal, Kansas
heartlandmill.com

MAINE GRAINS AT THE SOMERSET GRIST MILL
Skowhegan, Maine
mainegrains.com

RIVERBEND MALT HOUSE
Many micro malt houses are opening across the country and partnering with local, small flour mills, such as Riverbend and Carolina Ground.
Asheville, North Carolina
riverbendmalt.com

TOOLS

Sprouting Equipment

There are many companies, too many to list here, selling small and large sprouting equipment for both home and commercial application. Two that can get you started for setting up sprouting systems are:

THE MAIL ORDER CATALOG FOR HEALTHY EATING
healthy-eating.com/category/75

SPROUT PEOPLE
sproutpeople.org/sprouting-supplies

Home Milling and Pulping Equipment

To turn sprouted grain into mash or pulp, you can use any brand of meat grinder, hand cranked or electric, set to a medium grind. I use my Kitchen Aid mixer with its detachable meat grinder, but you will find many variations at stores such as Lowe's and Home Depot for hand-cranked units, as well as attachments for brands such as Cuisinart and Waring.

General Baking Tools

Sur la Table (surlatable.com) and The King Arthur Flour Baking Catalog (kingarthurflour.com) are still the gold standards for general baking supplies, but CHEFS (chefscatalog.com) also has almost anything you will need. Stores (and catalogs) like Bed, Bath, and Beyond; Williams-Sonoma; and even Walmart and Target have most of the basics too.

ACKNOWLEDGMENTS

As always, my biggest thanks goes to my wife, Susan, who supported me throughout this two-year process of research trips, all-night writing, and baking sessions with patience, advice, and great soups. She also made sure I got up from the computer every half-hour to walk around and, for the first time in memory, my back did not go out during the final push. For that alone, I will be eternally grateful!

The Ten Speed Press team was fabulous, as they always are. This is the third book I've done with my editor Melissa Moore, who is a wonderful collaborator. I wish her well as she moves into her new advocacy work in the non-profit sector, but hope we get to work together again in one way or another. Thank you also to editorial assistant Ali Slagle, who brought the final manuscript all the way home, as well as associate art director Katy Brown, who really grasped the essence of this book and came up with a beautiful presentation. My thanks also go to publisher Aaron Wehner, Michele Crim in marketing, and Kara van de Water in publicity.

Thank you to the photo team, headed by photographer Paige Green, who miraculously turned a bakery warehouse into a photo studio; food stylist Karen Shinto (this is our third book together!); food styling assistant Jeffrey Larsen; photography assistants Debbie Wilson and Morgan Bellinger; prop stylist Tessa Watson; and prop assistant Alexis Scarborough. Thank you to Heritage Salvage, who donated the photography surfaces. And a special thanks to copyeditor Jasmine Star on our fourth collaboration.

This was a tricky book when it came to testing recipes since many of the ingredients were not, at the time, locally available and needed to be shipped. I was fortunate to find the perfect tester, home baker Paul Scivetti, who went far beyond the call of duty, not only testing recipes but also catching measurement inconsistencies, making valuable suggestions, and using these formulas as a launching point for his own bread frontier explorations.

Peggy and Jeff Sutton, as well as Joe Lindley, were extremely generous in providing us with ample supplies of sprouted flour, as were Nicky and Keith Giusto, who not only provided sprouted grain mash but also allowed us to use their baking lab in Petaluma for the week-long photo shoot. Craig Ponsford was an invaluable connector and, of course, his breads totally rock!

Thanks also to the many experts, bakers, millers, and "next frontier" revolutionaries who let me interview them and pick their brains for information and recipes, including Michael Pollan, Mike Pappas, Harry Peemoeller, Bob Thornberg, David Haddock, Dr. Steve Jones, Dr. Harold "Dusty" Dowse, Janice Cooper, Mark Shigenaga, Joe Vanderliet, Bob and Maggie Klein, Peggy Furth, Paul Novak, Torey Arvik, Justin Wangler, Eric Frischkorn, Tucker Taylor, Jennifer Lapidus, and Alan Balshan.

Finally, thanks to Johnson & Wales University in Charlotte for providing a nurturing environment that allows me to forge these uncharted territories, especially President Art Gallagher, Vice President Tarun Malik, Culinary Dean Mark Allison, Baking and Pastry Department Chair Amy Felder, Laura Benoit (proofreader extraordinaire), and my many inspired colleagues on all four JWU campuses.

INDEX

Copyright © 2014 by Peter Reinhart
Photographs copyright © 2014 by Paige Green

All rights reserved.
Published in the United States by Ten Speed Press, an imprint of the Crown
Publishing Group, a division of Random House LLC, a Penguin Random House
Company, New York.
www.crownpublishing.com
www.tenspeed.com

Ten Speed Press and the Ten Speed Press colophon are registered trademarks
of Random House LLC

Library of Congress Cataloging-in-Publication Data

Reinhart, Peter.
Bread revolution : world-class baking with sprouted and whole grains, heirloom
flours, and fresh techniques / Peter Reinhart ; photography by Paige Green.
    pages cm
1. Bread. 2. Cooking (Cereals) 3. Cookbooks. lcgft I. Title. II. Title: World-
class baking with sprouted and whole grains, heirloom flours, and fresh
techniques.
TX769.R4148 2014
641.81'5—dc23
                                                    2014015090

Hardcover ISBN: 978-1-60774-651-5
eBook ISBN: 978-1-60774-652-2

Printed in China
Design by Katy Brown
Food stylist: Karen Shinto
Food styling assistant: Jeffrey Larsen
Photography assistant: Debbie Wilson
Photography assistant: Morgan Bellinger
Prop stylist: Tessa Watson
Prop stylist assistant: Alexis Scarborough
Surfaces donated by Heritage Salvage, Petaluma

10 9 8 7 6 5 4 3 2 1

First Edition